Abu Hamza:
Guilty

Abu Hamza: Guilty
The fight against radical Islam

Réda Hassaïne
and
Kurt Barling

First published in 2014 by Redshank Books

Copyright © Kurt Barling and Réda Hassaïne

ISBN 978-0-993000-20-1

A CIP catalogue record for this book is available from The British Library

Design by Carnegie Publishing

Cover image © AFP/Getty Images

Printed in the UK by TJ International

Redshank Books
Brunel House
Volunteer Way
Faringdon
Oxfordshire
SN7 7YR

Tel: +44 (0)845 873 3837

www.redshankbooks.co.uk

CONTENTS

Foreword by Kurt Barling   1

Introduction by Réda Hassaïne   19

Chapter 1: **Algeria: The Jihad Begins**   25

Chapter 2: **Trapped by the Algerian Security Services**   33

Chapter 3: **Londonistan Beckons**   41

Chapter 4: **Londonistan**   59

Chapter 5: **Safehouse London**   73

Chapter 6: **DGSE AGENT: Saving the World Cup**   85

Chapter 7: **Scotland Yard's Special Branch: Information Broker**   107

Chapter 8: **Trouble in Yemen**   121

Chapter 9: **A Tripartite Arrangement**   133

Chapter 10: **MI5 – Information Broker**   141

Chapter 11: **The Man Who Knew Too Much**   163

Chapter 12: **Journalist Unmasked**   177

Chapter 13: **From Secret Agent to Journalist**   189

Chapter 14: **Letter to the Americans**   197

Chapter 15: **Guilty – USA vs Mostafa Kamel Mostafa**   207

Bibliography – Alphabetical   219

Bibliography by Type and Date (most recent first)   224

Names and Organisations (by first initial)

Abassi Madani – FIS Leader imprisoned in 1991

Abdallah Messai – Algerian Community in Britain official (CBA)

Abu Hamza al-Masri aka **Mostafa Kamel Mostafa**

Abu Hassan (Al Yamani) aka **Abu Hassan Zin al-Abidin** aka **Abu Bakr al-Mihdar** – Former Afghanistan veteran who led Yemeni group Army of Aden

Abu Ibrahim – Algerian jihadi brought to the UK via the Yemen

Abu Mohammed – London linkman to Yacine and the DRS

Abu Omar al-Baghdadi – Leader of IS in Iraq

Abu Qatada al-Filistini aka **Omar Mahmoud Othman**

Ali Belhadj – FIS Leader imprisoned in 1991

Andrew Higgins – *Wall Street Journal* Correspondent

Athmane Oudina – *Horizons* reporter

Boualem Jolie Vue aka **Attalah Mohammed** – Abu Hamza enforcer

Colonel Benali – Head of Algerian Intelligence in the UK

David Heath – *Seattle Times* Correspondent

David Leppard – Correspondent for *The Sunday Times*

Departement du Renseignement et de la Securite (DRS) – Algerian State Intelligence Service

Edward Y Kim – State Prosecutor of Abu Hamza in New York trial

Front de Liberation Nationale (FLN) – National Liberation Movement and governing party after independence

Front Islamique de Salut (FIS) – Islamic Party

General Khaled Nezzar – Long serving military officer long held responsible for suppressing the 1988 demonstrations

General Mohamed 'Toufik' Mediene – Head of Algerian Intelligence Service (DRS) from 1990

Groupe Islamiste d'Algerie (GIA) – Islamist Military Grouping

Haroon Aswat – Former Abu Hamza follower now detained in Broadmoor Psychiatric Hospital

Jason Burke – Correspondent for *The Observer*

Jean-Pierre Chevènement – Former French Interior Minister

Jérôme – Head of French Intelligence in UK during 1990s

Joshua L Dratel – Defence counsel for Abu Hamza in New York trial

Journal du Francophone – Jihadist newspaper from the 1990s in the UK

Justice Antony Hughes – Trial judge in Abu Hamza's British trial at the Old Bailey in 2006

Katherine B Forrest – Judge presiding over the Abu Hamza case in New York

Khaled Bouchemal – Head of FIS Party list in Oran

Major-General Smain Lamari – Head of Department of Counter-Espionage and Internal Security from 1992

Margaret Thompson – Yemen hostage of Abu Hassan who gave evidence in New York trial

Mary Quin – Yemen hostage of Abu Hassan who gave evidence in New York trial

Michael Elsner – Lawyer representing the families of those killed in the 9/11 attacks

Mohamed Denideni – Elected as a FIS official in 1991, Managing Editor of FIS Newspaper *'El Balagh'*

Mohammed Abderrahmani – Assassinated Managing Editor of *El Moudjahid*

Mohammed Sekoum – London-based Algerian Islamist

Mokhtar Belmokhtar aka **Khaled Abou El Abbas** – Algerian jihadist post 2002 peace settlement

Mounir Boudjema – Deputy Managing Editor *Liberte*

Mufti Abdul Barkatullah – Chair of Finsbury Park Mosque committee beaten and intimidated by Abu Hamza's henchmen

Nadir Remli – Fundraiser in London for the GIA

Omar Bakri Muhammed aka the **Tottenham Ayatollah** – Founder of Al Muhajiroun (The Emigrants) organisation in UK

Oussama Kassir – Abu Hamza's link man in the Oregon jihadi camp affair and Abu Hamza's protective security at Finsbury Park Mosque

President Abdelaziz Bouteflika – Algerian President since 1999; presided over end of Civil War in 2002

President Mohamed Boudiaf – Algerian President assassinated in 1992

Rabah Kebir – Exiled leader of the FIS in Germany

Rachid Ramda – Convicted in absentia of involvement in 1995 Paris bombings. Extradited to France from UK after 10 years

Ramdane Zouabri – London-based Islamist and brother of senior GIA figure

Renseignements Generaux (RG) – Police Intelligence Service

Salafist Group for Preaching and Combat (GSPC) – Algerian-based terror group guided by Abu Qatada

Sheikh Mokrane – Formerly preached at Brixton Mosque in South London where shoe-bomber Richard Reid attended prayers

Sheikh Noureddine – Leader of GIA in Western Algeria

Stryker McGuire – *Newsweek* columnist

Supporters of Sharia (SOS) – Islamist organisation formed by Abu Hamza

Touhami Sebti – UK-based Algerian security service agent

Yacine Merzougui – Former *Horizons* colleague and DRS agent

Zacarias Moussaoui – Convicted of masterminding the Twin Towers attack on 9/11

Zinedine Zidane – Star of France's World Cup winning football squad in 1998

The Authors

Kurt Barling

A BBC journalist for a quarter of a century, Kurt Barling has worked at every level of BBC journalism. He has produced critically acclaimed documentaries, seminal current affairs programmes and been at the forefront of the news agenda since making a film in East Germany in November 1989.

As well as remaining a working journalist he is a Professor in Journalism at Middlesex University London. He was educated at the London School of Economics and Sciences Po Paris from where he received his PhD in International Relations before embarking on a career in journalism.

In 1999 he began an investigation into the management of Britain's mosques. What he found at Finsbury Park Mosque was deeply disturbing. Filming undercover in Abu Hamza's lair he discovered a world of deceit, jihad and terror. He also discovered the work of an honest anti-jihadi Muslim. They have collaborated on the story of terrorism since then.

The authorities were deaf and blind to his and others' warnings. He has won numerous British awards for his journalism that put explaining the plight of minority communities in Britain at the heart of his work.

He is married with three children and was born in London in 1961.

Réda Hassaïne

Réda Hassaïne was born in Algiers in 1961. He unmasked Abu Qatada and Abu Hamza in the British national press and fed information to the security services of Algeria, France and then Britain. He also cooperated with US law enforcement agencies to help the extradition of Abu Hamza. For this his life was constantly in danger not least from Abu Hamza and his supporters. Abu Hamza was held in prison in Britain and then extradited to America because of this threat. He has two children and now divides his time between Algeria and London.

Réda Hassaïne has worked as a freelance investigative journalist for *Newsweek, The Sunday Times, The Times* and *The Daily Mail* as well as French Television station France2. He also worked for the Algerian Daily newspapers *Le Quotidien d'Oran* and *L'Expression* as a permanent correspondent in London. Before moving to England, he was a journalist on the Algerian evening daily *Horizons*.

Foreword
by Kurt Barling

THIS IS THE story of Réda Hassaïne and his part in the downfall of some of the most dangerous men on the planet. **He was not in this for the money; he was in it for justice.**

The rule of law in the United States of America started to all intents and purposes in the Southern District of New York. The Judiciary Act of 1789 came in the wake of a revolution that freed patriots from the yoke of British Imperialism. It gave all free men access to justice.

Over 200 years later in Room 15A of the Daniel Patrick Moynihan Court-house in downtown Manhattan, 49-year-old Judge Katherine B Forrest began a month long trial of a man who has for decades believed and propagated that the United States and all it has come to stand for since those revolutionary times is now at the heart of what is wrong with the modern world.

Abu Hamza al-Masri is the 'nom de radical' for Mostafa Kamel Mostafa. Born an Egyptian, given British nationality, and tried in America he has called for a new revolution for over two decades; an Islamic revolution that overthrows the current world order and re-establishes a Caliphate** to rule over all Muslims. Whilst he could, he stopped at nothing to try and achieve that, including spreading terror across Europe and arguably attempted – as

---

* The concept of the caliphate derives from the first caliphate led by the disciples of the Prophet Muhammed. It is the political, social and economic system that governs the entire Muslim faithful (*the ummah*), ruled by a caliph strictly under Islamic law (*sharia*).

the indictments against him in the New York trial contended – to bring it to the United States.

The charge list was long and stretched back into the last century; conspiracy to take hostages, some American; conspiracy to support terrorists; conspiracy to propagate terrorist material over the internet; recruiting jihadists to fight in Afghanistan and providing material support to Al Qaeda and the Taliban.

This book is not an attempt to address these charges, the jury in this trial has now found Abu Hamza guilty, but it is an opportunity to explain how Abu Hamza has been in the midst of a battle of words and radical ideas for these past two decades.

He has espoused a methodology that has brought him into conflict with the authorities in Algeria, France, the United Kingdom and the United States of America precisely because he believed only violent conflict would bring about the ascendancy of political Islam by any means necessary.

But where did this man come from and what brought him to that courtroom in downtown Manhattan to face the jury's judgement in May 2014?

One man knows about Abu Hamza's rise to the forefront of the world of Islamic extremism in the West more than almost anyone else. From the beginning of his ascent to the helm of radical Islamism in Britain as a key recruiter for young men willing to train to wage war in the jihadi struggle, Abu Hamza has been watched closely by Réda Hassaïne, who tried to warn as Hamza took the helm and helped give birth to British jihadism.

This is Réda's story, of his singular fight to bring to justice the men and expose the methods that he held responsible for causing carnage in his Algerian homeland. It was his evidence that enabled the Federal Bureau of Investigations to pursue their case into those responsible for kidnapping American citizens in the Middle East and preparing for jihad on home territory. It was Réda's undercover evidence that helped build the case leading to Abu Hamza's prosecution in London's Central Criminal Court, the famous Old Bailey, in 2005.

The case began on 5th July of that year but was postponed as the bombings on the London Underground on 7th July 2005 filled the United Kingdom and its allies with revulsion. Two weeks later there was another attempt at suicide bombings by a team of four young British men who failed to detonate their devices. They were caught and all eventually sentenced to life in prison. All

FOREWORD BY KURT BARLING

of them had attended Finsbury Park Mosque at some point and lived just five stops up the Piccadilly Line on the London Underground from where they had been radicalised and put on the path to becoming suicide bombers in their own country. We may never know whether or not the timing was coincidental.

When the Old Bailey case finally resumed in 2006 Hamza was found guilty by a British jury. The judge in the case, Mr Justice Hughes, said before sentencing him:

> 'You are entitled to your views, and in this country you are entitled to express them up to the point where you incite murder or racial hatred. That, however, is what you did. You used your authority to legitimize anger and to encourage your audiences to believe that it gave rise to a duty to murder. You commended suicide bombing, you encouraged them to kill in the cause that you set out for them.'

(O'Neill, 2006)

For Réda Hassaïne, it has been a long journey, involving betrayal, death threats and disillusion. It has led to family breakdown, depression and a brush with madness. This is the story of his part in the downfall of some of the most dangerous men on the planet.

In a strange way Réda's story starts in two places; in Algeria and Berlin. The two places were far apart but the consequences of what happened in each place have had a profound bearing on how this story evolved.

On the evening of 9th November 1989 the Berlin Wall was breached without the firing of a single gun. That was a night of uncontained joy, which saw crowds singing heartily all night long, getting drunk and dancing on top of the Berlin Wall. It was a moment of profound liberation that pronounced the world had changed from a place of Cold War despair to a place of hope. But in the euphoria that followed the border guards putting aside their weapons, there were many people who warned that we should be careful what we hoped for.

So potent a symbol of the divided bi-polar world was this Wall that all the world's journalists, it seemed, descended on Berlin to try and get a grip on the shifting sands of the Cold War. The city and its bars hummed to the strains of freedom talk. One US academic described it famously as 'the end of history'. How wrong Francis Fukuyama would prove to be (Fukuyama, 1992).

All around Unter Den Linden, the legendary thoroughfare leading to the Brandenburg Gate and symbol of the Cold War divide, queues of people were travelling back and forth through the breaches in the Wall. There was a long snaking queue of Trabants also trying to re-enter East Berlin via the Brandenburg Gate after their brief foray into the West.

The fall of the Berlin Wall in 1989 precipitated the end of the Cold War. At first commentators focused on these momentous events in Europe without giving much thought to how this rupture might impact on the rest of the world. It was too early to predict how the structures of power might change.

Then in 1996 Samuel Huntingdon published a book with a controversial thesis. In *The Clash of Civilisations and the Remaking of World Order* he argued that religion is a central defining characteristic of civilisations and this meant that the new clash of ideologies would centre on religion.

Certainly, as this book bears witness to, pent-up theological forces were unleashed in Algeria. This galvanised political Islam and enabled radical interpreters of this tradition to undermine a regime that had been under-pinned by Soviet support during the Cold War.

I became a BBC journalist in the midst of all that euphoria and turmoil and reported on the consequences from different parts of the globe. Eventually, a decade after the fall of the Berlin Wall, and as a process of radicalisation was in full swing in some British Mosques, I made a film for Channel Four Television in the United Kingdom – *Trouble at the Mosque* – highlighting the issues and dangers of unregulated Mosques. It was during the making of this film that Réda and I first met and began to collaborate on exposing Abu Hamza's agenda and that of his fellow radicals like Abu Qatada and Omar Bakri Muhammed.

I had spent many years in Germany as a child in a society ridden by the angst caused by the silence of the majority in its period of political and military madness during the Third Reich. I am reminded of the verse in a poem by Albrecht Haushofer (a supporter of the Nazis who belatedly in the 1940s saw the calamitous direction they had embarked on).

"Madness grasps only what it is made to feel.
Madness alone lorded it over this country.
Its proud run finishes in fields of corpses and misery immeasurable rises up."

(Haushofer, A., *Dem Ende Zu, Moabit Sonnets, 1945*)

For me, what Abu Hamza and his fellow travellers were advocating had the tenor of a crypto-fascist *weltanschauung* (9/11 ultimately unleashed their madness). The darkness that fell over Germany* where the majority became paralysed and unable until it was too late to challenge a small clique of madmen threatened to overtake us too.

It deeply troubled me and I was perplexed by the British authorities' fractured and confused response. Making *Trouble at the Mosque* was certainly insomnia inducing.

In much of the developing world, still emerging from the yoke of imperialism, fledgling states were beginning to find their independent feet. Nationalist movements had often metamorphosed into authoritarian regimes to consolidate the gains of independence.

The early enthusiasm of independence had given way by the late 1980s to growing impatience amongst a younger, post-independence born generation. They wanted more accountability, more freedom, more everything, and this groundswell of pressure was making holding on to power an ever more fractious business for the generation that led their countries from the lowering of the French republican tricolore (or the Union Jack among other colonial dispensations elsewhere).

It wouldn't take long for the Soviet Union to quickly disintegrate under the combined weight of a collapsing economy, a failing war in Afghanistan, the consequences and costs of the Chernobyl disaster, and client states demanding their own freedoms in Eastern Europe. What was good for Europe presented a whole scale power vacuum when Soviet-supported regimes in the developing world found that the money and ideological support had run out.

Into that vacuum came the opportunity seekers – a plethora of flourishing freelance ideologues, many of them in the Middle East, encouraged and boosted by the belief that the Soviet Union withdrew from Afghanistan because of the strength of the mujahideen.

Into that space came also a resurgent political Islam propagated by Islamists, who called for the return of the Caliphate (see earlier explanation) proposing the unification of all Muslim lands under the central leadership of a religious and political leader. They sought to rally and radicalise communities around faith and assert the primacy of Islam in all matters to do with the human condition.

---

*   Fuller, E.A. (1945), *Darkness over Germany*, Longmans Green & Co

It is an argument and theological position which has gained traction in many parts of the Middle East. The latest incarnation, in late 2014, is ISIS in Syria (abbreviated to IS once they declared a Caliphate in Northern Iraq). The Islamic State of Iraq and ash Sham (ISIS) is led by Abu Omar al-Baghdadi (originally named Hamed Dawood Mohammed Khalil al-Zawi). IS has proven to be even more successful at attracting radicalised young people from the West. Is it just me or does this have a ring of the Spanish Civil War about it, when thousands of young men rallied to the cause of Republicanism in the 1930s? Young people chasing a dream, supporting a cause, committing to a revolutionary change. Of course suicide bombers never came back to directly threaten the home country and its citizens, but then, whilst the methodology might have been different we should ask ourselves was the sentiment so different?

Now of course there is more resolve to tackle the jihadists. But when President Barack Obama announced on 11th September 2014 that IS needed to be defeated and other world leaders agreed to find a way to curb the spread of IS's progress it was from the back foot. We are paying for the mistakes made over a decade ago. Mistakes Réda Hassaïne witnessed and warned against.

Radical Islamists have long wanted to change the world they live in and put political Islam at the heart of it. Out of that world emerged Osama Bin Laden. He recognised there was a craving amongst some of the dispossessed and angry, for action for change. With his small army of dedicated followers, he set about spreading a network of activists who chose to use the methods of terror. The goal was simple: to force the West to a resolution to evacuate the Middle East and other parts of the world where Islam was the dominant religion. As we now know, he was well placed to spread the message. Bin Laden had spent years refining his mission in the fight against the Soviets in Afghanistan and at first he was heavily supported, ironically, by the American security services.

Al Qaeda spawned many fanatics, none more fanatical than a former civil engineering student from Brighton Polytechnic turned jihadist and then spiritual leader to extremists in Algeria and Britain, Abu Hamza. Hamza boosted his reputation at his mosque in the late 1990s by recounting how he had lost both arms and an eye fighting for the jihadi cause in Afghanistan – claims later revised in a New York courtroom.

Hamza had in fact taken his young family to live in Peshawar on the

Afghanistan-Pakistan border in the early 1990s and then visited Bosnia several times during the war there to lend support to fellow jihadists.

It was in Peshawar that he built links with Zin al-Abidin Abu Bakr al-Mihdar, a Yemeni who when he returned to his country founded the *Army of Aden* under his jihadi nomenclature Abu Hassan. These links would also resurface in the trial in New York in 2014 (Thomas, 2003).

After the 9/11 atrocities jihadists used their indoctrination approach to foster wholesale panic in places where active cells began to operate. Spain, the US and Britain were just three early victims of this battle of ideas which had been translated by the methods of terror. The attacks on the World Trade Center in New York in September 2001, the Madrid train bombings in March 2004 which were widely attributed to a terror cell linked to Al Qaeda and the bombings on the London Tube in July 2005 were all manifestations of the jihadists' method. It is a method which this book claims was fostered by Algerian fighters who went to Afghanistan to support the Taliban and returned emboldened to carry on the fight as Algeria descended into civil war.

These young men, and sometimes women (and their successors), were trained to respect death more than life. Their worldview came to incorporate the belief that killing would take them to martyrdom and that life beyond earth would be more worthwhile than the hell that Abu Hamza and his fellow fanatics insisted was their future as mere mortals at the hands of the unbelievers.

The result was hundreds if not thousands of young people willing to give over lively intellects and creativity to training in espionage, bomb-making and ultimately self-sacrifice whilst they travelled on their journey to paradise. It remains unclear how many young people who were indoctrinated in this period remain in sleeper cells. These are dangerous and ideologically driven freelance operators who will remain a permanent challenge for security forces in America and Europe until the battle of ideas is won.

After 9/11, the evolving conflict, Western intervention in Afghanistan to root out Al Qaeda and then further Allied intervention in Iraq were the visible international responses to the threat posed by global terror.

That was the big picture, but all that strategic activity ignores the fight taken up by many individuals to expose the men of terror as their fanatical incantations drove a wedge between communities – and as Réda Hassaïne bears witness to in this book – fuelled terrible bloodshed in countries such as Algeria.

Réda Hassaïne was one such individual. He was born in 1961 when Algeria was fighting to gain independence from France. By the time he reached adulthood the country was emerging from its post-revolutionary rebuilding but slowly descending into a dictatorship. In this ultra-conservative country the young Hassaïne, who was a bright and able student at school, sought to find freedom of expression and a less-constrained life overseas.

Like many of his compatriots he had travelled to Europe in the early 1980s in search of adventure and a more liberating lifestyle. But observing dramatic changes happening back home, his dead-end job washing dishes in London restaurants made Hassaïne feel that his life lacked purpose. He returned to Algeria to train as a journalist and join in with the thousands of returnees striving to build a more robust civil society.

Algeria was, is and remains a very complex society, and despite an enormous amount of optimism the economic conditions continued to deteriorate. Now, however, the escape route overseas was becoming increasingly blocked as Europe retreated into its own fortress and put up more and more immigration barriers. In the late 1980s, like many young people, Hassaïne found it increasingly difficult to leave the country because of foreign currency restrictions.

As democracy failed to flourish, and the opposition to the descent into dictatorship in Algeria gathered momentum, Hassaïne was sucked into a world where theological fanaticism began to eat away at the fabric of Algerian society. As a working journalist he was forced into the world of espionage and became vulnerable to regular purges by the Algerian state, trying as it did with increasingly ferocious desperation to defend the power and resources it had secured. (This is explored further in Chapter 2.)

In Algeria, 5th October 1988 is a pivotal point in the descent into collective madness. The first widely recognised state-sponsored massacre of several hundred people at a legitimate demonstration escalated the internal conflict and the retaliations became ever more brutal after the cancellation of the planned General Election. The government's explanation was that it feared an effective Islamist coup d'état through the ballot box.

Algeria descended into a savage civil war pitching fathers against sons, siblings against siblings and families against each other in a descent into ideological and theological warfare. A quarter of a million people are estimated to have died in that conflict, many of them victims of a war of terror being orchestrated and justified by religious fatwas from beyond Algeria's borders.

To help the State identify the sources of support and funding for the endless cycle of brutality Réda Hassaïne left his country under the cover of the Algerian security services to investigate who was responsible for orchestrating the carnage, assassinations and murders from abroad.

Enter Abu Qatada and his band of followers in West London and a rival radical, Abu Hamza and his fast growing predominantly English- and French-speaking following, based in North London. It wasn't long after arriving in London that Réda encountered the Jordanian Abu Qatada, described by a Spanish investigating judge after the Madrid bombings as Osama Bin Laden's right hand man in Europe. (The indictment in the case against the Al Qaeda terror cell prepared by Spanish prosecutors after the Madrid bombings, named Abu Qatada al-Filistini [Omar Mahmoud Othman] as the spiritual leader of Al Qaeda in Europe as well as the GIA amongst others.)

Réda also witnessed what he felt was the alarming rise and brashness of a man with one eye and no hands, which at the time Hamza claimed had been blown off by a home-made bomb whilst fighting the Soviets in Afghanistan (Thomas, 2003).

This man was Abu Hamza. Up until Réda's arrival in London in 1994 it is clear the British security services had largely overlooked Hamza but he was most certainly on the radar of the French security services (see Chapter 6). The Irish Republican Army was still active and in the forefront of the minds of British anti-terrorism officers.

But with a growing interest in Hamza from the French, Réda decided to double up his role and work for both the Algerian and French Security services. It was his first opportunity to try joined- up thinking across the usual lines of demarcation for spies and feed useful information to both the Algerians and the French.

Hassaïne progressively infiltrated the coteries of both Qatada and Hamza putting himself at grave personal risk. The head of the French Security services in London (the DGSE) wined and dined him at expensive restaurants. Hassaïne's recollections of those meetings recount the inside story of how the French government feared the incompetence of the British.

Hassaïne helped foster the phrase 'Londonistan' to describe the active émigré networks in the British capital that were orchestrating mayhem in other parts of the world. It was as if the British had never given up their Empire. Instead of discouraging the organising of mayhem elsewhere the British, according to Hassaïne, made a pact, a so-called 'covenant of security', to allow freedom of action for jihadist political activity in the UK as long as no trouble and conflict was brought to British shores. (The interview by me for BBC with members of al-Muhajiroun on the occasion of the one-year anniversary conference of the 9/11 bombings at Finsbury Park Mosque confirmed this belief in a 'covenant of security'. With hindsight, this seems quite incredible.)

Hassaïne soon discovered the antipathy between the British and French security services. He found that there was no shared interest apparent between them in fighting what should have been a common enemy of radical Islamists in the final throes of planning a new wave of terrorism. 'Each to their own' was the unspoken motto.

After the carnage of the Metro bombings in Paris of 1995 the French authorities became even more convinced that Britain was ignoring the activities of those responsible for the bombings such as Rachid Ramda who lived in Wembley, North London and had become the London-based quarter-master helping to finance the jihadist bombing activities in the French capital.(Evidence to support this was presented to the extradition hearings of Rachid Ramda at the High Court in London covered by me in my role as a Correspondent for BBC News.)

The British continued to plough their own furrow, taking the attitude that as long as there was no trouble on their soil they would not interfere with the human rights of the radical Islamists nor with sacrosanct rights of freedom of expression. It is a tragic irony that whilst the British liberals defended the rights of Islamists to spread their message, they failed to recognise that the message itself was hateful and ignored the rights of just about anyone who disagreed with them – including, in some cases, the right to live.

Hassaïne has long argued that driven by a desire to help first his fellow Algerians, then the French, the British (and finally the Americans) he began acting as a conduit to pass information to all three security services as he infiltrated jihadist circles and posed as a follower and useful propagandist. He even produced a newsletter (see Chapter 6) for the supporters of the Algerian jihadist forces. He learned their philosophy, he understood their means and he watched them prepare for holy war.

Increasingly frustrated with a lack of action on the part of the British services he collaborated with a number of British, French, Algerian and American journalists including myself. He wanted Abu Hamza and Abu Qatada brought to justice.

Réda managed to raise awareness of the double standards being deployed in dealing with these radicals but he made precious little early headway in convincing the authorities to take action.

Réda was anxious to send a warning to the British government to act before it was too late. He reached out to American FBI investigators to help them identify Hamza's role in several of the episodes that led to his indictment by a New York Court in 2004 – kidnap and murder in Yemen, jihadi camps in Oregon. (See Chapter 15).

Still no authority in Britain reacted by cracking down on Hamza's endless narrative of hatred of the West and his allegations that Western values were corrupting the minds of young British Muslims in particular.

In the run up to the World Cup in France in 1998, the French interior minister, Jean-Pierre Chevènement, waited anxiously for reports from Hassaïne 'undercover' in Finsbury Park Mosque where Hamza orchestrated his propaganda output. Chevènement, a keen skier, would habitually wait until after Hamza's Friday sermon to decide whether to leave for the Alps for his weekend recreation. He was waiting on word from London of the latest Fatwa from Hamza, to see if security action needed to be taken to protect fresh Parisian targets. The French launched Operation Zidane (named after the Captain of the French Soccer team, Zinedine Zidane) to counter the possibility of disrupting the World Cup event across France.

By this time Abu Hamza was involved with people who seized hostages in Yemen in order to put pressure on the government of Yemen to release political prisoners. He provided them with a satellite phone and took calls from the kidnappers during the hostage crisis. Four hostages died – three Britons and an Australian. Two of those hostages released were American citizens.

When the kidnappers who survived the rescue assault were brought to trial, they were convicted and sentenced to execution. Abu Hamza reacted with militant anger:

> 'I believe it will ignite and spark something which the Yemen government
> can't afford. The sentence will make the Islamic Army of Aden pull together

and restructure. The sentence is totally unjust. Islamic law says that no Muslim should be killed for the blood of a non-Muslim.'

This international diversification led to a split in the London allegiances of the forces driving the Islamic revolt in Algeria. Abu Hamza became the de facto spiritual leader of Algerian jihadists and this began to take up the bulk of Hassaïne's time and energy. Abu Qatada was of lessening interest as he focused on the Arab-speaking communities in London whilst Finsbury Park Mosque was fast becoming a hub for émigrés from all sorts of war-torn regions.

Week in, week out, Hamza would declaim the Islamic texts (as evidenced at his Old Bailey Trail in 2006 and New York trial in 2014) from his platform in Finsbury Park Mosque – legitimising, he claimed, Muslims' call to arms irrespective of what atrocities were being perpetrated in the name of Islam.

Whilst Réda was busy monitoring the activities of Hamza – including involvement in Yemen and the bombings of American targets in the Middle East and Africa – news began filtering through to Finsbury Park Mosque that jihadists were planning a big event. This would change the rules of the game and the engagement between 'the Great Satan' of the USA and Islamist revolutionaries.

Time was running out for Réda Hassaïne however, to prevent an escalation of planned atrocities. Al Qaeda were very clearly beginning to adopt the methods and political ideology of the GIA in Algeria, their foot-soldiers instrumental in instructing émigrés in bases in Afghanistan. Algeria's form of warfare and theological struggle would infect the jihadists' global struggle.

Algeria's hardened practitioners became some of the most highly sought after recruits for jihadists in Afghanistan, Pakistan, Yemen, Chechnya, and Bosnia. There they would train young British, American, Canadian and Australian men who found their way to the Middle East, in the methods of carrying out terror attacks back in their home countries. It became clearer just how many when the Taliban fell and the United States started detaining foreign fighters before sending them to Guantanamo Bay in Cuba.

Hassaïne became increasingly convinced it was only a matter of time before the carnage came to London, Washington, Paris and other Western capitals. As he recounts, no one in authority wanted to acknowledge that what was really happening was the birth of a British jihadi movement.

All the tell-tale signs of the radicalisation and dispatching of young men overseas made him feel that what he saw at Finsbury Park Mosque and the Fourth Feathers base of Abu Qatada suggested that the murderous methods of suicide bombings, attacks on civilian targets and violent spectaculars adopted in foreign conflicts would soon be visited on the West; he just didn't know where and when. In this respect his recollections of the meetings with MI5 and Scotland Yard reveal a tale of missed opportunities.

Réda witnessed the emergence of Osama Bin Laden as a leading figure-head for holy war on the West and saw the recruitment of thousands of young men who were dispatched by Qatada and Hamza, and inspired by Bin Laden, for training in warfare and terrorism in Afghanistan and Pakistan. These young men were recruited from London and other centres of radicalism such as Luton, Birmingham, Manchester and Bradford in the UK.

Réda Hassaïne personally met the men responsible for undertaking reconnaissance in Bly, Oregon for a jihadi camp that Abu Hamza believed could be a useful venue to train American jihadists.

He was witnessing what in essence has become the method of attracting young Western educated people to the radical causes of Islam and then sacrificing their lives for those causes. First the process of radicalisation, then the travel to a conflict zone to gain experience and a fresh perspective. Some have returned with a greater sense of grievance which has led to suicide bombings and now increasingly, active engagement in overseas conflicts.

It was at this juncture, in the spring of 2001, that I had been commissioned to make *Trouble at the Mosque* which required secretly filming inside Finsbury Park Mosque among others.

A shocking picture emerged from my research for the documentary. It became abundantly clear that there was a significant problem in the management of many British Mosques. Each Mosque is sovereign and each imam is free to pursue his own theological agenda within that mosque. With no overarching regulatory ecclesiastical authority (think the Pope in Catholicism and the Archbishop of Canterbury in the Anglican tradition) there was no one to effectively police the debates going on in many fringe mosques that had attracted some radical imams like Abu Hamza.

Add to that the linguistic and cultural narrowness in some mosques where the imams had come from rural Pakistan and barely had a command of English. This meant the imams often failed to appreciate the cultural differences in the host communities that the British-born generation of Muslims were experiencing. There was an obvious growing disconnect between generations.

The preparations for 9/11 and the following all-out assault on the West were already long in the planning nevertheless they were still difficult to predict with any certainty.

In some parts of urban Britain there was another phenomenon that went largely unnoticed. I had been asked by the BBC to make a film about conversions to Islam amongst the Black British prison population in 1995. Many of these young men had no cultural experience of Islam in the home so came to it as a form of political engagement. Once out of prison some sought out the likes of Abu Hamza who put them not just on a spiritual footing but inevitably a jihadi one too. (Barling, 2008)

Since we first met in the summer of 2001 it was through my reporting on terrorism for BBC News that my relationship with Réda Hassaïne developed. He had become a reliable source of information which always stood up to scrutiny. He was also much bolder in his predictions than other people. He made it clear in our conversations whilst researching my many post-9/11 reports for the BBC that Abu Hamza had encouraged young British men to set up cells and plan attacks in Britain.

It was difficult to substantiate these claims at the time and under the threat of being sued for defamation I personally had to pull back on reporting allegations on several occasions, most notably in my documentary *Trouble at the Mosque*. For journalists working in the field of terrorism it is never easy to pin down the heart of the matter. You are aware of the smoke and mirrors play going on with your contacts on all sides. Being faithful to the audience takes a measure of audacity, shrewdness and faith in your own judgment.

One of the most difficult myths to overcome in reporting the story was the idea that Abu Hamza was 'just a clown' as so many people in positions of regulatory authority concluded. Some clown. But the thing that has always struck me about clowns is that it is their personality and routine that children and adults alike always remember most when the circus has moved on.

It is hard to believe but at the time the evidence we were presenting was seen as potentially inflammatory (even though it was true). I too came under suspicion of being an slamophobe by Hamza's supporters. But Ricin plots and tube bombings helped me to gain confidence in Réda's judgement. He had all but predicted these outcomes for years.

Réda was unusual as a source in that he understood the business of journalism. I won't pretend this didn't make me ultra-cautious at first because a poacher turned gamekeeper can play games with your storyline that you cannot necessarily detect at first sight.

He seemed to live a very chaotic life and it was very difficult to establish how he made a living or indeed if he shared his life with anyone. He was often unkempt, although always punctual, but never seemed to get enough sleep. It took some time to discover he had a wife and two children but by then his marriage was in meltdown. That was hardly surprising because his other characteristic was obsession. He was obsessed with Abu Hamza and his perceived wickedness and he didn't take kindly to being contradicted on this subject. The more I witnessed how Abu Hamza was conducting himself at Finsbury Park Mosque and in the media, in particular his insistence on carrying on Friday prayers in the street after the Charity Commission evicted him from the Mosque building, the more I recognised the grounds for Réda's frustration. Seeing the authorities seemingly in denial I grew to admire Réda's tenacity.

We began to trust each other and it was in this way that I became the first broadcaster to reveal his involvement with the security services, on a report for BBC News – something never denied by the authorities. The least I could do was to be a good listener.

Réda's fondness for good French red wine and our ability to converse in his native tongue of French meant we formed a better understanding of each other than some of his other journalist contacts. Curiously enough we were both born in the same year of 1961 and both shared a passion for a certain North London football team based in Islington. We had enough in common to not worry about the things that might separate us. Our relationship has endured the long years of bringing Abu Hamza and Abu Qatada to their latest reckonings.

Hassaïne was still attending Hamza's sermons as an undercover informant when, in the middle of 2000, supporters had decided to go to New York to raise funds to funnel to Finsbury Park Mosque in support of Taliban fighters in Afghanistan. This all came long after President Clinton had declared such activity illegal (4th July 1999), but one of the hallmarks of the jihadists is that they do not believe in man-made laws, unless – as in Hamza's case – it gives them the ability to claim human rights abuses by the British state. Indeed, in the attempt to prevent his extradition to the United States his lawyers made the case that his human rights would be abused.

After Mohammed Atta flew the plane into the Twin Towers, his inspiration was traced back to, among others, Abu Qatada. (Videos of Qatada's sermons were found in the Hamburg apartment of Atta when it was searched after the 9/11 attacks.

Abu Hamza's active interest in the Oregon camp at Bly, his financial support for the Taliban and the support of sending men to training camps in Afghanistan meant that he was appearing on the radar of American law enforcement too. The net began to close in.

As the pressure mounted on the jihadists so they became more paranoid about who might be informing on them. It is probable that Hamza and Qatada were in regular contact for their own reasons with the security service and, in this increasingly febrile climate, the suspicions of the jihadists also turned to Réda Hassaïne. Abu Qatada's loyal supporters decided to act. He was attacked and badly beaten and bloodied in an attack by Abu Hamza's bodyguard after Qatada's weekly prayers. Réda Hassaïne, knowing that many of the men he was dealing had little fear of death, was left fearing for his own life.

His life as an informant for the security services was over and he decided to actively pursue his campaign by exposing Hamza and Qatada in the American and British press. Hamza continued to spout his discourse of hate on the streets of North London after he was finally ejected as imam at the Finsbury Park Mosque when the Charity Commission decided he was in breach of his duties to keep politics out of a place of worship and was propagating extremist views. (Casciani, 2006)

Only after the US requested his extradition in 2004 was Hamza finally charged and subsequently convicted of terror-related offences in the UK. He spent the following eight years in a British High Security jail after the trial the Old Bailey. A considerable part of the evidence that was used to prosecute Hamza had been gathered through Réda Hassaïne's contacts whilst he was operating as a paid informant.

After fighting the extradition process all the way to the European Court of Human Rights, Hamza's appeals finally ran out on 5th October 2012. He was extradited the same day to face American justice.

Although in the intervening years Osama Bin Laden has been killed and much of the Al Qaeda hierarchy dismantled, the ideas they espoused persist and in radical circles there is still support for the values he propagated – as we see with IS in Iraq – the legacy is very much alive.

How else is it possible to explain the exodus of British born and educated young men – sometimes followed by their British wives – to fight jihad in the Middle East, most recently in Syria and Iraq. The Islamic State presents itself as a virtuous movement of liberation, using a London-accented jihadist to propagate its message over the beheadings of two American journalists James Foley and Steven Sotloff and British aid workers David Haines and Alan Henning. These public executions – for the benefit of an internet audience (and from there all other news outlets) – may have been designed to demonstrate the nature of the latest metamorphosis along the continuum from GIA, through Al Qaeda to ISIS but they also reveal what the battle is for as much as what it is against. This is why this story matters. It reflects how with certain radical sections of our community we lost the 'battle of ideas'. When Englishmen sign up to a force that celebrates the beheading of non-combatants in revenge for military strikes we must assume it is for an idea they believe in rather than just blood lust.

Now, the fragmentation of the jihadist cause has spawned ever more virulent strains, even Abu Qatada – one of the villains of Réda's story – says IS is stuffed with fighters who are the 'dogs of hellfire' and is a 'killing and destruction machine'. How he must have learned to be careful what you wish for!

Those ideas first gained traction amongst British born young men flocking to the jihadi flag raised by Abu Hamza. Estimates suggest several thousand Europeans have joined the fight including at least 400 from Britain. It was Hamza who roused the jihadi genie, and in my view his incompetent handling by the authorities, that allowed it to get out of the bottle. It meant the cause of jihad became legitimised for hundreds of young men who have taken up arms against a West that nurtured them but which they despise and reject.

What this eye-witness account illuminates is the process that began in the 1990s where the developed and developing world have become umbilically linked in this fight against theological extremism. To combat it we have to make sure that our interventions in the process of radicalisation and deployment are meaningful and don't simply alienate law-abiding communities and citizens further. Reinforcing the process whereby young people, who by and large emanate from these communities, seek a fresh identity and meaning in their lives in the battlefields of jihadi madness. The struggle against this new totalitarian ideology underpinned by theological dogma is likely to turn out to be a generational one.

Finsbury Park Mosque has been under new management for nearly 10 years. It is now a place of worship and peaceful sanctuary once again. The irony is jihadist networks and radicals no longer need to base themselves in mosques. The jihadi revolution has been privatised into the spaces where it is more difficult to monitor them and the freedom of the internet plays its part.

The New York trial of Abu Hamza marks another milestone in the Americans' efforts to put a senior member of the Al Qaeda network before the courts in America. The case raises as many questions as answers in Hamza's 25 years of waging holy war against the West. It has certainly not provided a solution to the pressing question of how we are to deal with those young people who have gone off to war. Will they come back to become murderers on the streets of London, Paris, New York or Algiers once again?

The story we tell here is of one man's two-decade-long struggle to see justice done. Not for glory, and certainly not for the pittance he was paid for his information, but for the justice that he felt was needed to account for the thousands massacred in his own country at the behest of ruthless and dangerous men.

It is about how Réda Hassaïne battled to warn others of the dangers and how we now are living with the legacy of uncertainty resulting from the indoctrination of thousands of European- and American- born jihadists who remain a threat to the peace and security of us all.

Professor Kurt Barling
Middlesex University London
November 2014

Introduction
by Réda Hassaïne

THIS IS MY journalist's story of my journey to enforced activism. It is a tale of clashing ideologies, a battle between jihadists and justice.

Terrorism thrives on manufacturing chaos and spreading fear. In the heat of battle it is sometimes difficult to make sense of who is fighting who, and why.

For twenty years I have felt like I was in a battle for survival in which I – an ordinary Muslim democrat – tried to face down jihadist theocrats who have a profound hatred of democracy.

My engagement with the men of terror started as I became the eyes and ears of the opposition to State terror in my homeland of Algeria and then to an emerging global jihadism. For nearly two decades it was my duty to take sides and I paid a heavy price.

This is my story, a tale of one Muslim's battle to overcome the evils of Islamist terror.

* * *

16th January 2013. A former follower of Abu Qatada, Mokhtar Belmokhtar, emerged from the wilderness of sub-Saharan Africa in the barren lands of Mali, into the midst of the Algerian gas fields and executed a deadly plan. Thirty-nine foreign nationals were summarily executed, in a fresh outrageous

ABU HAMZA: GUILTY

attack to prove to the world that the jihadists were still capable of a great spectacular.

Mokhtar Belmokhtar, also known as Khaled Abou El Abbas or Laaouar, is a forty-year old Algerian terrorist, a military commander of Al Qaeda in the Maghreb and leader of his own brigade ('Those Who Sign in Blood').

The Amenas gas field near the border of Mali in Southern Algeria contributes ninety-five per cent of Algeria's exports and sixty per cent of its revenues. It is hot, backbreaking work that is carried out by a mixture of tough Algerian and international staff. A normal day in the desert – 16th January turned out not to be, by any stretch of the imagination, a normal day for its international staff. Once again they were 'guilty' of being in the wrong place according to jihadists and became the targets of a fresh wave of hate.

The terror crafts learnt in Afghanistan by young indoctrinated jihadists were now being deployed in the latest episode of terror lunacy. It was almost certainly planned as a huge suicide mission. Firstly to send a signal to Islamists that their struggle should continue; and secondly, to remind the West that its citizens were expendable if they persisted in staying in so-called 'Muslim lands'.

For twenty years I have been saying to anyone who would listen that it is hard, almost impossible, to fully grasp the mind-set of the jihadist. I have discovered through bitter experience that the depths to which they are willing to sink for their cause are almost unfathomable to most people. But once you start to recognise they believe they are engaged in a theological struggle in which their ends are justified by any means and that their targets are chosen just to spread fear, you realise there are few grounds on which to broker a compromise. Nevertheless, the Almenas spectacular had all the hallmarks of a terror attack designed to achieve multiple objectives. It targeted an apostate government, it killed a large number of foreigners and it sacrificed the lives of martyr fighters.

Many of Belmokhtar's fighters died in the attack on Ain Amenas – but not the one-eyed commander himself. It is believed he remains active in the countries that border the Sahara desert. The Ain Amenas attack was a propaganda coup that reverberated around the world, particularly amongst Islamists. Every perceived victory emboldens those who have chosen this path. This was no defeat in battle – this was another step to winning the war against the infidels and apostates. For jihadists it was one big fat win.

It happened as Kurt Barling and I were writing the first draft of this book. It came as no surprise that once again my country was caught at the heart of the global terror nexus. Since then it has re-emerged in Iraq with ISIS and pursued women and children in Northern Nigeria with Boko Haram. For me it has been a huge case of déjà vu.

* * *

Roland Barthes once wrote some good advice about writing biography. He said, 'above all, don't try and be exhaustive'. Therefore I have pruned out the undergrowth of my past to leave you with my view of the landscape of Islamist terrorism as I witnessed its evolution from the early 1990s. Beyond that in this book we have tried to graft my story on to the broad sweep of history so it makes sense of a phenomenon that has made us all potential targets, wherever we are.

What is true and what is not true is always open to debate; what is undeniable is that the historical record shows terrible things have happened in the name of my religion. By writing my story I am trying to explain, from a personal perspective, why I think these things happened and that ordinary Muslims like me are just as outraged about these things as anyone else.

In my experience most people in the West have been fortunate enough to lead sheltered lives. Only those thrust into adversity and situations of war will truly understand how crazy things are when the 'lunatics take over the asylum'.

What happened in my homeland of Algeria in the 1990s prompted a dramatic set of consequences. It fed the idea and machinery of terror. This did not happen by accident. I know that because I witnessed it. I remain convinced that I did something along the way to combat the terrorists and warn others of how serious a threat they faced. I started with a warning to my fellow countrymen. When it felt like I wasn't being heard, I reached out to warn the French. When that felt increasingly ineffectual I reached out to the British. But it soon became obvious that the real targets of the jihadists' anger and scheming was the United States. So, I tried to get the message to those in America who I thought could help combat the scourge of terror.

In my deepest and darkest moments of desolation and depression I would remind myself of the crimes committed by the French during the wars of independence. We Algerians had overcome that I told myself.

I also remembered the massacre at Bentalha in 1997. Amnesty International estimated up to 200 people were slaughtered, many women and children, mostly butchered with knives. When Abu Hamza gleefully claimed responsibility for this depraved act of violence from the pulpit at Finsbury Park Mosque I knew absolutely what I was fighting against, more importantly I knew what I was fighting for. The memory of Bentalha and its people, animals and culture should never be lost.

When I recently returned to Bentalha I was saddened and disgusted to find that there were no physical remains, no plaque or monument to the erasing of this once peaceful community. I felt like screaming 'shame on you Algeria for trying to erase the memory of such terrible times and crimes'. It wasn't just the French colonialists who were bastards. We must face our tragic past, even where we were culpable, to build a just future.

However, I believe the real lesson of Bentalha, for us now fighting the scourge of terrorism, is that the basest human instinct for revenge can unleash, despite all its terror, the highest instinct for justice. Despite the terror unleashed at Bentalha it became a propaganda coup for the democrats, because everyone was able to see that they had a just cause. Bentalha needed to be remembered and avenged.

* * *

As my story will show, Algeria and its machinery of internal security and then in turn its most violent opponents – the Groupe Islamist d'Algerie (GIA) – sought to impose their own 'climates of terror' to control people. It was terrifying to be in the middle of that firestorm of pitiless blood letting.

But, of course, as my story will demonstrate, it did not stop there. The men (and sometimes women) of terror went on to seek out new places to refine and export their methods of terror. Jihadists from Algeria found willing collaborators in the mountains of Afghanistan amongst the kindred fundamentalist spirits of the Taliban. They decided that what was learned in Algeria could be a way of showing the West and the 'Great Satan' of America that they were willing to fight and achieve martyrdom for the cause of ridding 'their' lands of apostates.

I could never fathom their thinking. Like most ordinary Algerians I wanted to be able to get on with my life in peace. I was disgusted to the core of my being, and it wasn't long before I was wedded to justice for all those innocent people who were sacrificed on the altar of jihadist righteousness, either of the state or the GIA and its many faces.

But my story puts a face on the faceless terrorist. It unravels their craft – such as it is – and shows the mistake of firstly not taking them seriously and then ignoring them, whilst they busily organised themselves. This gave them confidence to mount more and more outrageous acts of violence. It's about how we need to see the dangers present in extremism and not combat it with our own version of violent extremism. It comes back to the central premise of democracy; a battle of ideas that needs to be won.

* * *

Looking back I recognise I was naïve enough in 1994 to believe that I could somehow get the three security services of Algeria, France and the United Kingdom to work together to combat those who used border control paranoia to evade prosecution and conviction. I assumed that if the security services had the right information they would act accordingly. They did not. Soon it became clear that the fanatics were so focused on causing harm to the United States that I would need to try and use my journalism networks to make the Americans see the dangers too.

At the start, all a jihadi terrorist had to do was to cross an international border and find a more laissez faire regime to continue their work. Naïvely, I thought that by using my intelligence-gathering instinct and doing their joined-up thinking for them, I might actually help thwart terror attacks in my own country. My instincts told me that the terror would spread as it did to the Paris Metro in 1995, but no one could have imagined the scale and impact of 9/11 and then the 7/7 bombings on the London Underground.

To this day I regret that my constant ravings to the British security services, including Scotland Yard, were only heeded after the mass slaughter on the tube. I was profoundly depressed in its aftermath (in fact doctors said I was close to a breakdown). I still believe the tube bombings of 7th July were preventable.

Why didn't they listen to me when I asked them? 'For what reason do you suppose these young British men are being sent to Afghanistan?', I asked of my handlers on many occasions.

Of course they had their own value system which made it hard for them to believe a foreigner like me, even one from terror-bedevilled Algeria. They repeatedly told themselves suicide bombings in London were impossible. They didn't understand that British boys in the hands of terrorists would adopt a value system of hatred, annihilation and martyrdom. I did understand. I had been in Algeria and seen the corrupting force of terror first hand. In retrospect perhaps they didn't value the information I gave them. There were clues in the fact that they paid me a pittance, which I should have recognised as a sign of them not valuing my information. I believe Britain paid a heavy price for the contempt they held for a so-called snitch.

* * *

My mantra was simple. Anything is possible – it can happen. Moreover it will happen if you don't do something about these fanatics. It was a mantra that literally sent me to the edge of madness. I told the security services and eventually anyone else who would listen, 'They are being trained to come back and murder as many of you as possible'. My greatest fear in all that I did and said was that I wouldn't be believed and I would be taken for a madman. As the record shows, I very nearly succeeded in fulfilling my worst fears.

Finally in Britain I found journalists courageous enough to publish what I said. But then it was almost too late to prevent full-blown terror attacks. The genie had been let out of the jihadist bottle.

I have decided to share this story as a witness to history. I want others to know that the evidence of terror was not hidden. Many of us could see how the spirals of terror fomented by the state in Algeria and the reciprocal terror of those that opposed them in the GIA inevitably became so ferocious that the fates of hundreds of thousands of ordinary people got mangled in the process.

In these circumstances you either joined in, you opposed, or you got mangled. No one makes their way through these killing fields unscathed.

Not everyone has the voice or opportunity to warn others. This is my warning.

Réda Hassaïne
Algiers, Algeria
November 2014

CHAPTER 1

Algeria:
The Jihad Begins

OCTOBER 1988. I had been a journalist for nearly three years. It was a vocation – something I'd inherited from my father and he from his father. The Hassaïnes were committed to the revolution and I was a natural.

However, the world was changing fast and my generation was beginning to find its voice. We had been raised in a time when the revolution had been consolidating. We no longer saw the revolution as political in the same way as our parents had. For our younger generation what was now needed was a social transformation. Twenty-six years after a bitter war of independence liberated the Algerians from the French, we young Algerians wanted to be liberated from the stifling government of the ageing regime of revolutionaries. That too was natural.

Then, over the Sahara desert rolled the storm of political dissent. It was a Wednesday when things began to happen. In Algiers, as in other cities across the country, young people had taken to the street in protest against the dead weight of the *ancien regime*. The whole country was experiencing a popular movement of discontent.

Fed up to the back teeth with promises, the younger generation attacked all the symbols of authority and State they could lay their hands on. They burned and ransacked public buildings and seats of local government and, in particular, targeted the offices of the National Liberation Front (FLN – Front

Nationale de Liberation), which had taken the fight for independence to the French. All the while they chanted anti-government slogans and put fear into the hearts of those who governed.

The President of the Republique was no longer revered. For the first time public admonishment and insulting of the Head of State was heard in the chants of the demonstrators 'Chadli assassin'.

After three days of mayhem General Khaled Nezzar brought the tanks out onto the street. The result was an infamous massacre in which dozens of people died. According to the authorities one hundred and sixty people died. Other sources like the Association of the Victims of October (AV088) claimed more than 400 citizens lost their lives. Worse still it was soon discovered that torture was widely used against those demonstrators who were arrested. This was the beginning of a period of turmoil that only today in 2014 are we beginning to overcome.

In the corridors of the newspapers *El Moudjahid* and *Horizons* rumours began to circulate about where all this might lead. There was talk of fresh investment capital being available to launch new newspapers and many of my colleagues began to plan how they could take advantage of the situation to branch out and set up their own enterprise. My head was elsewhere. I could not shake off a sense that the state should pay for what it had done. AV088 expressed the need for a reckoning with the system governed by the men of the FLN, the most obvious symbol of the State. That is the consequence of the system that had come to be dominated by one party.

International events then overtook us in Algeria. The end of the Cold War, symbolised by the fall of the Berlin Wall, meant the world's attention was focused on other things rather than the tanks of the North African country of Algeria rolling against its civilians. We were not news. The end of the Cold War of course meant the loosening of decades-old friendships between Algeria and its Soviet supporters; this plunged Algeria's revolutionary leadership into an uncertain future.

* * *

In that uncertain international climate, in Algeria we approached our own moment of glasnost on 12th June 1990. In my home neighbourhood I saw a mushrooming of political organisations to put forward people for the proposed electoral lists. It was the first version of the Arab Spring seen in 2012–13.

Amongst these organisations was the Front Islamique du Salut (FIS – The Islamic Salvation Front). The FIS quickly gained ground and popularity, particularly because it wasn't tainted by the sins of our revolutionary fathers.

For decades, following the lead of our former French colonial masters, Algerian society had been politically secular. The Cold War had consolidated the idea that politics was for politicians and not for the old world of tribal allegiances and religious affiliations. Of course unlike the Soviet Union, The FLN had never banished religion. It would have been impossible anyway; the mosque was far too central to most people's lives. Even many lapsed Muslims (in the sense of taking part in Friday prayers) were wedded to the idea that Islam was part of their lives. Now the end of the Cold War would once again let the theological genie out of the bottle.

I had always been the competitive type. I liked being a winner and therefore in the political sphere I was going to choose an electoral winner on the political list. I guess I was what is known as a political opportunist. This was a political ballot – so I put my name forward for the FIS. I hadn't a clue about their ideology and took no interest in attending their meetings to find out if they even had a political manifesto. I was immersed in the world of journalism, football and the good life. I liked going out and partying and I liked living life to the full. I had never been interested in politics up to that point – far from it.

My immature ego got the better of me. It was more out of a sense of vengeance than political conviction that I let my name go forward. It was a chance to take revenge on the FLN and also my boss, which amounted to pretty much the same thing at the time. Most of the managers in the national press were solid FLN supporters, or even card-carrying members, as a consequence of the famous 'section 120' of the party's charter.[*]

In any case I was also being driven by a sense of citizenship. I wanted to help my local district and, more broadly, my neighbourhood. For me it was just a question of who would be the Mayor, whether it was FIS or someone else hardly mattered – the most important thing was to do something for the people. In my defence, I even considered becoming the Mayor although

---

[*] Section 120: Access to positions with official responsibility are reserved for members of the Party. Formatted: English (United States).

being a journalist was a better fit with my own ambitions.

On the day of the election the FIS hit the jackpot and I found myself elected in my commune. It was all a little strange. On the evening of 12thJune 1990 the news flew around the newsrooms of Algiers, and I took part in the raucous celebrations of the FIS in my neighbourhood.

* * *

The following day I was to get my first taste of an Islamist approach to politics. A meeting was arranged to bring together all those newly elected representatives. To my utter surprise the meeting was not held at the Town Hall but instead at the mosque. I was categorically against this approach and I made my opinion known to all those FIS militants present.

I gained the impression that the decision to hold the meeting at the mosque was orchestrated to send out a signal that there would be a new way of conducting affairs in our commune. Their plan seemed to me to be to take over all public spaces and turn them into places of worship. Some militants wanted to go one step further and declared that those who made community-wide political decisions would do so using the mosque as their guiding light.

I began to realise the reality very quickly and discovered to my own cost the real face of these people with whom I had joined forces without taking the trouble to get to know them. It was a brutal awakening from my political naiveté. I was already beginning to get an unpleasant taste in my mouth – I had made a mistake. I met the Mayor on the way out of the meeting and told him about my concerns. He advised me to talk to the man who led this group, Abassi Madani. Good idea I thought, be direct. I got in my car and went straight to see Madani at his home, turning up without an appointment at his house in the fashionable district of the Heights of Algiers.

The red-bearded Sheikh welcomed me into his home with open arms. He was courteous and likeable. I was a journalist and knew how to put people at ease. I was also used to being blunt. I told him what had made me so angry. He listened to me calmly as I continued to ask him to clarify exactly what his policy was.

To my surprise he told me to 'return to the Town Hall and we will organise for you to become the next Member of Parliament'. He even authorised me to go back and speak on behalf of his movement the 'El Djab'ha' – the Front. As much as I was reassured by his wise and serene demeanour, I was also filled with a sense of foreboding. I already smelt politics and behind his sophisticated and fatherly front I sensed a hidden puppet-master pulling strings. How would he arrange, for example, for me to become the next MP I wondered? By the end of our meeting I wasn't sure he could be trusted.

The Algeria I wanted was free, full of energy, life and spirit. An Algeria built on the solid foundations of justice, free will and free enterprise. Unshackled from the misadventures of the past, resolutely focused on the future – modern. I wanted an Algeria that would conquer injustice, where people could live well, where everyone could work and where politics would no longer constantly dwell on nationalistic ambitions. Whether it be in the mosque, the church or the synagogue everyone would be free to choose their place of worship.

Madani himself, from the evidence that soon emerged, was light years away from sharing my dreams for the future of Algeria. He seemed to be surrounded by very strange companions. I went to a press conference with a group of people who appeared to have stepped right out of the middle Ages, dressed in long Arabic robes, beards down to their navels and eyes ringed with khol. They made me feel the fear of the unknown. A BBC journalist, who was based in Tunis and had come along especially to get an interview, said to me in passing that this whole gathering had a strange air about it.

Seeing these gentlemen it was clear that you didn't need to see their hand to know what cards they were going to play. I realised that at best they would replicate the FLN but with theology replacing Marxist-Leninist ideology as their central driving principle. It didn't take a genius to work out that this would mean less freedom.

Madani was expecting me at that meeting and had reserved me a spot on the top table for the upcoming parliamentary elections in eighteen months time. But the FIS's top man had misread me – as soon as I walked out of that house of his I had made up my mind, I would leave the FIS. My name and my position as a journalist had given me plenty of advantages. It was fashionable in those quarters to hide behind someone with my credibility. They could use it to legitimise the Islamist Party. It was clear that I was the only journalist who had been elected in these elections. It put me in a precarious position.

After my interview with Madani, I left to see the head of the FIS party list, Khaled Bouchemal. He was making his preparations to take over as the

Mayor of our commune, Rais Hamidou. I told him about my visit to the home of Abassi Madani and brought him up to speed on what ground we had covered. To my surprise, he launched into a tirade of half-veiled threats. 'You had better watch out. We know your type. You'd better make yourself scarce fast in this neighbourhood if you know what's good for you'. He even openly accused me of being an agent of the dreaded military security.

Stunned by Khaled Bouchemal's allegation, I asked myself where he could have picked up such nonsense. I didn't have time to dwell on that because if you give a dog a bad name it usually sticks and that's what Bouchemal did for me. It was hard to shake off his false allegation that I was an agent of the state. For the people where I lived this became a self-fulfilling prophecy. I had the head for such work so why wouldn't I be doing it?

I took these threats to heart and knowing I wasn't in the mood to fight such drivel from the inside, I went straight to my boss at the newspaper and asked for a year's sabbatical, which he gave me without hesitation. I went to the Air Algeria travel agent and bought a ticket for Stockholm, travelling onward to eventually land in Paris. Chastened, it was in France that I settled; it was Autumn 1990.

A well-paid job in a removal company meant that I could afford to live comfortably and things were going well until February 1991. The first Gulf War changed the mood – coming as it did off the back of the Soviet withdrawal from Afghanistan and the Allied decision to defend Kuwait against Iraqi aggression. A wave of anti-Arab sentiment swept through Europe; the racists raised their heads. We were undesirables and the work I was doing began to drop off. When I rang on the bell of a French household I was welcomed with distrust. The boss decided to tighten his belt and I was given the sack. I returned to Algeria, back to square one, in March 1991.

* * *

Things at home had become more difficult. The Cold War long departed, a new Gulf War underway, the Islamists agitating against the infidel's invasion of Muslim lands. A mess abroad seemed to contrast with a political renaissance at home.

I took up my job again at the newspaper *Horizons*. More precisely, I was able to indulge my passion for sport. I narrowed my field of view to football and in particular Mouloudia FC the oldest of Algeria's football clubs. At home we were all MCA supporters. I had played in Mouloudia colours from nursery through school. It was a congenital virus I'd inherited from my family. My grandfather was one of the founders of MCA; my uncles played for them and my father had been part of the back up support team. One thing I took care to do was to keep myself well away from political discussions.

The one party political set up had finished, so had the one way of thinking. Algeria was basking in the glow of democratic renewal. Quite naïvely I thought that the secret police that kept an eye on the press had given up the day job and moved on to new pastures. However, I discovered that actually there wasn't now one set of eyes on journalists, there were dozens. Fellow journalists had jumped on the payroll of the secret services. Some took their instructions from the police and their secret friends others with the local police through their communications specialist Colonel Hallab. The smarter colleagues went all the way and built relations with the mythical military intelligence. It became almost a badge of fashionable honour to have links with the military as a journalist.

I saw one amongst them, who had a long ponytail, hanging around one of the mosques in Algiers. Mounir Boudjema was to become the Deputy Managing Editor of the daily *Liberte*. He was very proud of his network of contacts amongst the Algerian intelligence agencies.

In such a polluted and feverish atmosphere, where the intelligence services were crawling all over the media I was beginning to feel my passion for journalism waning. I would need to find a clean and unblemished newspaper or even start one of my own so I wouldn't be dragged into the manipulations of all these external agencies.

With an old childhood friend and colleague at *Horizons*, Athmane Oudina, I decided to set up a regional weekly newspaper called, *Ici Algers*. It was a new title to add to the kaleidoscope of papers in the new Algeria. Mounir Boudjema, the mouthpiece of the security service agents who pulled his strings approached me when he threw a party at his girlfriend's house. He advised me not to throw myself into this new intellectual venture. 'Reda, do whatever you want. Open a pizzeria or something but don't throw your money into a newspaper. You will get screwed'.

I was pretty sure he was not just offering me friendly personal advice. The Algerian secret services had just had their own perestroika moment and reconfigured themselves as the Departement du Renseingement et Secu-rite (DRS – Department of Intelligence and Security). It was clear that they would not take kindly to a former elected official of the FIS starting up a new independent newspaper just at the moment when they were struggling to curb a plethora of Islamist publications. That was a rod I'd made for my own back.

Stubborn as I was, the friendly warning from Mounir far from discour-aged me, but the harsh reality was that without any serious links or patronage from the army or the police my newspaper had no chance of sinking its roots into the emerging media ecology in Algeria. I had no influential personality supporting me so that I could take advantage of the advertising revenue that flowed from the State's advertising conglomerate ANEP, which had a monopoly on advertising placements. ANEP was busy cultivating around a dozen new publications with pages of advertisements. But marketing people in private businesses would not place their copy with me knowing that I was out on my own. The risk was too great. *Ici Algers* withered on the vine.

At the age of thirty, I no longer had a salary and I now had to find a way of finding the resources to start up my own business. My intuition told me that there must be some way of making money in this virgin territory of the media. I just had to find out what it was. I moved back to Paris.

CHAPTER 2

Trapped by the Algerian Security Services

I N PARIS I quickly teamed up with an Iraqi political refugee Al-Ayach. Exiles together trying to survive and still have an impact on the political chaos back home we decided to set up a press distribution service. It was – with plenty of hindsight – a bit ambitious given our means but we had been offered a great business deal by one of the largest distribution agencies in France.

They were keen to give us a substantial amount of help; access to signage, billboards, advertising and a distribution network second to none. As a sweetener they proposed selling us *Paris-Match* at twenty-five per cent of the cover price. That was a potentially lucrative contract. In my wildest dreams I never thought I would get such an opportunity, I felt I was in the right place at the right time.

All I needed to make the whole thing work was approval by the Algerian authorities. I returned to Algeria to see if I could seal the deal. The first step in doing this was to make contact with the Algerian police to go through the right procedure to establish a business. For this they would have to conduct their usual enquiries. Establishing the paperwork for the business would run through the office of the Renseignement Generaux, commonly known as the RG.

On 29th July 1994 shortly after my return to Algiers I was summoned to police headquarters. Being a Friday it was prayer day in the city. I thought the request to see me was a little bizarre. It made me nervous to be honest. But I told myself when the country was in such a state it was only normal that the police would want to conduct their business when and where they thought it necessary. Even on a bank holiday.

I took the view as I had nothing to hide there was no reason not to go and meet with them. I assumed, of course, that my business enquiry needed some detailed questioning to establish exactly what I was proposing to do. If you want to set up a foreign press company in Algeria you had to expect a more detailed level of scrutiny.

I was even more surprised when the RG officer Mohamed suggested we move to a café opposite the central headquarters. A strange way to conduct official business I thought.

A journalist I knew really well accompanied Mohammed. He had been a colleague of mine in a past life, the sports correspondent in the east of the country in a town called Skikda. I couldn't for the life me work out what Yacine Merzougui had to do with all this. Our paths had crossed over the years as I had moved around the country on assignment, but what intrigued me was he had always been a regional journalist and I never realised he had operated in the capital city, mostly in Sétif, Oran and Constantine.

After some brief small talk, the officer suggested that we go over to his offices to continue the conversation. As I stepped across the threshold of this building I had no idea I was about to enter a parallel universe. Yacine was still beside us like a stalker and his presence was beginning to bother me. What the hell did he have to do with my business enquiry I asked myself? I was in for a real shock.

As soon as we got to the office where I was going to be interviewed, Yacine turned to the RG officer Mohammed and told him rather brusquely to leave us alone as we had some business to discuss. It was clear who was in charge. Mohammed left us and wished me luck. I was dumbstruck. Suddenly, Yacine, the correspondent from the daily newspaper *Horizons* metamorphosed before my very eyes.

He sat down behind the desk and started to remonstrate with me. I was struggling to get a grip on this changing situation. I was also shocked by his lecturing tone. It was as if we had never known or worked together before. This was a guy who'd worked on some small-time journal and was now putting on airs and graces talking to me like I was an imbecile. I could feel my blood pressure rising. The penny dropped. This was no longer a journalist in front of me but a hardened cop. What kind of mess had I landed in here I thought to myself. Yacine soon enlightened me. 'You do realise that a couple of days ago the police were coming to arrest you, don't you? It was only because I intervened that they decided to leave you alone for the time being. I told them that I could guarantee you were a man of good character. I told them you come from a really good family'. They must have been watching me from my arrival at the airport. I had been completely oblivious – that was about to radically change.

'What are you talking about? Arrest me, for what? What am I supposed to have done?' Yacine dropped a complete bombshell. I was accused of conspiring to assassinate the Mayor from the Islamic Salvation Front (FIS) in my borough, in Algiers. My jaw dropped. I mean I clearly didn't like the guy, but murder? Yacine knew this was completely fabricated.

It got worse. He said there was incriminating evidence against me and added that my name was on a list of those involved in the bombing of Algiers airport in August 1992 which left dozens dead. He claimed that I had been seen with one of the masterrminds of the bombing, Hocine Abderrahim. As God is my witness, I knew this fellow no better than Adam or Eve.

Yacine seemed to sense that I could see through these stories and he continued, 'Even if you think you can save your skin in these matters, there is something else out of which no expensive lawyer can get you. In this you are really facing trouble'. What was my alleged crime? The person I had decided to set up business with in my press distribution service was a very dangerous man indeed, according to Yacine: 'Mr. Al-Ayash is an Iraqi political refugee who is well known as an agent for the Israeli secret service'.

That was barely credible, but from my point of view sitting in this office it was catastrophic. In a country as sensitive to the Palestinian plight as Algeria, almost anything could be forgiven but not collaboration with Mossad. Supposedly this fellow's father was a political refugee in Algeria along with his entire family. None of what Yacine was telling me made any sense – it was all nonsense.

The ordeal went on for two solid hours. The rant was full of menace and threats of violence and progressively I could feel my blood running colder. I was so overwhelmed I could feel myself close to fainting several times. I began to have visions of myself being arrested and shoved in one of their notorious underground prisons. My subconscious was playing tricks; I started imaging what streets I could run through in Algiers if I managed to get away from these thugs once the ordeal was over.

While Yacine continued, I kept asking myself if I was in some kind of nightmare from which I would suddenly wake up. His monotonous voice was deadening my senses and I was no longer listening to a word he was saying; all I could think of was how to get myself out of the police headquarters in one piece. I was totally confused.

I figured a punch to the head might stun him long enough to get out of the building and then I could report the incident to my friends in the media. But then I realised they might be like Yacine – they might pull out a gun and shoot me. That gave me the idea of pulling out his gun and shooting him with it. But where would I flee to once I'd killed him? Join the underground movement of the GIA? I might fall in with the wrong group and be eliminated by them. What had I done to get myself in this damn mess? All I had wanted to do was set up a little distribution business and live quietly.

To think that I'd thought I would just come here to answer a few innocuous questions and fill in a couple of forms to get authorisation. Instead I was being accused of some of the most dreadful crimes possible. I could certainly no longer see myself getting off the plane from Paris with an armful of magazines to distribute across Algeria to make some money.

So finally after softening me up with threats and intimidation, our friend the so-called journalist got to the point. Agents from the DRS had infiltrated terrorist networks and they now knew where to collect bundles of cash collected by overseas fundraisers in particular from London that were destined for the GIA's underground operatives in Algeria. London had become the epicentre of the Islamists in Europe and the revolving door for terrorists going into and coming out of the field of operations further afield like Afghanistan.

From the fog and confusion in my mind a clearer picture was emerging. They wanted me to travel to London and Paris in order to pick up these funds on behalf of the Mukhabarat. The Mukhabarat was an alternative name for the General Intelligence Service (RG) or the main arm of the Algerian Security Services. 'Look we know your business and you have a credible back story because you already have a British visa. You are the ideal man for the job,' Yacine said with a smile.

Instinctively my answer would have been no. But those were not the words that rolled off my tongue. Instead I asked Yacine, 'Who the hell are you? Are you a cop or a journalist?' He burst out laughing with such gusto that I could practically see his tonsils. 'Neither one nor the other,' he said.

I no longer understood anything about what was happening. He hadn't been a journalist for all those years I'd known him as a sports correspondent. But wasn't it me who had counted the words in his copy to decide how much he should get paid? He wasn't a cop even though he was sitting opposite me during an interrogation in police headquarters. Now I was getting my senses back and I continued to press him. 'So who are you then? Who is it that wants me to go to London to pick up these bundles of cash?'

With a mischievous smile and a puffing up of his shoulders he gave me a wink and whispered in a soft voice, as if delivering a state secret. 'We are the *Greens*. The others are the *Blues*.' Now clarity was returning to the proceedings. What he was saying was that he was part of the army of agents that serviced the Secret Police of General Tewfik, the DRS nicknamed the Greens because of their military fatigues. The *Blues* were Chief of Police Tounsi's men. They wore blue uniforms.

* * *

Since the early days of Algerian independence an alliance had been created between the separate intelligence services of the police and army. At times it was an uneasy alliance, even a competitive one, but together they created a formidable network of spies who kept tabs on tens of thousands of people. Often it meant that people were spying on their own families.

By telling me his great secret and real position, Yacine no doubt assumed that I would be seduced by the offer to work with the DRS. To be fair there were plenty of people who had been seduced down the years by the prestige of working for the security services – even those who fantasised about being asked. Not for me. I wanted no part of their little game. I didn't see myself being involved on either side of this espionage game. What, I asked myself, was the point of a man like me without any problems entering into this kind of environment at a time like this? Frankly I had already dabbled in politics and had seen how badly burned I had been by that experience. I was now more convinced than ever that Algeria was on a downhill slope. I, for one, had no idea what the end game was likely to be so with my preference for picking winners there was no prospect of me calling that here. I now had one single thought in my head – how do I get myself out of this mess?

I was starting to reason properly again. It made sense that all the allegations that Yacine had made were so over-blown, so exaggerated that they would never stand up in a courtroom. What gave me pause for thought, though, was the hardly veiled threat that the day after tomorrow I might be going about my business and a sixteen-year old street kid could murder me instructed by the service, answerable to no one. The bottom line was my life was now in his hands and he was relishing it, I could see that in his eyes. I remembered what an unpleasant person he had always been. Now he was in control I concluded I was on a hiding to nothing.

Given the atrocious reputation of the Algerian secret service, I couldn't ignore his threats. In short I had little choice at this stage but to agree to help them, even if a little voice in my head was advising me to go into hiding or immediate exile.

How would I get out of the country to extricate myself from the mess? My mug shot would be everywhere, at a time when the country was in a state of general collapse. My name would be on every border guard's list at every airport or sea crossing. The country was obviously in free-fall and these thugs were taking advantage of that fact. The State was slowly losing its authority, terror was everywhere and had reached alarming levels.

In these circumstances who was left to protect human rights and stop abuses by the State in the name of upholding their authority? Kidnappings, summary executions, arbitrary arrests (of which I now had first-hand experience), were all part of what filled the vacuum. When the state fights back and hands power to lunatics in the middle of this end game, what was to stop a small journalist like me falling off a cliff? They had a ready-made excuse. It was the GIA. Another atrocity committed by the Islamists.

Back to Yacine. The more I sat there staring at him the more I was putting the pieces of the puzzle together in my head. I recalled crossing his path a few months earlier in December 1993 at police headquarters when I had come to report those death threats against myself from the Islamist brothers of the FIS. He made all sorts of excuses at the time that he was visiting a policeman friend. He also mentioned he was about to go to Sweden on business.

It suddenly clicked in my mind that the GIA journal and central organ,

Al-Ansar, was published overseas in Stockholm. It seemed logical that in my last days in journalism at *Horizons* I was probably surrounded by a whole cast of snitches like Yacine. Back then I had only from time to time had dealings with the Office of Preventative Security (BSP) – the arm of the ruling party that acted as military security.

Yes, all those journalists were indeed great sources of intelligence, a veritable mine of information but at the same time they had the tendency to be incredibly indiscreet. They started to be seen as spies in the service of those in power. It was no surprise to me that politicians and public opinion started mistrusting journalists and the media.

Yacine could sense I was reluctant. I had taken too long to say yes. So he changed tack. He started remembering the times when we had been colleagues; he must have decided this was an easier way to buy me off. 'We can give you everything you need, forget about going abroad,' he told me. The ordeal ended with him laying out two stark alternatives: collaborate with them and I would get be rewarded or refuse and no one could guarantee that I would still be alive the day after tomorrow. As we say in Algeria, 'What would a dead man do in the place of a gravedigger?'

Leaving police headquarters I felt the rush of warm air on my face. I was trembling all over. I felt my legs about to buckle underneath me. Now I had entered the world of paranoia where it was hard to know whom to trust. Who knew what these men were capable of? Having walked, or more accurately, stumbled into the lair of the devil, I realised that my life would never be the same again.

The conversation with Yacine had ended with me being told that I was to go the Mustapha Hospital in Algiers to meet someone who would hand over money destined for the GIA. I had no way of knowing if another trap had been set for me. Furthermore the next part of the bargain had already been decided. I would make several trips to London to collect money on their behalf and if I did the job well I could live the rest of my life the way I wanted to. As a bonus, they suggested I could get a newspaper of my own.

It now became clear that all along the arch manipulators of the DRS had sprung a trap to get me to go to London to track down where the funds for the GIA were coming from.

The Algerian State had its tentacles everywhere.

CHAPTER 3

Londonistan Beckons

YACINE CERTAINLY MADE me think hard about what life had come to in my own country. It also made me come up with a plan – fast. I had been asked to go to London to pick up the GIA's money which I saw as a chance to get a one-way ticket out of the mayhem. The problem I had was this: if he could not guarantee I would come back Yacine would never sanction me going in the first place. I could end up an embarrassing witness to the fact that the Algerian secret services were heavily implicated in manipulating the GIA.

A full week elapsed between my encounter with Yacine and the mission to the hospital. It was a desperately uncomfortable time for me. I could feel a change in myself but had no grasp on what was happening. I distrusted just about everyone. I no longer knew who I could trust. I was in the grip of a terrible paranoia where I saw potential assassins at every turn. Bearded assassins, assassins dressed in qamis (Islamic traditional dress), assassins in suits, assassins just hanging around where I lived. I saw GIA disguised as assassins and assassins disguised as colleagues. It was one of the worst times of my life. Everyone and anyone was armed with a weapon tucked up their shirt or in their belt. The only questions in my mind; was it a regular weapon or worse, a machete that would inflict a slow, painful death.

I was completely enveloped in this paranoia when Yacine called me. I wasn't expecting his call – I didn't honestly want it either – but it was better than a bullet or a slice of a machete. He fixed a meeting the following day for the early morning, Monday 7th August 1994.

He was quite relaxed when I approached him and he had a kind of fixed smile. The smile of someone who knows they have you in their control. He took hold of my arm and steered us towards a small coffee house opposite the post office. I had psyched myself up to discuss the trip to London, but to my surprise he wanted to talk about a job that needed to be done that very afternoon. I trusted Yacine least of all. 'At one o'clock you will need to go to the Mustapha Hospital and meet a fellow from 'Beznazzi.' He works with the militia. He'll give you a load of cash which is supposed to go to the group led by Emir Abdelhadi.'

'What – today?' I asked clearly in a surprised tone. 'Yes, today'. 'And this Beznazzi fellow is he going to know exactly who I am?' 'It's easy. You will be waiting in front of the Mustapha cardiology clinic. You will recognise him by his yellow shirt and red tie. He'll be carrying a large bag and in the other hand he'll have a bunch of keys. You take hold of the bag with the money in and you go home. You then wait for my telephone call. It couldn't be simpler.'

* * *

I figured that if I survived this encounter I might just find a way out of this mess. I pulled on a jacket and headed over to the Place 1er Mai to check out the location where I was going to meet 'Beznazzi'. I won't feign the fear I felt. I had to draw on what remnants of courage I had left and after spotting a man in a yellow shirt and a red tie I tried hard not to make it too obvious I was absolutely terrified. I had good reason to be fearful, as I had to assume that this fellow was an agent for the GIA.

I was in such a state I was trying to remember the code that Yacine had given me but my mind had gone blank. The fellow frowned at me suspiciously saying that the code I had given was incomplete. I gritted my teeth ready for him to pull out his weapon and shoot me dead on the spot.

Breathless and my stomach knotted with fear, all I could muster was a feeble excuse that Abdelhadi had only given me the details of what he was wearing. Abdelhadi being our fake 'Emir'. The fellow looked at me even more suspiciously and suggested we go to grab a coffee and later that evening he could try and make some calls to see if I was who I said I was. I followed him as far as rue Kelifa Boukhalfa.

He entered into a craft shop and I followed him. Pretending to look at one of the items to buy it, he held out his hand without looking at me and passed me the bag containing the money. I took it as calmly as I could as if nothing had happened. We then both left the shop and went our separate ways.

As soon as I turned on my heels I darted into the maze of back alleys in Algiers. I knew them well enough to make sure if anyone was following me I could lose them. For once I felt my local knowledge was an advantage. I ran as far as the Bab El Oued, taking twists and turns for a good thirty minutes. From there I took a taxi towards Pointe-Pescade where I arrived home in one piece. I locked myself in one of the bedrooms and started to count the money inside. I wanted to check if it was counterfeit notes or even just newspaper clippings. It was real all right. I knew then that the situation was real too and I was in deep up to my neck. But at least I wasn't dead yet. I was also checking frantically – by now I could feel the sweat trickling down my back – to make sure I wasn't carrying a bomb or some explosives.

Once the bag was empty I could feel my heartbeat returning to normal whilst I counted the notes, forty million in local currency. That was a king's ransom, enough in Algiers to buy a nice little car or even a small apartment.

Why had I been chosen for this kind of mission? Why would they trust putting me in charge of such a small fortune, particularly when they knew I was up to my eyes with financial problems? More importantly why would I be trusted to know about their secret relationship with the GIA? And if the trip to the hospital was a test, what of the plainclothes operatives I thought I saw staking out the hospital? Was that all my paranoid imaginings or reality?

I was pretty convinced that whatever was going on, there was no way that someone like me, who wasn't on the payroll, would be sent to pick up a bag stuffed with cash from a supposed terrorist without monitoring it very closely indeed. For all I knew they could have already intervened after the transaction, which was set as a trap to catch someone who was a real GIA activist.

Paranoia kicking in I also thought perhaps it was a way of setting a trap for me. What if someone had been taking photos at the point I met the fellow with the bag and then followed us to the craft shop?

I figured if I didn't come back from London, it would be easy for them to send a photo to Scotland Yard of my liaison with a terrorist and it would be a simple process to get me locked up and extradited. If there had been a bomb or weapons in the bag I would be completely done for. The very next day I would be headline news in the Algerian papers or splashed all over the television. In my experience it was common practice to see people suddenly appear all over the media guilty before trial. I'd be made an example of, confessing my links to terrorists and goodness knows what else. Perhaps they would force me to confess to assassination attempts or even confessing it was me who assassinated President Boudiaf.

To try and calm my nerves and distance myself from this mess, I began to scribble down a few hurried notes. These are the same notes that have now enabled me to retrace my steps through this sad, dangerous and terrifying part of my life all these years later.

'Yes, Réda,' I told myself, 'you are really in trouble here.' I didn't dare step out the door or even peer through a window to see if our house was surrounded – to see how many agents had turned up to arrest me for belonging to a terrorist group. There were phantoms everywhere. After all, they had enough circumstantial evidence to suggest my links to terrorism.

I'd been elected a FIS official in my hometown. They had pictures of my contact with 'El Beznassi' and I was now in possession of 40 million in local currency. What more evidence would they need to deport me to the south and one of their camps for tens of thousands of undesirables?

The more I thought about it the more my heart and morale sank. They had all the evidence they needed to take me to one of the special courts for hearing terrorist cases. The charges were mounting against me. They could practically invent anything they wanted and even the greatest lawyers in the world wouldn't be able to save my neck from the guillotine. It was just as Yacine had described the scenario to me in that first meeting. His words, 'you are screwed' kept spinning around and around in my head getting louder as the minutes passed.

But, perverse as it might sound now, I wanted to know what I had done wrong. I may have been elected as an official of the FIS but, as quickly as I could, I had moved myself away from having to take any decisions as an FIS official as I began to see the writing on the wall. Unsurprisingly, I had never been invited back into the political arena. Then I reminded myself of how this whole business started with the promise of a business venture made in Paris coming back to Algeria. Maybe that's where the root of the anxiety lay. What I planned was potentially embarrassing.

Then the telephone rang. It was Yacine. The conversation was very brief. He asked me if I had collected the bag of cash. I told him 'Yes.' Yacine hung up immediately, saying 'I'll call you later tonight.' This only fuelled my anxiety. It was obviously over for me. Yacine was simply mocking me asking if I had received the loot. He knew very well how things had gone with his network of spies in hot pursuit. I was not so naïve to think I had fooled my tail and that I wasn't filmed, photographed and followed all the way home despite my best efforts at evasion.

✳ ✳ ✳

Everyone knows how omnipotent the secret police were at that time with their noses in everyone's business in everyone's home. The prevailing wisdom was you weren't even safe going to the toilet. At which point in my thinking I ran to check my own toilet, crashing the door open as if that would crush the agent against the wall like an errant spider. I ran through the house checking the wardrobes, under the beds anywhere from where someone could spring a surprise ambush. But there was no one. My head was in a spin. They had me where they wanted me – fearing and believing I was now a terrorist in their eyes.

At 11pm, Yacine rang again. He just barked down the phone line, '10.30 tomorrow morning same place', and hung up. 'Just leave me alone,' I said in my head before replacing the handset.

That night was like a blank sheet on which I painted the conversation I had had with Yacine and all the images that now tumbled from my head of every conceivable unpleasant thing that could happy to me. Through all this I had completely ignored my wife who was busy in the house caring for my young son. I was so immersed in my own problems I barely registered the baby crying. It was if I was at home all alone, disconnected from the rest of the world. Things had become so desperate that I even suspected my parents – who lived close by – and wife of working for the secret police.

How was it that the mission to London which I was being asked to do would be combating the terrorists of the GIA, when they were practically GIA themselves. Who the hell would I be able to trust? If I were to join the secret police it seemed tantamount to joining the GIA. How the hell did I get into this mess when I just wanted to start up a small business and have a quiet life with my wife and kid? I had to remind myself this was Algeria in collapse.

Waiting for the next meeting at the post office I was extraordinarily impatient. What an idiot. I was forgetting I had a wife and a child. How could I forget my own son? What a true mess had befallen me. It was Salim's crying that morning calling for his mother that had brought me rapidly back to reality. I had no right to give up on them. I had no right to leave him as an orphan. I had no business to fulfil the Algerian saying: 'He lived without possessions and he died without handing anything on.'

From that reality check just a few days into my ordeal I began to pull myself together. I needed to get a grip and remember I had come from good stock, I was intelligent and Yacine was an intellectual imbecile so I had to play the game to my advantage. I would have to work out my own destiny. I needed to toughen up and show some courage so that I avoided being arrested and getting sucked into their little cabal. My blood after all would be a tiny drop in the ocean of Algerian blood that they had already spilled.

I left the house at 8.15 that morning without having washed. I had no appetite for breakfast. In fact the previous two days had seen me eat hardly a crumb of bread although I had been smoking one cigarette after another. I went out onto the terrace and took a good look around to see if there were any agents from the DRS or terrorists lurking around the house. If only I could get on one of those boats and cross the Mediterranean with my wife and son, I said to myself. Or perhaps just swim across to the coast to the north. 'Patience,' I told myself, 'get this meeting over with and just get a good lie of the land, then decide.'

I left my house and hailed a taxi and jumped in looking to see if I was being followed. The entire journey I kept looking through the back window to see if anyone was following, goodness knows what the taxi driver made of my paranoia. I repeatedly told him he was driving too fast for my liking. As we approached the Hotel Aletti I asked the driver to stop. The last 500 metres I wanted to walk. I walked into the café where I would be meeting Yacine. At least there were plenty of people having an early morning coffee and cake. But even in this gentile place of tables and cups of coffee I asked myself how many of the people at the tables were spies or terrorists.

I ordered a strong coffee and then waited for Yacine. One hour passed and still Yacine failed to materialise. Two further hours and still no Yacine. My eyes were riveted on the entrance and I stared at everyone who came through that door just in case Yacine turned up in disguise. After downing three cups of strong coffee and smoking at least a dozen cigarettes I was ready to be peeled off the ceiling. Two and a half hours of waiting was my limit. I got up and walked out of the café. I would find Yacine in the crowded streets somehow.

I walked back and forth from the main post office and Place Audin by the coffee house and took great care not to be seen on Boulevard Amirouche because that was where the notorious police headquarters were. I was almost tempted to make a detour via the police station but I thought better of venturing into the lions' den.

There was every possibility that if I found myself there again I could be kidnapped and who knew what could happen then or if anyone would ever find out. I'd be another name added to the already too long missing list. My wife would then join the other families of the 'disappeared' who held regular protests. She, like me, was a journalist and had the power of the pen at her fingertips. She could warn the international organisations like Amnesty of our plight and raise awareness of the abuse of human rights. She could make a lot of noise.

Of course the only problem with that strategy would be that she could then disappear and Salim would be orphaned twice over. No father, no mother. Then my parents might disappear. My father was also a well-known journalist in his time. If the DRS agents didn't pick them up then there would be a good chance that the thugs from the GIA would take care of them. So, I reasoned, better not to take the risk in the first place. I returned to the main post office and continued my wait for Yacine.

It was now 5pm. Five hours – never had anyone kept me waiting that long. I was sure that he had calculated every part of his move that day. He wanted to introduce me to slow torture of my morale. I wished he would just come and get his money. I didn't want to be found with such a princely sum in my possession, too many questions would be asked. And the trip to London – did I need to prepare or was it all just nonsense? Was I now officially an agent or not?

There was no time to be lost in fighting terrorism and this past four hours was lost time. I decided eventually to go home. I was not looking forward to another night of anxiety and nightmares, my head awash with all those unanswered questions. As for Yacine, he had clearly followed my progress since my days at the old newspaper *Horizons*. He had studied what I was about without me realising and now he wanted to recruit me but for what exactly?

Now it was the 8pm news. I could hear in the distance the tired and stale news programme. I'd lost faith in listening to that fatuous nonsense. Every day it was the same format. First there would be men standing up spouting nonsense, trying to defend the regime against those who condemned it. Then men sitting down pretending to do something as government ministers, all sitting around on armchairs, nodding wisely. Finally, it would end with all the men laid out as the day's fatalities, always described as victims of terrorism taken to their final resting place. That was the only narrative that Algerian television seemed to understand. Victims of terrorism they might have been, but it was never clear whose terror.

✱ ✱ ✱

For the next few days I didn't receive any calls, not even from Yacine. There I was, waiting at the end of the line. I was exhausted with hunger and a profound lack of sleep. I was a walking wreck again. Each subsequent day that passed Yacine would phone to say, 'Tomorrow, same time same place,' and hang up. No wasted words, never quite enough time for me to spit out the words yes or no. The telephone was almost certainly bugged. Exhausted I had laid flat out on my bed – I was dreaming.

After several days like this, I calmed myself sufficiently to gather my thoughts. I steeled myself for the 10.30am meeting at the post office. I took the same route I had played over and over in my mind. The same anxieties and the same apprehension with the taxi driver filled me with fear as he took me from la Pointe Pescade to the Hotel Aletti. From there I counted every step towards the café – three hundred and twenty two. But no sooner had I sat down than I caught sight of Yacine getting out of a white Renault van. As soon as he stepped inside the café he motioned to me to follow him urgently. We jumped into the cab of the van. It was a very tight squeeze in between a giant of a driver and a surly cop. Yacine introduced him to me under the pseudonym Abdelhadi – it seems a lot of agents are called Abdelhadi.

'I'm a little puzzled by this whole Abdelhadi business. This fellow doesn't look like much of an Emir to me', I thought to myself. I was also puzzled because to me the driver wasn't your archetypal looking terrorist. He was a handsome fellow, light brown hair; a huge physique, blue eyes and fair, almost white skin. Funniest of all, he had rosy cheeks. I guessed he must have been a Berber. Dressed in the usual blue jeans and t-shirt with blue stripes he looked like a Breton sailor. He seemed quite shy and he uttered not a single word apart from the occasional grunt to agree with something Yacine said. I had no idea where we were going.

Yacine was armed. It was the first time I'd been in such close proximity to someone who was armed since I had done my national service. He had a Kalashnikov under the front seat and his sidekick had a sawn-off shotgun (commonly known as a mahchoucha), a typical Algerian weapon used by terrorists. When I saw Yacine fiddling with his Kalashnikov I was terrified.

All my fears came flooding back. I was an embarrassing witness. I'd discovered the loot. At the very minimum I had discovered that the DRS and GIA was at times one and the same thing. So here I was with the Emir Abdelhadi with his henchman Yacine. I'm unconvinced this is an Islamist plot. That 40 million was my Achilles heel. Some poor mug had passed it over thinking he had been had by the GIA. But now their game was becoming clear. I'm about to be liquidated, rubbed out, nullified. Tomorrow the press headlines would scream 'Réda Hassaïne, former journalist on the Horizon Daily, has been assassinated by the GIA.' Another fiction created by the secret state. Another journalist becomes a martyr to freedom.

Appropriately, we had arrived at the Boulevard of the Martyrs. Not only were they professional but poetic too. We were now very close to the main Algerian television station. Abdelhadi parked the car with great care and Yacine told me to jump out. We both walked towards the television building. Now I was certain. Before the kill they were going to make me confess like other terrorists had done on primetime television. That would guarantee a clean kill without the need for physical torture.

It was all psychological torture in line with what I'd been subjected to the past dozen infernal days. Much worse, I'd convinced myself, than the use of electrical currents, wet blankets and suffocation. I was now ready to confess to any crime. I was washed up, finished, kaput. I was hoping for one last wish that the broadcast would be live. Then I would scream as loud as I could – 'I am innocent, I am innocent, the GIA and DRS are in cahoots. I don't want to die'.

Of course I knew they would instantly go to a black screen and cut the sound. The announcer would interrupt the broadcast. *'Dear viewers we apologise for the interruption to our broadcast due to circumstances beyond our control.'*

Meanwhile, I would have been dispatched efficiently, swiftly and silently.

Or perhaps they would execute me live on television. Why not? They did it with President Boudiaf. Why not with me too, a simple terrorist? My execution would serve as a warning to other embarrassing witnesses to their complicity in jihadi terror in the same way as the assassination of the unlucky President Boudiaf had reminded his successors as Head of State that he should follow orders.

We passed the television station. All these gibbering thoughts started to be replaced by other less attractive ones. So now they are going to hole me up in a secret flat. My family is not even going to get one last chance to say goodbye. Another added to the list of the disappeared.

When they ask what has happened to me they will be told that I have joined the GIA underground. The proof is right at home they will be told. Where did that 40 million come from that Yacine has now come to reclaim? He wasn't even going to talk to me about it. He would just go and fetch it after my execution to hold it up as a trophy, shaking his head at the proof that I was a GIA agent. He would take the loot and then bring out the guy who passed it to me, softened up to squeal, '*It was him, Réda Hassaïne was GIA scum.*'

I don't know where this was getting me but I had lost all sense of perspective, my senses completely overtaken with fear. To my astonishment, Yacine invited me into a pizzeria. I really didn't feel like pizza. The three of us sat down. Three coffees were instantly produced. I was clueless as to what was going on. All I know was that I was in a trance-like state. It was as if I had been drugged. Perhaps it was the coffee or they had managed to stick a hypodermic needle in me in the squashed cab. I was, metaphorically speaking, floating outside myself looking back on this poor forlorn creature at the mercy of circumstance. My life could never be the same after all this. How could it be?

Yacine brought me back down to earth and out of my dream with a thump by handing me a wad of used notes, saying that I should take them and buy a ticket to London. 'I suggest you reserve a place for next Friday,' he ordered me, as if I was some kind of subordinate.

'I'm not out of the woods yet,' I thought leaving the pizzeria. We got back into the Renault and after a few hundred metres Yacine dropped me off, warning me not to forget what we had discussed.

Crazy, I said to myself. Not once did he ask about getting the 40 million.

He never even broached the subject. As soon as I got home I rushed to where I had hidden the bag with this cursed devil's haul. I asked my wife if anyone had stopped by the house asking for me.

I insisted she tried to remember if anyone had come by. 'I've been here all day. Do you think I am deaf or stupid?' I grabbed my passport and ran to the travel agent. Air Algeria flight to London, open return for Algiers, even though the trip was anticipated to be for 48 hours only. I had no intention of coming back to this madhouse once I set foot on British soil, I would stay there before I became tomorrow's news. I had a full week to prepare to get my wife and son out of the country. All other plans could go on hold. The trip to London was my path back to sanity and salvation; a way to put this nightmare and almost certain death behind me, once Yacine had played his game out.

* * *

12ᵗʰ August 1994 was my thirty-third birthday. I felt fifty. At quarter to eight the telephone rang. Yacine wanted to meet me at noon on the dot at El Biar, Kennedy Place. So much for freedom Mr American President (if only a name could demand righteousness). He wanted me to bring the 40 million. Finally. All I could think was what a relief, finally I can get rid of this golden burden which in my eyes was nothing more than a large finger pointing at my links with the DRS's version of the GIA.

At exactly midday Yacine turned up in the same Renault Express van, shadowed permanently by his sidekick Adbelhadi. I got in the car and placed the bag with the 40 million on my lap. Yacine took no notice at all, carrying on some secret conversation in coded language with Abdelhadi. No time for small talk just, 'Hello, get in.' I noticed that there was a bundle of computer equipment in the back of the vehicle. Both the guys were armed with automatic revolvers tucked into their belts, with no obvious effort to conceal them – that was on top of the Kalashnikov and sawn-off shotgun they still had from my last trip in their murder taxi. Yet again I had no idea where we were heading. This was undoubtedly part of their psychological warfare. Silence is golden until you fill it with dark thoughts on the way to your execution.

Al Biar, Chateau-neuf, Frais-vallon, Climat de France, Bab El Oued, Saint-Eugene were all in the rear-view mirror and still I was given no inkling of the destination. When we arrived at Deux-Moulins we took a right fork on to a deserted alley.

In front of a rather beautiful villa, Abdelhadi stopped the car just behind the Vogt cinema. Yacine and Abdelhadi got out. Beyond the great gates that guarded the villa was a truly magnificent building with stunning grounds. They lugged the computer equipment from the back of the van inside the house and beckoned me to follow.

Once they had finished that little task Yacine winked at me and smiled. I was not in a smiling mood. 'If you want to start up a newspaper we have all the material you need here.' I had to hold my tongue. I would have responded, 'What do you take me for? Starting a newspaper with you is not on my agenda.' I quickly chased the idea of responding away before it reached my tongue. I also didn't want to expose my plans of escape by saying something I might regret. All I could think of between Al Biar and the Deux Moulins in the van was how soon would my wife be able to get her visa to travel to England. Would it be quick enough so these bastards would only find out when I was already far beyond their clutches in London?

She obviously couldn't apply for the visa whilst I was in Algiers because the security services might see her going to the British consulate – then my plan would be exposed. We would have to hatch that plan once I was in London. It would be a nerve-racking few weeks.

There was danger in my palpable relief. Having left the villa and got back into the car I knew they had no intention of an interrogation with torture or a bullet to the head or that I would open my mouth and say the wrong thing. I was safe and sound for the moment. Relaxation has a marvellous way of rekindling clarity.

Now I was actually entertaining the thought that I would have to go through some initiation ritual to be allowed to travel to London –killing someone for example. The idea of assassinating someone almost terrified me more than being shot myself. I felt sick in the pit of my stomach thinking about it. The thought, for the first time, almost brought me to tears. It was just too awful, the idea that I was going to be asked to kill someone as part of some sick game. I could never do it and I would be exposed as a gutless and unworthy agent.

Thank God I was never actually put to such a test. I later learned that this was a key method to expand the ranks of the GIA by implicating reluctant recruits in murder. You shoot someone you don't know and this way you fall headlong into the messy business of being a ruthless jihadist. Your only option then is to join the underground where you would be an authentic terrorist and even then you would end up being controlled by our brutish friends in the DRS like Yacine.

Now we were driving in another direction which gave me no better idea of our destination. There was a deathly silence apart from the purr of the engine and the occasional stone that caught the undercarriage of the van, sounding to me each time like a gunshot. Occasionally the two guys exchanged seemingly inane comments, talking of a vehicle in front which had false registration plates. Perhaps they were just trying to impress me with how omnipresent the secret police actually were.

After an hour suffocating in the endless traffic jams crossing Algiers on roads that were struggling to contain the City's expanding population we stopped at a restaurant that looked over the city not far from Hotel Saint-Georges which had a reputation for opulence.

I still don't quite know where the courage came from to start a stream of questions which had been swirling around in my head since Yacine re-entered my life. I started by asking how it was I was implicated in the murder of Khaled Bouchemal that Yacine laid on me in that first interview cum interrogation.

That was an assassination that had in actual fact been attributed to a murder squad led by Abdelhak El Ayada, first Emir of the GIA. I persisted, 'Why Khaled Bouchemal, the former Mayor. Is he supposed to have threatened me? Was it because he forced me to leave my neighborhood? Why have you left it until now to accuse me of this assassination?

He looked at me, leaned forward and in hushed tones said, 'You were actually accused of having offered up Khaled Bouchemal to the Islamists for being an agent of the DRS. A Captain in our unit told us that after he had infiltrated the FIS. Believing you were an official within the FIS he was too fearful of exposing himself so he kept quiet about this DRS question so he didn't blow his cover.' Abdelhadi fidgeted in his seat, he seemed a little uncomfortable that Yacine had let the cat out of the bag.

When you know the truth you just have to look in a man's eyes when he is lying to you and you can see it. Yacine had made up a hastily improvised lie on the spot and I could see it. They had nothing on me. He was hiding his unease poorly and showed that he hadn't really anticipated that I would ask him such a direct question. I had actually never doubted that Khaled Bouchemal had been a paid-up member of one of the secret police agencies. I hoped he paid for it at some point.

It was clear that they were not interested in being involved in an honest conversation. I asked Yacine what he actually thought about the state of the country, what he thought the future held and whether the bloodshed would end soon. Yacine suddenly metamorphosed into a Political Science major and launched into a boring and ill-informed monologue on the state of the nation.

All I can really recall of the endless stream of nonsense was that terrorism was very close to being eradicated. That for me took the biscuit. Here they were fomenting terrorism, my presence at the table was proof positive of that, and he claimed this phenomenon was in decline. As if to convince me of his (flawed) thesis he concluded 'after terrorism we will live in the shadow of organised crime for a while.' Given the company I was in at the time I could well see organised crime being a new and profitable enterprise for the DRS.

Having fostered terrorism under the cloak of religion nothing could hold them back on the organised crime front. They had already been busy building up their organised crime balances. The 40 million that fell out of the sky for them into my unhappy lap was as much as I needed to see. And I was just about to take a trip to London to collect a whole lot more. That was surely only the visible part of a very large iceberg.

Finally, Yacine grew tired of his game for today and dropped me at rue Didouche Mourad and I handed over the bag containing the 40 million. He didn't bother to look or count the notes. I said, 'I used 2000 dinars to settle some urgent expenses.' 'Just make sure you pay me back next time we meet,' he said.

As I walked in my front door I felt the pressure of the previous fortnight lifting off my shoulders and my head felt like I had just stepped into a cool breeze. I tried to distract myself playing with my four-month-old son who I'd utterly ignored for that whole time. For the first time in two weeks I talked to my wife without snapping her head off. She had been under enormous stress and anxiety seeing me in such a state. She hadn't dared speak to me because she could see I was on such a short fuse. Now she asked me if we could visit her sister together and it made me realise how negligent I had been. She would have peace of mind for a few days.

For the first time in my life, I was no longer the master of my own destiny. I had no idea what tomorrow would bring. I had no idea what would become of my loved ones and me the day after tomorrow.

Monday 14th August. Despite a few days re-immersed in the warmth and security of my family, the fear started to work its way through my system again. How could it not? I had no idea how much of this would be destroyed by the lunacy of someone like Yacine from whom I was awaiting a phone call. Some people might have said I was close to a nervous breakdown.

I felt caught in a stranglehold by the DRS which was barely distinguishable from the GIA in my mind and I was beginning to ask myself just who was responsible for the deaths and disappearance of so many of my fellow journalists. I had certainly convinced myself that on this issue the GIA and the DRS were not at odds. From that moment on I was firm in my belief that there was an unfolding plan to liquidate journalists by that organisation that had become a state within a state.

Being a journalist was now to live with a death sentence. What is known as being between a rock and a hard place? Some of my erstwhile brothers and sisters of the pen might have chosen the rock camp because it was aligned with power. But they had in effect sacrificed their freedom and their credibility. This has always been the lot of journalists operating in authoritarian regimes. Now those who chose to throw their lot in with the Islamists either paid with their lives or several years behind bars. Frankly the thought of being in either camp was out of the question for me.

* * *

It had been another rough night and I was rattled out of my sleep by the shrill ring of the telephone. Yacine was at the other end of the phone. '12.30 – same place, I will see you there,' was all he said and slammed the phone down.

Yacine actually turned up on time for once and this time he was accompanied by someone I hadn't met, but had seen, before. It was an agent from the offices of the Renseignement Generaux (RG) who I'd actually seen before in the press centre downtown but also on the day I had gone to the Police headquarters some years back to complain about death threats I had been getting.

Yacine got straight to the point. He said everything was in place for me to go to London. He told me precisely what I was expected to achieve whilst there. I was to remain in the English Capital for two days in order to pick up a valuable parcel. As soon as I arrived I should telephone the Algerian Consulate but apart from that I should keep my head well below the radar. It was a quick encounter and Yacine arranged another meeting for two days time, same place to give me a virgin passport for a contact in London. I walked home to clear my head which was now full of fresh questions and projects.

But now I had a firm plan up my sleeve on how to banish these demons that had surrounded me and sucked me in. My priority was to leave and not come back; then to organise getting my wife and son safely to London. There, a new life could start to take shape beyond all the foolishness and turbulence in Algeria. I had been given a last chance to escape from this nightmare. No more meetings with this cursed DRS officer.

Of course this now meant almost the most difficult part which would make us immediately more vulnerable. I had to tell my wife about what needed to be done and how little time we had to do it. I went to pick her up from her sister's where she had been staying for a few extra days respite from my increasingly manic mood swings. She needed to be put in the picture. She had no idea what the past month had been about. I hadn't wanted to risk telling her in case she flipped and made our predicament even worse than it was. It's a golden rule of being up to your neck with this intelligence service nonsense that you tell no one, don't even talk to yourself out loud in your own toilet for fear of being overheard.

You don't have the right to tell anyone. You speak, you die is the motto. My wife was obviously beyond worry having seen me metamorphose into a nervous wreck over such a short period of time. She knew something was wrong, but she knew better for her own safety and that of our son it was better not to ask.

In all that time, she never said a word. Never probed, never ask difficult questions, just let me be. For my part, I had kind of expected her own journalistic instincts to get the better of her (we had met as journalists working on the same newspaper) and to torment me with hidden questions. I really wanted to know what she made of this dramatic change in my behaviour. But I knew it was better for both of us if we avoided the subject entirely.

I would only discover the depth of her anxiety and thoughts some years later when I read her own recollection of how that tension was shredding, what had been up to that point, a loving relationship. This is what she wrote.

'The atmosphere in our home was unbearable. Too much was being said in a kind of double-speak. I could never be sure what he meant. Too much mystery and certainly too many night terrors. I simply no longer recognised my husband. It was someone else, impulsive, chaotic, distracted. He was there in body but not in spirit. To preserve my own sanity I took increasingly to spending more time with my sister.

A week after going to my sister's for the last time, on 17th August 1994 to be precise, my husband came to fetch me and he told me bluntly on the drive home that the day after the next he would be leaving for London. At all costs he continued within the following week I would have to join him in London. He gave me no explanation. He had lost weight terribly and became so embittered I could barely recognise him as the man I married. He would panic at the slightest noise and he was scared witless and clearly increasingly distressed.

I remember on the journey home from my sister's he was looking this way and that as if someone was following us. When we got home the atmosphere could have been sliced with a blunt knife.

After asking so many questions and then adding another flurry and saying I would refuse to follow him to London unless he told me exactly what was going on, he told me about the secret police, the death threats, the GIA. All of which I found difficult to follow and believe was real.

On the day he left he had to take a flight at 1pm and as I'd refuse to go with him he left the house in a state of high agitation at 9am.

To say I was confused is an understatement. I didn't know which way to turn. I went to see his mother and she helped me see the story more clearly and put it in the context of Algeria's decades of turmoil. I confided in her that I thought my husband had sunken into a world of acute paranoia. That he only seemed to think that everything was now impossible. He saw evil everywhere.

I also told her about a huge sum of money I had found in his business affairs and that it had then gone missing the following day. Add this to his secretive actions and strange telephone calls and his increasingly bizarre behaviour it made me desperate.

And now as if that weren't bad enough he expects me, out of the blue, to pick up my baby without any preparation and go somewhere I have no experience of....

My mother-in-law urged me to do what my husband asked, but conceded that she had noticed how strange his behaviour had become recently. How he was no longer the same. So without really being convinced it was the right thing to do I went to the British Consulate with all the necessary papers to apply for a visa.

Unfortunately the diplomatic mission was closed because of the bombing of the French Embassy some time earlier. In an emergency I was told I would have to go to Morocco or Tunisia and wait until 3ʳᵈ September when the consulate would eventually re-open for business.

I was in the middle of breastfeeding my baby so the idea of travelling was out of the question. I preferred to take my chances and wait until September. But a sequence of events which could not have been foreseen meant that the consulate would not open for business for years!'

When I finally read that years later, I felt all the guilt and shame I should have felt at the time, but my priority back then was saving our skins and getting us to a place where I believed the three of us would be safe. There was no time for tears and sentimentality in that world. Londonistan beckoned.

CHAPTER 4

Londonistan

1 8ᵀᴴ AUGUST 1994. The day I flew to London it was as if a nightmare was nearing its end. I needed to draw on all my reserves of patience and sang-froid in my last meeting with Yacine. I couldn't afford to give him any inkling of what was about to happen. This time the 10.30 meeting was in front of police headquarters.

To my utter surprise, Yacine, who seemed very at home at police HQ, was brusquely stopped at the entrance by a security guard. At first he tried to blag his way in by rolling off his tongue a list of officers that he had come to see. The officer on the door was not in the slightest bit interested and held out an outstretched palm.

'It's Friday. Time for prayers. Obviously there is no one here,' said the officer not even making eye contact. Confused, and feeling a little humiliated in front of me, because his passage to police headquarters had been barred by a lowly police officer, he fumbled around in his pockets for his identity pass. He whipped out his unmistakable pass and the officer stood to attention, giving him a crisp and respectful salute to the temple, this time he looked straight at him. Yacine's honour was restored.Climbing the stairs to the floor where the RG conducted its business he threw me a quick glance and a smirk. 'You see how all these boys in blue are idiots? You just need to show them who's boss around here. I can go wherever and whenever I want in these offices and see whatever files I need to.'

And just to make sure that I wasn't heading in the direction of such a small agent he whispered in my ear, 'It's better like that. It makes me feel more at ease. I'm not entirely cut out to be a secret policeman. Probably just as well as it helps me pass myself off easily as a real terrorist in the underground movement.' I believed it. He was the spoiled child of the DRS who easily moved in and out of the GIA underground. By day he was a police officer in the town and by night he would slip effortlessly into the Boufarik underground in the surrounding countryside.

At the floor where the RG lived, we entered into an office where Mohammed (the officer I encountered right at the beginning of this saga) was waiting with his team. Without missing a beat he stood up and went to a filing cabinet to pull out a blank passport. He advised me to conceal it carefully in my luggage amongst my clothes. Just as I opened my bag to put the passport in it, the agent I had last met with Yacine came in the room and saluted me. He asked me 'Where are you off to today, Réda, looking so dapper?' I replied in as matter of fact a way as I could to disguise my nerves, 'To London.' Yacine stared at me with disgust. He told me later that I should not tell anyone where I was going. 'If someone asks if you are going to the East, you tell them you are going to the West. No-one needs to know your true destination.'

'I assumed he would be aware.' 'Never assume anything Réda, there are always secrets'. 'But you guys are all in the same boat aren't you?' 'Look, I told you the other day as clearly as I could we are the *Green* team and they are the *Blue* team. They have no business knowing what we are up to. They do our bidding and for the rest they can shut up.'

We quickly left the building and jumped in a waiting car. I couldn't tell what team the driver was on, blue or green. I could not follow their machinations. Mohamed sat beside the driver whilst Yacine and I sat on the back seat together. I could see the road signs pointing us in the direction of the airport. Relief.

En route he reeled off a list of instructions for me to follow. 'Take care of yourself and make sure you are on time for all the meetings that you have to make, etc.' I took no notice of him. My head was elsewhere. He got my attention back by handing me a fifty-pound note for expenses during my stay in London. Surprised at such a paltry and ridiculous sum, I told him this would not be enough in such an expensive city. 'You're only going there for a few days. It will do. At least it will have to do.'

Not wanting to cause a fuss, I kept my mouth shut, because in reality I was happy to go without a penny. The key point for me was to flee from hell. I put the note in my pocket and returned to my daydreaming.

On the way to the airport I no longer felt any fear. Mohammed's presence in the car reassured me. I had no reason to think that all wouldn't now go to plan. After all I was an officer of the RG with the reputation of a young man from a distinguished family. According to all my references I had always conducted myself properly.

At the airport there was no fussing at the check-in or customs or passport control. My companions saw to it that I got exemplary treatment and took me straight to the departure lounge. But as long as I was on Algerian soil I had to watch my every move and distrust everyone. To reassure myself I kept telling myself, 'Patience Réda, only a few more minutes and the skies will clear overhead.' I had not a single official document in my possession. No mission orders, not the slightest proof that I had been detailed to accomplish some dirty deed in London. I had signed no docket that justified whatever money this was about to cost.

In fact, it reinforced what I already knew. The secret police were accountable to no one but themselves for such an operation. I'm certain the money that I had handed over to Yacine was not logged anywhere. It was like a bank account without a credit and debit department. It was like a secret service economy underpinned by money filched from terrorist networks and from rackets extorting money from people under the banner of GIA terrorism.

Who was going to tell an agent that he should declare one sum rather than another? There was a complete lack of accountability. They were a law unto themselves. Much later you could see where the money ended up when one of the bosses was roaming around in a Mercedes Benz. I imagine those vast sums ended up directly in the pockets of the bosses.

* * *

As soon as I landed in London I started to hunt for a safe house. I needed to prepare the ground for somewhere secure for my family to stay. My mind had been made up I would not be returning to Algeria. I would leave the country to its DRS and its cops (both the *Blues* and the *Greens*) and the GIA; all of whom could slug it out amongst themselves and then let one devour the other.

By a stroke of good fortune I met a childhood acquaintance from my old neighbourhood on the plane. He regaled me with all the people he knew in London. God must have been smiling on me. As soon as we arrived we met up with some other friends in common whose presence in London I had clearly previously overlooked. What a small world it was turning out to be.

That sense of solidarity amongst émigrés meant I very quickly found my feet. My friends instantly took me under their wing and fed, watered me and put a roof over my head. On my third day they offered me a small job. I had to post leaflets for a pizzeria through the doors of local homes. I got fifteen pounds a day and a free pizza from the boss. It was a time of pure happiness. By the end of the week I had found a room to rent for thirty pounds a week and I moved in and settled down like a Lord of the Manor. And the cherry on the cake was that by going to the local mosque at Finsbury Park I was able to get my hands on a false French identity card to help my stay in the United Kingdom.

In London it soon became clear that people of my background could take on virtually any nationality they liked as long as the paperwork endorsed it. It was a counterfeiter's paradise. False passports, false identity cards, false and stolen credit cards. You could buy a false identity card as easily as walking into a shop and buying a spare phone card. In truth the identity card I picked up would be of little use to me, at least for the moment. My plan was working like clockwork. It just remained for me to recover my duchess and my baby and then life would be back to its full beauty.

I completely put to one side the business of the funds collection from whoever the GIA link person was. I had no space in my head for anything other than saving my little family from this Algerian trap. I knew my wife was terrified and I'd been unable to explain everything to her for fear of putting her in even more danger.

But she of course suspected something was up. When she saw me under so much pressure, anxious, terrorised, turning white as a sheet over the slightest noise, she knew all was not right. When I drove my car I was looking left, then right, and then left again all around. In less than a month I'd lost nearly two stone. All things considered it was never going to be possible to hide everything from a woman's intuition. It was clear she was not going to follow me on that path to hell. I was at the point of a psychotic breakdown, consumed by paranoia. My married life had been suspended.

Unfortunately things were not that simple back in Algeria. My wife was trapped in Algiers. After the attack on French embassy staff in Algeria all the western diplomatic missions shut up shop. The British consular services had decamped to Tunis with the promise of reopening in September. So there was nothing for it but to wait until September. I hadn't called Yacine as we had set up to do. My wife had to handle his extreme harassment on the telephone. This is how she described it when she committed her recollections to paper.

'A man calling himself Yacine rang nearly every day to ask for my husband's contact details in London. He kept asking after the welfare of my son. From time to time he even changed his name but he couldn't disguise that voice. Sometimes someone else called but refused to give a name.

Three days in a row when I went out someone followed me. At first I thought it was a coincidence. But on the third day I took a diversion and the person was still following me. I began to believe that what my husband had told me was perhaps true. I was starting to feel the fear coursing through my bones. Practically every day I was stopped and asked for my papers and where I was off to.'

My plan quickly foundered. Because of the deteriorating security situation in Algiers the western embassies decided to play a cautious game. The British consulate failed to re-open as I'd hoped. It decided to transfer its services permanently to Tunis. It was no longer possible for my wife to join me in London. I would be forced to return to Algiers and try and organise every-thing from there. But in order to do that I would have to accomplish the mission for which I'd been sent to London.

I was resigned to getting my wife to pass on my numbers to Yacine. After ten days of radio silence, I was once again on the line to Yacine. My suffering started once again. Yacine was enraged. From the moment he opened his mouth I could tell he would dump all his own anxiety on my head.

- 'What have you been up to, why didn't you call? What got into you?' he ranted.
- 'Look it's taken me a week to find somewhere to stay and I still haven't got a fixed phone line for you to reach me.'
- 'What are you talking about, you can't get a telephone number.'
- 'Remember all you gave me was a lousy fifty pounds. I told you that

wouldn't do the job. That wouldn't even pay for a room in a flea-bitten hotel for a single night.'

- 'So Réda, what are you up to right now.'

- 'Thanks to some friends I've found a place where I can use a phone.'

My response seemed to convince him. In a calmer tone he asked if he could call me the next day on the same number to give me more exact details on how to successfully conclude my mission. Before hanging up and as if to make his peace with me so that there would be no bad blood between us at such a distance, he told me. 'There's some good news here in Algeria. When you come back all will be made clear.' To hell with Yacine and his claims of good news, the only good news I was interested in was that the British consulate in Algiers was reopening so that my wife could get her visa.

Thursday 8th September 1994. Yacine rang me at 9am from Algiers. He gave me a telephone number which he said was a telephone box so I could get in contact with someone called Abu Mohamed – real name Nadir Remli. He said I should ring the number at midday on the dot. That's precisely what I did.

- Salaam Alaikoum. Abu Mohamed?

- Yes.

- My name is El Beznassi. Where can I meet you so that you can hand over the receipts?

The voice at the other end had no trace of an Algerian accent and had a classical Arabic cadence. The man on the telephone suggested a time and left it to me to decide a venue. I suggested the Pizzeria Gogo in Lordship Lane in Wood Green in North London. Not far from Finsbury Park Mosque.

At 9pm I arrived at the meeting point accompanied by a cousin of mine who had lived in London for a long time. Whilst my cousin waited in his car, I went and stood in front of the Pizzeria. Within a few minutes a red Ford Sierra pulled up on the opposite side of the road.

It was definitely the car of the fellow on the phone as he had described it to me during our brief conversation. The driver stayed behind the wheel whilst his passenger, a man with a substantial beard, got out and walked in my direction. He recognised me from the orange cap I had warned him I would be wearing. He shook my hand.

- Salaam Alaikoum. My name is Abu Mohamed.

- Alaikoum Essalem. My name is El Beznazzi. How are you?
- Very well, El Hamdoulillah. Where do you want me to follow you to make the swap?
- I'm in a car. You can follow me in yours. We won't be going far.

I rejoined my cousin in his car and led us in convoy to where I was living. I invited Abu Mohamed to come in. He was holding two parcels. He put them down and asked me for a password. I said 'tir ellil' (night bird). He repeated the same words to me and said, 'Here are your goods.'

He thrust his hand into the right pocket of his jacket and took out an envelope and some bank notes. On the envelope he had written in Arabic 'to the families of the mujahideen.' He told me, 'It has two hundred pounds in it.' He also gave me a hundred US dollars, ten Dutch florins and six hundred pounds sterling. In return I gave him a blank passport which I was given in the police headquarters in Algiers. As soon as the transaction was finished Abu Mohamed left. Nothing was said, no explanations were offered. Everything had already been sorted out by telephone.

The man Abu Mohammed presumed was the Emir Abdelhadi had put in place the logistics to make it happen. In short I was a simple office boy running an errand. More for safety than anything else, I cast my eye over the two packages. I opened them to make sure they were neither weapons nor explosives. I was dealing with terrorists not choirboys. There was nothing to say these packages weren't some kind of entrapment or filled with compromising materials.

To my huge relief one contained a laser printer and the other a fax machine. I also opened the envelope to make sure it contained cash and not something else. I ripped it up after taking out the contents. I wanted no compromising documents. It was plain stupid to walk around with an envelope with 'to the families of the mujahideen' written right across it.

I had quite recovered my senses when Yacine called to make sure that the operation had gone according to plan. At the same time he ordered me to make the necessary arrangements for me to fly back to Algiers on Sunday, 11th September.

I did my very best to procrastinate and delay talk of a return to Algiers so that my wife would have enough time to get a visa out. Then I would be able in a flash to postpone my return to Algeria indefinitely. I was thinking on my feet and I was trying to think of a line he might just swallow. 'The problem is, I already checked flights and it seems those for the 11th are already full. I will try and get one on the following Tuesday.' I bought myself two days which I hoped would suffice. The thought of returning to that mess terrified me.

I was beginning to regret having met Abu Mohamed and having shown him my safe house. Abu Mohamed knew Yacine and he could perfectly easily point out where I could be found. Whereas I should have thought first about my safety in London, I had delivered myself into the lion's mouth again.

The sense of security under London's drizzly autumn skies made me think long and hard about the experience I was living through and how London could rescue me from my predicament. The recurring question was why didn't they just finish me off after the 40 million operation? Why lead me to their contact in London? Why let someone whom they didn't really know they could trust in on such an important secret? Why show me how they had infiltrated these networks so that these same networks believe they are dealing with the GIA underground?

They also knew that I was a journalist by trade. That everything they had confided in me could be turned against them in time-honoured journalistic fashion. I fell asleep that night in a whirlwind of conjecture.

The following day I woke up with what seemed to me to be a fantastic idea. At least it was an attempt at saving my skin. I put pen to paper and wrote to the editor of *The Sunday Times*. In this letter I pretty much spilled out the guts of my story. I told him of the twists and turns in the nightmarish journey I had been forced to travel. I sent him copies of the notes I had taken in Algiers which I had bought with me as a kind of insurance along with the registration number of Abu Mohammed's Ford Sierra.

I put the letter in a sealed envelope and invited my landlady into my room for a chat and handed her my testament. 'Margaret, I beg you to do me this favour. If I don't return in a month's time please post this letter.' She looked at me and then at the letter and was clearly perplexed. Pointing to the equipment on the floor, I added, 'Madam you are a Christian and I a Muslim. Despite our differences we still believe in one God.' She appeared to nod in agreement. 'So please, on behalf of the God in whom we both believe, please take a note of this equipment that I am taking back with me, a laser printer and a fax machine. I have nothing more.'

Mrs Margaret was clearly taken aback. She had no idea what I was going on about. I gave her a hint that I was in serious danger swearing that under normal circumstances I would not choose to return to Algeria but I had to go to save my wife and child. I showed her a picture of Salim and I could see in her confusion she had tears in her eyes.

She took the photograph and placed it on the mantelshelf above the fireplace in the lounge. 'He will be here soon.' It was an amusing way to stick two fingers up at the all powerful Major-General Toufik, the boss of the DRS, who through his minions wanted to turn me into a dead terrorist and my son into an orphan who would be ashamed of his father's past.

Before asking my landlady to leave I showed her the bundle of notes that Abu Mohammed had given to me and told her that in the letter addressed to the editor of *The Sunday Times* that was now in her possession, I had named her as a witness to the fact that I had left with the monies stated in the letter.

A sense of relief came over me. I believed that in the event of a cowardly assassination the truth would come out. All I would need to do was warn Yacine that in the event that I was assassinated, the whole world would know that it was the Algerian secret services that ordered the crime. My assassination would not be attributed to the GIA.

Sunday came and my hope that my wife would get her visa, before I had to return to the country, vanished. I had no other choice but to resign myself to take the Tuesday flight back to Algiers. Waiting for the day of the flight to arrive Yacine called again. I was to fetch yet another parcel from Abu Mohammed. A meeting point was arranged at midday at Ealing Common just at the exit to the underground.

This time his six-year-old daughter accompanied him. He was much less cold this time around and invited me for a coffee. The atmosphere was much friendlier. We sat down in a coffee shop and chatted for over an hour about events in Algeria and life in London. But not a word about his activities or what his plans were. I had no idea whether he was a poor stooge who was acting in all sincerity for the Islamists or was an agent of the DRS.

As far as the purpose of our meeting was concerned he gave me the massive sum of ten thousand pounds, an audiocassette and four books, which were all highly compromising, and I would never risk having in Algiers on account of their seditious and subversive text. As usual Yacine called me that evening to reassure himself that everything had gone well. He told me that everything had been arranged at Algiers airport for me to hand over the material and the cash.

Tomorrow I would have to take the most dangerous flight of my life. Would it be my final one? If they sought to ambush me everything was there in one place; computer equipment, subversive literature and audiocassettes as well as foreign currency which hadn't been declared. Fear seized me again.

* * *

Tuesday, 13th September 1994. My cousin came with me to Heathrow airport. He said his goodbyes and left me to my own sense of rising panic. I could feel my stomach knotted as I walked into the departure lounge. The flight was like being in a parallel universe living someone else's life of stress and psychological torture and looking back at myself and asking what kind of fool I was for going back to mayhem.

Walking down the steps at Houari Boumediene airport in Algiers and touching the tarmac was perhaps the most terrifying experience of my life. I handed my passport to the border control officer and I could barely control my body which was trembling all over. My legs were on the point of giving way. The police officer asked me to wait for a moment, and a few moments later he returned with two plain-clothes agents who asked me to follow them. The first one was tall and dapper in a navy blue suit, blue shirt with yellow stripes and a smart sky blue tie. He had green eyes, a freshly shaved head and the physique of a middle distance athlete. He had the face of a B movie actor and a physical presence that completely overshadowed his partner, of whom I cannot remember a single distinguishing feature.

In a state of terminal distress, I just imagined the worst. Then I caught sight of Yacine, waiting and giving me the once over looking particularly at my hand luggage. He greeted me with a smile as if to say, 'Don't worry, I am here now.' He explained the greeting party was a way of speeding up my passage through customs without unnecessary questions. He gave me a wink.

True to his word we went through customs without so much as making eye contact. With one of the fellows who had come to greet me, Yacine and I jumped in a Fiat Tipo which was waiting for us at the airport. The atmosphere became surprisingly relaxed as the journey progressed towards police headquarters.

En route Yacine asked me, 'how are the coconuts over there?' That was their nickname for the Islamists. I answered casually, 'As you can see, everything went according to the plan.' I was feeling relaxed enough to slip a few more anecdotes into the conversation. 'In London anything is possible. Everything is for sale there.' I showed him my fake French identity card as a way of confirming how I had come back with more intelligence than he might have imagined. My time had not been wasted. It was my pre-emptive defence before the threats started.

I was about to warn him that if anything untoward were to happen to me, I'd already taken the precaution of leaving a letter for the editor of *The Sunday Times* in the hands of a safe postman. He cut me short, reacting to the story of the French identity card. Sarcastically, he said, 'Oh is that all. You can get one of those from the Prefecture in Paris. I've got one I use all the time when I have some dirty business to do over there. If I'm ever caught, no one will ever be able to point the finger at the Algerians. We all belong to France!'

A few kilometres later I was back to square one. We arrived at the police HQ. The chap who met me at the airport turned to me as he jumped out of the car and asked me for the money I had brought back. I gave him the notes whilst Yacine was watching. He didn't even bother to count them. He slid them into the pocket of his jacket. He went into the building for a few minutes presumably to deposit the cash and then rejoined us. Whilst we were waiting Yacine enlightened me on the good news he had spoken to me about on the telephone while I was in London. It was about the release of Ali Belhadj and Abbassi Madani, the leaders of the FIS imprisoned since 1991. Frankly I didn't care, as I was more preoccupied with the need to get my family a visa for England. It was obvious that was now an impossible escape route to engineer from Algiers. This was worrying my wife even more as her anxiety-ridden notes scribbled at the time reveal.

'Because it was impossible to procure a British visa in Algiers my husband decided to come straight back. He arrived back late on the Tuesday evening. I was on the balcony waiting for him in a state of high anxiety. He insisted on coming back from the airport under his own steam. Around 10pm I saw him arrive accompanied by two strangers, in a Fiat. Getting out of the car he took two large packets out of his luggage and left them in the car. He was still so distressed and almost unrecognisable.

The following morning we both went to the British consulate in Algiers hoping that we'd be able to sort out my papers there and then. We were both disappointed to find it closed. We both then went to the Ministry of Foreign Affairs to see if there was a chance they would give us a visa to leave Algiers without necessarily wanting to leave the country. They cut off all hope, which left us with no alternative but to plan to make a trip to Tunis. After a heated telephone conversation with the British consulate in Tunisia we managed to arrange an interview for the Friday morning.

The Air Algerie flights from Algiers to Tunis were all full. It was impossible to get a flight for the Thursday with a return late on the Friday. It was only by calling in lots of favours and going through contacts that we were able to get a one-way flight only to Tunis on the Thursday. We would have to hustle there to find a return flight. We only picked up our tickets on the day of the flight at the airport itself. All very skin of the teeth stuff. An acquaintance would then ensure that our return flight would be sorted out successfully.

On the morning of 16th September, my husband and I arrived at the British consulate. After having filled out the required form for interview my husband decided to go in my place. He went into the visa office alone, armed with a complete file of information including all our official documentation. He emerged three-quarters of an hour later. He was pale. He had failed to secure a visa. They had also failed to consider our child.

I decided that I needed to go in myself to try and convince them. It was quite daunting to enter that building a second time and try and convince them to give us a visa. Without even giving me a chance to press my claim the officer who was dealing with me said categorically that I would be refused a visa. The reason for this is obvious from what he then said to me. 'Look you are a journalist. I can't give you a visa. You are certainly more in danger of dying than I am. It's obvious that the purpose of you going to London is to stay there. You are hardly going to come back to die. Your husband has almost certainly prepared the ground for you and your son. Once you get there you will apply for political asylum.

It was clear I had no chance. Despite this I decided to go ahead and take a chance on applying through the usual route. I went along for the interview at 3pm. I already had half an idea in my head; I would make use of my husband's French identity card....'

Of course my wife didn't ignore the fact that this identity card was fake, purchased by me, of all places, at Finsbury Park Mosque. But backed into a corner she thought this might be her trump card. She had nothing to lose and she was willing to deploy any tactic to save us all. It was our last chance, and despite the bogus nature of the papers, she was willing to try anything.

'At 3.30pm without even getting his interview underway, the interviewer started to give me all the reasons why my visa application would be refused. Before he finished I asked him where he got his fixed idea that I was going to go to London to seek political asylum. That's the point I deployed my trump card. I told him that my trip to London was just to sort out my affairs, that I had no interest whatsoever in living in England and that as a francophone the best place for me to be and settle easily would be France where my husband was a citizen. At that point he winced and took a time out. He asked me what proof I had of my claim. With that I pulled out of my file the photocopy of the French identity card. He asked me for the original and I told him he could have it but that I would need to get it from my husband who was waiting outside.

After thoroughly examining and re-examining the official French document, he suggested I return on Monday. I told him that would not be possible because I had left my baby who I was in the middle of breast-feeding in Algiers and it was impossible to leave him for the entire weekend. My baby-sitter was expecting me back on Friday and what was I supposed to do with my baby.

With great difficulty I managed to convince the officer. He finally gave me a visa for six months with my son's name on it. Relieved I went outside to tell my husband and we left for the airport. It was nearly 7pm and we made the flight by a whisker.'

I remember well we cried with relief.

* * *

The following day, Saturday 17ᵗʰ September, I had a meeting with Yacine. From the outset he let me know that he knew all about my Tunisian adventure, that I had been closely followed. All the same I had an excuse prepared. I explained to him that my wife was a bit overwhelmed with everything of late and we thought a visit to London and a change of environment for a short while would see her right. Of course, my feeble yarn did not take him in.

He had clearly understood my desire to leave and not come back. Out of his pocket he took a fifty-pound note (almost certainly from the haul I had brought back with me) and handed it to me saying, 'Go. Maybe it's the best way of making sure you stay alive.' He added a few words of advice. 'In my opinion, it is better that you leave alone first and your wife joins you later. In that way if anyone begins to ask about you, I would be able to say you fled.'

In a way, looking back, I can now see how I owe him my life. But at that point he seemed a little strange and preoccupied. He confessed to me why he was so anxious – something I read in his eyes. 'The day before yesterday I had a very eventful day. I only just escaped being killed.' He patted me on the shoulder and wished me good luck. In my heart of hearts I knew we would not see each other again and I can't say I'm sorry. But that conversation did change the course of my life. I never saw Yacine again.

CHAPTER 5

Safehouse London

A LITTLE WHILE AFTER settling my family and myself in London I set out to find Abu Mohamed. All the information I had been given by Yacine pointed to him being the GIA's linkman in London. I was quickly able to work out his real name, Nadir Remli. He had lived in London since 1983 and married an Irish woman giving him the right to British nationality.

Despite now being far from the madness that had become Algeria, I couldn't just turn my back on that trauma. My mother and father, brothers and sisters, uncles and aunts, cousins and friends were still all there. I owed it to them to try and help stem the flow of resources to the GIA and a regime bent on driving the country to ruin.

Tracking down Remli was a first step. Until war broke out in Algeria in 1992 he had led a perfectly normal working life. He had gone about his business without, to all who knew him, any theological baggage. In fact his London mission bore no relation to scripture as such. His job was to ensure a firm link between supporters in the United Kingdom and the GIA underground. I don't know if he even thought much about where the funds he was raising, from generous FIS donors and passing on, ended up.

In London no one was hiding so it wasn't difficult to find Remli. The world at large in London was not even listening to their politicking and fundraising calls. No one in Britain seemed to care about a war in North Africa. All I needed to do was to go and watch Remli where he held court in the confines of the Regents Park Mosque. It was one of the largest mosques in Europe, built with Saudi Arabian finance. He didn't care about that. It was a home from home. To be sure, to find him all I had to do was to go on the main prayer day – Friday every week. It was a shock to be somewhere again where you could be with fellow Muslims without having to look over your shoulder every five minutes, fearful of an assassin's bullet.

At the end of collective prayers I stood at the main entrance to the mosque and waited. It didn't take long before Remli came out brandishing a placard with photos of people who'd been killed in Algeria. He invited the faithful to part with their cash and give alms to benefit the mujahideen. 'Help your brothers in Algeria fighting to establish an Islamic Republic', he proclaimed. The bucket was filling with cash donations so he was obviously convincing.

Remli flanked by two 'militants' was easily recognisable. His jet-black beard contrasted with the bright white of his gandoura (a type of long robe worn in North Africa) and the prayer cap that covered his hair, the official uniform of the Algerian Islamists. I let him get on and finish his affairs before approaching him.

- 'Salamou alaikoum, Abou Mohamed.'

He was clearly surprised to see me. It took him a while to recover his composure and greet me with the usual Islamic salutation 'Walaikoum essalam.'

In contrast with our two previous encounters, this time Yacine hadn't warned him of my arrival. He was struggling not to show his surprise. He was searching for a way to find out what the purpose of this meeting was. 'Wach El Beznazzi kach affaire.' (Well, sir, what kind of business are you proposing to do today?)

I asked him if his goods had arrived at the right destination. He said they had and expressed his gratitude using the words of Koranic scripture to drive home the point. I couldn't keep my mouth shut. I stopped his sermon and told him the truth about where his money went. I told him that the money that he was raising was not going to the GIA underground but to the secret police who were intercepting the payments. I told him his so-called friends were not the real mujahideen but officers of the DRS and the police. There was a stunned silence. He was lost for words. He stammered a few inaudible words and looked me straight in the eye.

- 'Are you sure you know what you are talking about?'
- 'For sure. There is no shadow of a doubt. Your contacts are secret agents. I only need to check a few details. What would help is if

you would record your next telephone call with them. I could then listen to the tape to confirm everything. It's important to verify the position.'

- 'No problem my brother.' He replied, if a little sceptically.

He had a reassuring tone and gave me his telephone number so I could call him directly to arrange our next meeting. Before leaving him I turned to him and suggested that he keep our conversation secret for the moment from his supposed 'Emir.' He made a promise that as God was his witness he would keep things between us for the time being.

* * *

Saturday 26th November 1994. Once again I spotted Nadir Remli at a sit-in outside the French Embassy. On this occasion it had been organised by a group of Pakistani Muslims who were protesting against the exclusion of young girls wearing the hijab in French schools. Remli was obviously there to show his support for the sit-in. Discreetly I sidled up to him and engaged him in conversation.

- 'So did they call you from Algiers yet?'

To this simple question he began to extol the virtues of his Emir Abdelhadi who he believed was a devout and honourable Muslim. He applauded the Algerian underground and their just call to arms. He stressed the important role he personally was playing in the struggle against the infidel and the corrupt powers in Algiers.

- 'According to my information he is a very pious man. Our brothers
  who made a number of enquiries about him have confirmed to
  me that he is a man of the utmost moral integrity. They have also
  confirmed his strict observance and unwavering commitment to the
  cause of Islam. There is no question mark over this man's character;
  the Muhajideen themselves have sanctioned this information.'

By now he had adopted an incredibly pompous tone. There was little point contradicting him. I asked him if this Abdelhadi knew me. He retorted that he even knew my brother. 'In fact it was he who told me you had come to London,' he added to convince me. The truth of the matter was I was an only son so I had no brother – pious but a liar or misinformed.

I asked him if perhaps my Emir and his was not one and the same person and there was perhaps a misunderstanding. I told him I thought we had made a deal and God was the witness. I asked him again if he would at least record the conversation the next time he made contact. At least if he brought me the cassette I would be able to say if I recognised the voice and then the deal would be concluded.

A few days later, I met up with Nadir Remli in a coffee shop in Ealing Common – the scene of our second meeting the first time I had been in London on the DRS mission to retrieve money, fax machine and printer. I wasn't very happy with his demeanour and I sensed a certain hostility, even that he might begin to cause trouble. He held out a Walkman and a cassette and invited me to listen to the telephone conversation that he had had the day before with the Emir Abdelhardi. It went something like this.

- 'You know El Beznazzi is here in London. He says you are an agent of the secret police.'

- 'Don't listen to him do you hear me. This man is dangerous. He killed three of our brothers and a fourth one is in hospital.'

An immediate shock convulsed my body. I fixed my eyes on Remli and started swinging the machine to see if I could find an appropriate response to this departure from our bargain. Remli had not kept his word. He was too busy reporting to his 'Emir' the accusations that had been made against him.

He'd not taken the time or the care to verify the information with his other contacts or even those officials of the FIS whom he said he knew. As far as I was concerned the case was open and shut. He was obviously on the payroll of Yacine otherwise he would have been a lot more cautious about how he broached the subject with the 'Emir'. So not only was he a GIA man but he was a stooge of the secret state too. It was a reminder I would need to be careful. Some militants wouldn't hesitate to give me a beating if he ordered it. I know it was my paranoia resurfacing but this fellow knew where I was living with my family so now I had another problem to solve.

- 'So was it him or not?' he asked me

- 'No. It wasn't him,' I lied, 'There must have been some crossed wires somewhere. I think that almost certainly your conversations must have been intercepted and exploited by the Algerian secret police.'

I was absolutely sure that the voice I had just listened to was one and the same 'Emir', Lieutenant Abdelhadi who was Yacine Mezougui's sidekick. I knew I couldn't trust the snake Abdelhadi and this character was no more trustworthy than the handsome assassin with the sawn-off shotgun who had terrorised me for months. Now Abdelhadi had damaged my reputation by accusing me of being a killer of Islamists. Once again the Blues and the Greens were on my mind. As Yacine had said, you cannot trust anyone.

I suggested to Nadir Remli that he might facilitate a meeting with Rabah Kebir, one of the leaders of the FIS in exile. I figured that whilst I had this man in my sights I should exploit the contact to get better access to a broader network of people in exiled Islamist circles. I needed that if I was going to find a way of disrupting their fundraising activities supporting jihad in Algeria.

Strangely, Remli didn't seem to want to check the information that I had killed three mujahideen and wounded another as the 'Emir' had advised him. Perhaps he didn't want to think about how dangerous I really might be. He seemed more interested in making it clear to me that he was not in league with the DRS.

Three days later I returned to Ealing Common not far from where he lived. From a telephone box Remli dialled a number in Germany for Rabah Kebir. I stayed outside the cubicle and kept an eye on who else might be watching us. After a brief chat he called me into the cramped box beside him and handed me the telephone receiver. If it wasn't such a serious situation I could have laughed. Two men squashed in a telephone box talking about terrorism.

I got straight to the point with Mr Kebir – I recognised his voice from his many press conferences so I was confident it was him – 'I must tell you that the money you are collecting here in Europe for the mujahideen is going to neither them nor their families. It is ending up in the pockets of the secret services and making them rich. Brother Remli, can confirm that a little while back he gave a sum of nearly eleven thousand pounds to someone he believed was an 'Emir' for the GIA. Let me assure you the person I gave the money to was a 'moukhabarate' (nickname for the intelligence services).

Rabah Kebir made no attempt to disabuse me of what I had just told him, 'It's true we too have our doubts about some of the groups we are dealing with. We will make enquiries about what you have just told me and we are sure God will lend us a hand in flushing out these hypocrites.'

I reminded Nadir Remli that I had grave reservations about the authenticity of this so-called 'Emir'. I admitted to him that I had put my hand in the same fire that he was playing with. The honourable Captain in God's army was no more than Lieutenant Moukhabarate. Remli flew into an instant rage. I was pleased to step out of that highly charged telephone box.

He had good reason to make a fuss. I later discovered that Yacine Merzougui had recruited Nadir Remli the year before I arrived in London in 1993. He was tasked with providing a key link between the DRS and the militants of the FIS in England. He was to provide the money collected to general intelligence (RG) and above all the names of Islamist activists based in London.

Remli did all that and more. He published a newsletter called *Ettabsira* which was used by the DRS to publish what was in effect their list of current assassinations, but attributing them to a group called 'Al Baqonne ala el ahd' (loyal to the oath), a GIA proxy.

After that telephone conversation, Rabah Kebir wasted no time in cutting off Remli from speaking on behalf of his group or acting on behalf of the FIS. Needless to say from that moment on I became persona non grata for Remli. It was a very useful lesson in how I had access to information that could in fact disrupt the activities of these people funding assassinations, murder and massacres in Algeria. It gave me courage to press on.

To keep himself off the hook meanwhile, Remli began to spread rumours that I was an undercover agent and I was extremely dangerous. Let's not forget he now believed I had killed three and left one more for dead. That hostile reputation gave me some breathing space.

* * *

I had, of course, rather naïvely believed that in taking my family and myself into exile I would have put a healthy distance between myself, the DRS and the GIA. What I found in London was a hive of activity for both sets of supporters.

Blues, Greens and every other colour were continuing their mischievous plans without the slightest inconvenience from the forces of British law and order, and that meant I had them all snapping at my heels. There was no need to hide your beliefs in London, it was a safe meeting point for those supporters of terrorism in other parts of the world. One difference in London was that they were all bearded and dressed in white cap and robes. That would have been too obvious back home.

I had no political, ideological, theological or even sociological axe to grind. As far as I was concerned I was a straightforward citizen who fled his country to save his own skin and those of his family. I had already made my application to the British for political asylum.

The best way of camouflaging my real purpose in London was to take refuge amongst the enemy – the Islamists. I had one big problem though, in this world of political chameleons how the hell could I tell the difference between the real and fake Islamists? Everywhere I went I was suspicious of them. They were wary of me too, especially with Remli's rumours doing the rounds. Here I would have to operate on my own, watch my own back, think of my own plans, and take huge risks.

I worried that in extricating my wife and child from the mayhem in Algeria I might actually make them just as vulnerable in London by deciding to play this dangerous game. I couldn't afford to let myself fall into a false sense of security because it appeared a much less dangerous game than the one Yacine had been playing with me in Algiers.

I decided family comforts would have to wait. I knew for my family I should get a job and make sure we could feed ourselves, but this took no account of my obsession to get these fanatics to stop their dirty war that was killing my people. My wife bit her tongue, but I think she knew then that it would cause us real difficulties.

✳ ✳ ✳

Curiously I found my salvation through a very influential man in Islamist circles in London. His name was Mohamed Sekoum. For me he would become a key person in helping me discover the networks of itinerant Islamists across the capital. It was Sekoum who helped most of the Islamists arriving in London to regularise their status so, unsurprisingly, he was the font of all credible knowledge.

When we first met I made it my business to raise the subject of where the money collected in England was ending up – with the mujahideen or the DRS. In confidence he shared with me his doubts about Nadir Remli saying how surprised he'd been to see a man who had no religious background suddenly emerge self-proclaimed as the key official of the FIS in the United Kingdom because he had such a good contacts list. Even more surprising was his claim to be in direct contact with the GIA underground in Algeria, when he hadn't set foot on Algerian soil since 1983.

These two men were effectively rivals in the London Algerian community. It was clear that Mohamed Sekoum had good evidence pointing to Nadir Remli's collaboration with the DRS. Moreover few people doubted him. That made him a powerful ally to get close to those distributing their murder funds to terrorists back home in Algeria. Sekoum would often have to remind people that the many claims made by Remli of crimes committed in the civil war were those events that mostly favoured those in power. These people he would say are always trying to find an alibi or issue a fatwa to legitimise what had happened.

There was clearly a pattern of people using the crisis in Algeria to build their own power base in London. It was one of my most upsetting discoveries on arriving in Londonistan that many Islamists leaders fuelling the conflict back home had nothing to do with Algeria culturally. People were being murdered to make a theological point.

I soon came to know that the most belligerent activist was Abu Qatada Al-Falistini. Later in 1996 when the GIA engineered a 'coup' at Finsbury Park Mosque and effectively installed Abu Hamza Al Misri as its Imam he joined in and overtook Qatada's belligerence. This also coincided with a split in the GIA with Hamza taking over from Qatada as the spiritual leader of the GIA.

These two radical imams, were always the first to applaud the crimes of the GIA with their 'take-away' fatwas. There was no blood spilled in their speeches but plenty of throats slit as a consequence of them.

Sekoum seemed to be very interested in the information that I had been able to share with him. He suggested a series of meetings so that I could meet some of the leading figures in the fundamentalist diaspora in London. I was introduced to a former FIS Member of the Algerian Parliament who went into exile after the Algerian government dissolved the organisation of the man I had deeply suspected when I stood for election for the FIS, Abassi Madani.

The man's name was Mohamed Denideni. He was elected unopposed during the 1991 elections in his hometown of Sidi-Aissa about 200 kilometres south of Algiers – the same election where I had been bloodied. He was also the managing editor of the FIS party organ, 'El Balagh'.

On Friday 6th December 1994 just after communal prayers I met Mohamed Denideni along with my new friend Mohamed Sekkoum and a number of other figures for the Islamist movement including Abdallah Messai, Kamel Rebika and Nadir Remli. Three of them ran an association called the Algerian Community in Britain (Communaute Britannique Algerienne – CBA) and were all outspoken supporters of the FIS. I quickly realised that Denideni did not hold Nadir Remli in particularly high regard. He confided in me that, 'Remli should no longer present himself as an FIS militant. In any case a decision will soon be taken on what to do about him.'

By 19th December things were beginning to move. I met Mohamed Denideni at the exit to Holborn station before going on to a meeting he had arranged with Abdellah Messai, the leading light in the CBA and editor of a propaganda sheet, *Ettabsira*.

Sitting down in a fast food restaurant, Abdellah Messai launched a series of critical questions and from his tone I could tell he was trying to intimidate me. His questions were all centred on the use of funds collected by his group in London and repatriated to Algeria. It was more like an interrogation under the watchful eye of Denideni. The tension mounted by the second and Messai's tone got more belligerent with it.

I understood that the CBA guy had come with pre-conceived ideas; he feared being undermined in front of Denideni. He was doing his best to let me know he didn't trust me. He wanted to introduce me to one of his moles in the DRS; clearly the man lacked serious intelligence. If he was genuine then adopting that tack was simply a route back to helping Yacine in Algiers profit from his endeavours. It was obvious that the meeting would achieve nothing. Denideni walked outside with me to say goodbye and said he would call me soon. Messai left with his tail between his legs.

Of course the encounter reminded me of all the questions gnawing away at my own conscience. Who is with whom? Who is killing whom? As a brutal reawakening, news came through that Mohamed Abderrahmani, my former Editor and Managing Editor on *El Moudjahid* had been murdered.

This despicable act had the effect of giving me more clarity on the question of who was taking sides with whom. I saw the Islamists in London rejoice and claim his assassination. In their unmasking they were shameless. It was clear to me that Mohamed Abderrahmani would not have been killed by the Algerian secret services. He was one of the journalists who had compromised his liberty and credibility by working for the regime. What was the point of the state killing him? The man had never made enemies in his profession and he was widely regarded as a good and honest man, even if he had adopted the path of least resistance in continuing to ply his trade.

Who else would take his life other than the Islamists who had made all journalists their sworn enemies? For them all journalists were lackeys and apologists for the regime, the mouthpieces of a vile power. That meant that come what may they all deserved a death sentence.

Watching a band of bearded men in London so jubilant as a result of the assassination of the Managing Editor of *El Moudjahid*, I realised they disgusted me and I felt hatred for these 'mad mullahs'. Of course I had been closer to the belly of the beast than any of them and that gave me a more privileged perspective. I had seen for myself that the DRS and the GIA could be one and the same thing. But here in London I had quickly discovered a multitude of opportunists who made Islam a means to a commercial end. They had no qualms making the most of the dirty business of Major-General Smain Lamari (Head of Algeria's Department of Counter-Espionage and Internal Security from 1992) and General Mohamed 'Toufik' Mediene (Director of the Departement de Renseignement et de la Securite [DRS] from 1990) and their respective teams of 'Blues' and 'Greens' (nicknamed as such because of the colour of their uniforms).

* * *

That night at Finsbury Park Mosque the truth of their theological meanderings was revealed. Not only was the Mosque the epicentre of Islamist London, but Denideni revealed his dark side. He had nothing but harsh words for assassinated Algerian journalists. Mixing up his French and Arabic in a tumult of abuse he asserted, 'The majority of them who have been assassinated deserved it. I am in London and I am not afraid to say it.' Clearly the irony in that observation was lost on a man blinded by theological rage.

That phrase dissipated all my doubts. They were all of the same mind; ignorant and bloodthirsty, and yet at the same time protected by distance and the ignorance of the authorities who gave them a safe haven. First it becomes a habit, then a passion. Then it escalates to an obsession and now I could see the disease. I searched for meaning in the deep recesses of my political science education. The American political scientist, Harold Lasswell, who specialised in the influence of the media in political life, described the 'hypodermic sting' – a metaphor for the impact of the media on public opinion.

That metaphor was never more appropriate than to describe the way news from Algeria of Islamist assassinations galvanised the faithful at Finsbury Park Mosque. All the more so when the surrounding social and political climate in London meant the sting went unchallenged.

As for me it was probably the same. That day at Finsbury Park I was stung badly too. From the first day with Yacine that had led to my mission in London my life had been turned upside down. I had forgotten my projects, my ambitions, my family and my health. All I could focus on was this parallel life that I had stumbled into. I viewed this mysterious life with trepidation because in it I could only see a secret war between thugs and suicide bombers.

All those months before, when I left to pick up the parcel at the Mustapha Hospital in Algiers, I learned a terrible truth about spying. Only later when I started to replay the film in my mind of that crazy day, did I become excited by the thrill of it. With hindsight, I revelled in those moments of absolute danger. The truth of the matter is once one overcomes a fear of death and learns to accept it, fearlessness can fill the void. Switching to my natural role of investigator helped. It was the journalist in me that drove me in this direction.

Distance can turn complacency into a hellish impotence. How could I pursue a normal life when miles away tragedy was befalling my countrymen, women and children? I wasn't interested in nostalgia – I was living the Algerian tragedy in my bones. How could I go out and socialise, party, take advantage of nature's beauty in London's parks? Denideni at Finsbury Park Mosque made me realise that I had to get to the battlefront in some shape or form.

Thousands of miles away a new the battle for Algiers was raging,* but here in London there was a full-scale battle too, only it was invisible to the

---

* The Battle for Algiers was a defining moment in the Algerian war of Independence from the French taking place between 1956–7 and reconstructed in a celebrated 1966 film.

authorities and the general British public. Different languages and cultures meant they were insulated from these entire goings on. Over there was the *maquis* underground in the back-country. Here in London there was the Finsbury Park Islamist underground.

Ironically what my experiences and fear in my darkest moments with the DRS and GIA had taught me, was that I had never felt more alive than when I feared death the most, because then I learned about the real sanctity and value of life. A bombing campaign in Paris would soon bring me back to life and remind me whose side I was on.

CHAPTER 6

DGSE AGENT:
Saving the World Cup

DESPITE DEVOTING CONSIDERABLE efforts to their London operations the Algerian security services were gaining very little traction in England in the mid-1990s. Official relations between the two countries were seriously weak and whilst my Algerian contacts were incredibly well informed, they were powerless to intervene. Relations with the British were wafer thin and the situation in Algeria was getting grimmer by the day.

By late 1996 after nearly two years in London I was intensely frustrated that any information I gathered for my contacts linked to the Algerian security service station commander, Colonel Ali, based at the Algerian Embassy, seemed to enter a vacuum. It clearly couldn't stop the likes of radical Imams Abu Hamza who had taken over the reins at Finsbury Park Mosque in 1996 – after the GIA split – and Abu Qatada at the Fourth Feathers community centre, plotting and spreading their poison. For me in any case there was no difference between the new grouping – the GSPC – and the established GIA. Ultimately they both were intent on death and destruction in Algeria.

I always consoled myself that for my countrymen living through hell, it was better that I tried to do something by gathering information and passing it on to try and undermine their activities, rather than twiddle my thumbs doing nothing.

I was reluctant to go to the old enemy – the Algerian security services – but given my spoken English was still so poor I felt it was something I should consider. Then Fate intervened to make me see life in a different way. When I held my new daughter Sonia in my arms it made me think of all the terrible things that had happened in Algeria, which I had left to give her a better chance. I couldn't take my eyes off her lying in the hospital bed. She was born in Britain on 24th October 1996 but she was still Algerian and it concentrated my mind once again on our uncertain immigration status.

At this time I was still waiting for an appointment for the Home Office to interview me about my asylum application. The last date had been cancelled at the last minute with the excuse that the officer was sick. A swift complaint to my immigration lawyer secured a fresh date but that too was cancelled the day before it was due to take place. My natural paranoia was beginning to take over and I concluded that something was going wrong with my application.

This sense of anxiety was only heightened when one of my Islamist contacts joked that the reason they kept cancelling on me was that Scotland Yard were going to pick me up to interview me very soon about my Islamist activities. I still feared that the same Islamist contacts, amongst the most fervent supporters of Abu Hamza and Abu Qatada, would discover my true identity. I was walking a delicate line between friend and foe. Sometimes it is difficult for your enemy's enemy to know that you are really a friend.

In my heightened state of anxiety I scanned the man's face and assessed his body language. Was he joking or did he really have inside information. Was he in fact a police informer? This thought had plagued my dealings with the two mosques, which had become centres of radicalisation.

Perhaps my imagination was over-active, but I felt as though I was in some Cold War double-cross situation. I no longer had my key insider to advise me on what to do since Colonel Ali from the Algerian Embassy had returned to Algiers. To be honest I was lost, isolated and increasingly scared.

The information coming through the grapevine, at what was clearly a base for the Groupe Islamist d'Algerie (GIA) at Finsbury Park Mosque, of the spiral of sadistic violence in Algeria, was giving me nightmares, not least because I felt that at any time I could be deported back there with my young family. I began to think that my family might actually be better off without me around.

I could not see any glimpse of light at the end of a very long and dark tunnel that our country had entered and it seemed to me that Britain was giving refuge to increasing numbers of fanatics and murderers. Looking back it is easy to see how I had begun to feel that everyone was against me in

Britain. Whilst I was struggling to get my status sorted, it seemed to me that ever more Islamists were entering the country and getting free board and lodging courtesy of the British government.

For me it made no sense for Britain to welcome assassins, terrorists and criminals if there wasn't something they received in return. I had now spent over a year, week in week out, observing their activities, much of it under the nascent tutelage of Abu Hamza. It was obvious to me just how dangerous they were. The man who had helped me to keep my information in context, Colonel Ali, was no gullible man and he was under no illusion that they were busy fostering a terror network to be used against the West in order to widen the war they had started with the secularists in Algeria. But now he was gone.

In all this and despite the new addition, Sonia, it was easy to forget about my family. From one moment to the next I felt that my head was pounding with rage. Every day I argued with my wife. She would complain about me working late into the night and quiz me about all the Islamist newsletters she came across. She was increasingly focused on the children and I was becoming more obsessed with the tragedy unfolding in my country.

We had both been through difficult times and now she wanted to get on with her life peacefully. She was there when we were both caught in the cross-fire of a battle between Algerian police and terrorists in central Algiers. She was pregnant with my son at the time and we had to hide under a car to save our lives. She was terrified and I was terrified for her. It was that incident that made us realise that if the right option came up it would be better for our safety to leave.

But now my obsession was driving us further apart. My wife was worried about my weight loss and my increasingly erratic behaviour, but it was impossible to explain to her that there was actually a secret civil war going on right here in London. She simply didn't believe me when I told her that the GIA effectively had a base at Finsbury Park Mosque run by the radical imam Abu Hamza.

She insisted I was getting paranoid. The British would never allow that to happen – he would be arrested. She would not hear of my protestations that the British seemed more willing to accommodate the Islamists than we refugees from terror. It felt to me that she, too, was turning against me.

* * *

My New Year's resolution, as 1997 began, was to sort my head out. I made an appointment to see my doctor, as I had no one else to talk to in confidence. I told him that my head 'was not working right and was ready to explode.'

I was admitted to a clinic where I was given a thorough assessment. It was all I could do to explain to the doctors there that I was in the middle of a web of intrigue involving the security services and terrorists. They were sympathetic and stressed that they had heard similar stories before and then prescribed me medication to relieve some of my symptoms of anxiety. There were a lot of sick people in this clinic and I knew it was the wrong place for me but I needed to rest in order to start thinking straight again, to make my next move.

I was able to do a little writing every day and slowly I convinced the doctors that I was not psychotic or unhinged – just worn out and at the edge of a nervous breakdown. Slowly, with the rest and medication, I felt my equilibrium and energy returning. But I realised that it would be impossible for me to return to the family home. Part of my anxiety was the risk I was putting my family at. If I was going to continue in this world I would need to create a distance between myself and my wife and children. So in early 1997 I moved out of the family home with the view that now I could concentrate on finishing what I'd come to England for. Looking back now, it was my family that suffered for my obsession.

A two months stay in a National Health Service facility gave me plenty of space to get my thoughts together. I reminded myself constantly in that time that I had embarked on a course of action having left Algeria and I had to make up my mind if I was going to continue to make a difference.

I needed a new Colonel Ali with whom to share the Abu Hamza and Abu Qatada story but I was now convinced that my plan had to involve making contact with the security services of a country closer to the action and perhaps with more power. I decided I would approach the Direction Generale de la Sécurité Extérieure (DGSE), the French equivalent of the CIA.

The situation back home in Algeria was going from bad to worse. I was picking up much of my information from the notice board at the Finsbury Park Mosque. Unlike the newspapers that were either unprepared to speculate or unable to print because of self-censorship of graphic information, the Islamists positively gloated over the massacres unfolding in Algeria as if they were some kind of holy triumph. I was sickened by their attitudes but I could not reveal my disgust or I would no longer be able to sit with them. These were difficult times for me.

* * *

By early May 1997, my personal recovery was progressing as well as could be expected. I put whatever residual doubts I had in my mind to one side and took a trip to the French Embassy in Knightsbridge. At reception, the sceptical woman behind the glass window informed me that my contact Charles would see me. I only really intended it to be an exploratory visit and had no idea where it might lead, if anywhere.

Charles turned out to be a perfect gentleman. As a pretext for our meeting I raised the vexed issue of my seeking to establish my French nationality. I made the point that as I was born under the *ancien regime* before Independence on 5th July 1962, 'I will always be the son of France.' He looked at me with slight disbelief. I think he could see that my argument wasn't entirely consistent with my age and the fact I had held Algerian citizenship from the beginning. It broke the ice though, and it set the tone for my next gambit.

'Listen, Charles, I have some really important information about the Paris bombings on the Metro two years ago. I have the sort of information that could lead your enforcement people directly to some of the perpetrators of the 1995 attacks, who are hiding here in London.' I had in mind people like the alleged quartermaster of Parisian terror on the Metro, Rachid Ramda.

I could see Charles was a little inexperienced and, in my judgement, was a little intimidated by the situation. His hands were starting to shake. But my gambit worked and he asked if I could leave a telephone contact number. 'I will need to talk to some of our people here to see if this is something they want or are able to follow up on.'

I left the Embassy feeling there was a good chance I would be hearing back from them. In fact I didn't have to wait long. Within twenty-four hours Charles had called and invited me along to the Consulate in order to talk to the 'fonctionnaire' (French civil servant) responsible for civil registration, Patrick.

In fact Patrick had a more detailed role; he was rather more interested in the civil status of Islamists. Here was another perfect gentleman showing me great courtesy. I've always found that the French mask their general hostility to well-educated Algerians with an air of respect. Patrick was nothing if not to the point and he kicked off the conversation by quizzing me intensely about the Islamists based in London.

I was not overly concerned that he had forgotten to grill me on my initial request to have French nationality reinstated. I needn't have been worried in any case. It was clear that he was interested in a trade that might need a reward. 'Of course I cannot promise anything but we can certainly look at doing something for you. We need to hook you up with someone from the Embassy. I'll get them to phone you on the number I have here.'

I understood that they were interested in the intelligence I had access to and, more importantly, that if I accepted to play the informant game I might get French nationality for services rendered. The French are punctilious and Patrick promised that I would receive a call within forty-eight hours.

True to their word, two days later, my phone rang with an unfamiliar number in the display. 'Is that Réda Hassaïne?' asked a cultured French voice at the end of the phone. 'It depends who you are,' I joked. 'I'm calling from the French Embassy. I wondered if you could make a meeting at 10am sharp tomorrow. Just ask for Jérôme on your arrival at reception. I will have warned them you are expected.'

Coming out of Knightsbridge tube the following morning I gazed absent-mindedly into the windows of the famous Harrods store. The two worlds of plenty and poverty raced through my mind. It reminded me of the absence of good fortune back home and now how my journey to disrupt the Islamists was taking a curious turn into the world of Western espionage. By sheer coincidence my arrival coincided with that of the newly appointed Ambassador to the Court of St James and the Queen of England, Daniel Bernard.

The security detail that day was particularly intense. They had their eyes on any tomfoolery that the Islamists might try and deliver on such an important occasion. It reminded me that all we Algerians come with a stigma. It was a slightly less friendly welcome than I had anticipated, quite frosty in fact. It was a reminder that we are all tainted in some Western eyes. I was un-welcomed by the rather officious gendarme on duty that morning. When I told him I was here to see a M. Jérôme, he looked me up and down with intense suspicion.

'Il n'y a pas de Monsieur Jérôme ici. Comment vous vous appelez monsieur?' ('There is no one here by this name, sir, who did you say you were?').

'Sorry, not M. Jérôme, just Jérôme', I said checking myself. Of course Jérôme was quite possibly a pseudonym for a security service operative. The gendarme took a look at a separate register and beckoned me to sign in.

A man who looked to me to be of Mediterranean origin approached me; for some reason I was struck by the elegance of his suit. He put out his hand and offered an extraordinarily firm handshake that brought me back to reality. We went through the final scanning machine and passed along a corridor before entering a huge meeting room with tables and chairs arranged very neatly.

I was so focused on meeting Jérôme that I hadn't really given much thought to the circumstances I was leading myself into. I knew nothing about the French intelligence service other than its reputation. It was like a leap in the dark.

Another man appeared through a door at the other end of the room. He was not of athletic and muscular build but had a rather intellectual air. Frankly I couldn't imagine him in hand-to-hand combat or pulling the trigger of a hidden weapon to protect the honour of France. This man was Jérôme. It was all a little underwhelming in a way. Paradoxically, this feeling gave me confidence.

Jérôme appeared charming, despite the fact that he insisted I would not be allowed to smoke – a cigarette always calmed my nerves. He started with the subject of my request to acquire French nationality.

'Let me make it clear, Mr. Hassaïne, all I will need to do in order for French nationality to be possible is to write a letter of recommendation and place it in a file with your name on it. It will immediately be prioritised. If it is done in this way,' he banged the table with his fist for added emphasis, 'there will be no questions asked.'

I watched his body language intensely but it betrayed very little. 'So what will I have to do to convince you it is worth writing such a letter of recommendation?' I asked. I wasn't going to divulge that I wasn't particularly concerned with getting a French identity card. In the circles I had been mixing in, pretty much any identity you wanted was available.

Jérôme elaborated. 'France is under the threat of terrorist attacks. It is clear you know their milieu, their habits, how they think, how they communicate, you speak their language. What we need from you is to infiltrate the hard core of GIA exiles in London.' Now he was smiling. 'How well do you know the Islamist circles in London?'

He needed to know that I was well placed to help them. So I rolled off a few names of the key players and lesser known individuals. But I also let him know that I was already familiar with the work of spies. 'You know that it was probably the Algerian intelligence services that were probably behind the attacks in Paris?' I suggested to him. Jérôme's expression turned serious.

I continued, 'I know this is perhaps hard to believe but I know for a fact that a few days before the attack on the Metro at St-Michel station a very important meeting was held at the Algerian Embassy in Paris. One of my former contacts here, the head of the security office at the Algerian Embassy had gone along to the meeting. The purpose of this meeting was to establish a plan to coordinate a massive fraud in the upcoming 1995 Presidential election in Algeria. They wanted to ensure a comfortable majority for the Army candidate General Zeroual. The head of the Algerian security services in Paris chaired the meeting.'

'That might be circumstantial evidence,' said Jérôme. 'Although I admit it is a pretty strange coincidence. Our information is that these atrocities were the work of the hard core activists of the GIA.'

I was pretty sure we had established enough of a rapport to make a start on building a working relationship. Jérôme asked me if I could meet him in a few days' time. 'I'll try and find somewhere a little more relaxed for our next meeting. Let me call you.'

I gave the head of the French spying team in London my contact details and left no wiser about how exactly we would work together. I was still a trifle nervous about putting myself in harm's way. I consoled myself with the fact that it was nothing compared with what was happening back in my homeland.

* * *

The massacres in Algeria were coming thick and fast and no matter how positive a message the Algerian government put out, all we exiles knew that back home people were entering a new period of terror.

On 27th July 1997 the electricity went out in the Si Zerrouk neighbourhood in the southern part of Algiers. During the following night a number of guerrillas armed with shotguns and knives, stormed into the area and started breaking into homes and cutting the residents' throats. When the killing spree had ended 50 people were dead and a number of houses had been blown up.

Further massacres in Souhane, Oued El-Had, Mezouara killed hundreds during August 1997 and provoked an exodus to the relative safety of the towns. Each time reports from survivors described the murderers dressed as 'Afghans' and some even claimed to recognise the leader of the militants as Aoueb Abdallah, known as Sheikh Noureddine, the leader in Western Algeria of the GIA.

How all this lunacy added up to the work of people driven by faith was entirely lost on me. My brush with a madness of my own in a North London hospital had driven me to a renewed effort to play my part in trying to end the carnage.

Within three days I got a call from Jérôme arranging a meeting at a very pleasant French restaurant in Knightsbridge called Victor. I liked the irony of the hotel name. It made for a surreal atmosphere. Jérôme chose the table carefully so that he could see who else was entering the restaurant and more importantly make sure we were out of earshot of other potential spies.

The conversation needed lubrication and a generous bottle of French red relaxed us both. The French often find talking to Algerians tough. There is so much love and hate between our two countries and, as a consequence, so much distrust that it is like negotiating your way through a maze. If you both reach the exit at the same time then discussion becomes possible.

Jérôme insisted that the Algerian Army High Command had no connection with the group of collaborators that I had mentioned to him in our first meeting. 'It is our view that those who knew us best during colonial times are the ones who have now become our worst enemies. Algeria, Cambodia, Vietnam – there was simply too much bad blood that we couldn't gloss over after independence.'

Talking to Jérôme felt like playing chess with a grandmaster. I made sure that I only gave him the kind of information that I knew I could afford to give. My reporter's instinct kicked in and I bombarded Jérôme with questions about his view of the current state of play in Algeria and the state of relations between our two countries.

He was incredibly knowledgeable and I found my respect for him growing as the conversation proceeded. His responses were direct and showed he was a man of intellect. After a few more glasses of red wine during our meal he became more animated. I couldn't make out if his liking for wine was a weakness or he was simply eager to impress me with his encyclopaedic knowledge.

Jérôme appeared in no hurry to deploy me on DGSE's behalf. We were approaching the summer break and he told me that when he returned from leave he would make contact with me again and then we could get down to the serious business of infiltrating the Islamists. I supposed even spies need holidays.

* * *

The mayhem continued in Algeria. The massacre at Rais on 29th August 1997 was one of the bloodiest in the entire war. Rais was a village just south of the capital Algiers. Although the figure given by the government at the time was 238 dead, it was reported later at the much higher figure of 800.

When first reports got to me in London the description made me physically sick. I cried myself to exhaustion. Hooded attackers had arrived in the dead of night armed with shotguns, knives, axes and hand grenades. They continued the killing until sunrise. Men and children first and old women were the first targets. They spared the young women from death to abduct them and subject them to goodness know what torture and humiliation later. They cut throats once they ran out of ammunition and burned corpses. In some cases they left severed heads on doorsteps.

In the neighbouring town of Bentalha, 200 were murdered on the same day. Then on 22nd September explosions tore into Hai el-Djilali in the south-west corner of Bentalha. Attackers poured into the village from the orange groves. It was an unprecedented methodical slaughter, moving from house to house, leaving no survivors. Throughout, a helicopter circled overhead.

From a few of the survivors it was reported that attackers were dressed in dark combat fatigues and the Islamists' trademark kachabia, with balaclavas and beards. They even recognised some of the locals, calling them by name. That didn't stop the killing of babies and raping and killing of women.

* * *

Towards the end of September 1997, I was getting more anxious as the violence in Algeria seemed to be escalating. I could feel myself stepping once more on to the edge of the precipice which had put me in hospital before.

I was relieved therefore when Jérôme called me to arrange a meeting point opposite the Sheraton Hotel near Knightsbridge. From there we walked the short distance to the Pizza Express on the Green. They often played fantastic jazz there and it had the kind of ambiance that soothed my soul and made me less inclined to focus on Islamists.

At this point, Jérôme admitted that he wasn't a simple diplomat and was actually the Head of French Intelligence in the UK. He told me that after his recommendation Paris had given him the green light to recruit me as an agent for the DGSE.

I feigned a sense of gratitude but told him that I hoped he was selling me fish that had already been caught. 'I want this to be a fair bargain. If you are to take me under your wing I want to be sure that French nationality is still on the table.'

'Réda,' he responded, 'It is not so easy to obtain French citizenship. It very much depends on the service you are able to provide. The stronger the intelligence you gather the more certain it will be that my recommendation will be successful.' Jérôme reinforced his point by banging his palm on the table.

'And what about my financial reward for putting myself at risk?' I was keen to remind Jérôme that a man cannot live on promises alone.

'That depends, too, on the quality of information you supply and how much we actually ask you to do. I cannot predict that at this point. It will be cash in hand. At each meeting you will brief me and I will give you an envelope. It will be up to three hundred pounds per envelope. But you will have to sign a waiver.'

'I still don't know what it is you want me to do or who I am to target?'

His primary objective was the GIA and its activities in what he described as 'Londonistan'. I was to infiltrate their circles and gain as much insight into their activities and plans as I could. The prime targets were Abu Hamza and Abu Qatada.

At the top of the agenda he placed targeting Abu Qatada's makeshift mosque at the Fourth Feathers community centre in Lisson Grove. It was a stone's throw from the Central Mosque at Regent's Park that had received millions of pounds of funding from the Saudis. The Fourth Feathers had become a venue for those disaffected with the direction of the Central Mosque.

In late September 1997 the French had also become acutely aware of the danger posed by Abu Hamza who had effectively taken over control of the

North London mosque. This mosque in Finsbury Park had also been funded by Saudi money and opened by the heir to the United Kingdom throne, Prince Charles.

These men were recognised as the two most virulent preachers of radical Islamism and spiritual leaders of terrorist organisations in London. The French were particularly concerned because they were hosting the World Cup in 1998 and didn't want a repeat of the Metro carnage at such a global sporting event.

Jérôme proved once again to be well informed and began citing dozens of names. I was not sure of many of them so asked him to show me their photographs so I could pick out the ones I was familiar with. When I spotted someone I vaguely recognised I made sure I pointed him out even if I was a little uncertain. We needed to get off on the right foot.

The Islamist hub in London transfixed the French. Jérôme told me that he had it on good authority that Jean-Pierre Chevènement (the French Minister of the Interior) could barely sleep for fear of the consequences of an attack. They were stunned by the emergence of suicide bombers who conducted their attacks in the name of Islam. They recognised the implications – if they lost the intelligence war hundreds if not thousands of civilian lives could be lost.

Jean-Pierre Chevènement had good reason to fear the Islamists. Jérôme told me. 'These people there will stop at nothing. They are not afraid of death. In fact, it is the opposite – they are willing, happy and able to die because then they will enjoy eternal martyrdom. Meanwhile we will have to clear up the mess.'

'We understand that they are planning a number of attacks to disrupt the World Cup. This would be an absolute disaster for La France. We must do everything to try and prevent this eventuality and putting the Islamists in London under close surveillance is a key part of this fight.'

I understood the French fear. So far I had seen very little in England to persuade me that the Islamists were having their activities disrupted by the British. The French knew from bitter experience that Islamist terrorism would strike at the heart of their cities and they had a rational fear that the British were too complacent and ignorant of the capabilities of the Islamists.

The British were still focused on their battles with the Irish Republican Army who they saw as their primary threat. Jérôme and his security service were deeply concerned that the British security services had arrived at a tacit deal with the growing ranks of Islamists seeking asylum in the UK. There was some veracity to this fear. Some years later in 2002 after the 9/11 attacks Omar Bakri Mohammed claimed that the British authorities had previously entered into an unwritten 'covenant of security' with Islamist forces in the UK if they refrained from pursuing targets in Britain.

Jérôme's assessment of the British was that they took an attitude of, 'Do what you want, write what want, insult who you want, as long as you do not attack our territory'. He added, 'as far as the Rosbifs* are concerned if shit happens somewhere else it is the internal affair of that country. It is a crazy way to try to tackle these fanatics. They are just worried about their own skin.'

We discussed the different view of the British which tied in with my experience of them. This was that the British wanted to keep the Islamists under surveillance and make sure that they provided enough information to the home countries of many of the suspected terrorists to have them arrested and kept in jail in their country of origin.

My head was bursting with all the information being fired at me. I could feel myself losing concentration. I think Jérôme recognised I was tiring and made one last request for me to put Brixton Mosque in South London on my list of targets too.

An Algerian imam called Sheikh Mokrane led prayers in this makeshift place of worship in an old gymnasium. Word had reached the French that it was actually a place where stolen goods changed hands. It was not clear who was benefiting from the exchange. The French were paranoid and, as far as they were concerned, anyone Algerian who was acting like an Islamist was a potential enemy.

* * *

I left Pizza Express on the Green with a thumping headache. I had secured what I wanted. I now had the resources and the motivation to try and stop these fanatics killing my people, but also the realisation that this was a dangerous undertaking. Sometimes you are so focused on reaching your goal that you forget what is likely to be on the other side.

---

* French slang for the British.

I was now in the pay of one of the most powerful security services in the world and Jérôme was confident that he could get the intelligence he needed to prevent a catastrophe in the World Cup the following year. Now the Islamist circle in London would no longer be out of bounds to them and, more importantly, they would not have to rely on the British, whose competence they doubted.

That night I called a journalist contact to ask his advice on the prospects of MI5 finding out about my new relationship with the DGSE and what the implications of this might be. He was rather sanguine about it. He suggested that the Algerians might give MI5 cause for concern but they would invariably turn a blind eye to the activities of the French.

I was a touch perplexed by the idea that the British would ignore evidence that could potentially cause them harm too. But burying heads in the sand was not an exclusively British condition. Jérôme and his Paris masters also had their blind side. As far as they were concerned the threat was focused on the Finsbury Park Mosque. They believed, rightly or wrongly, that the Paris bombing campaign that they feared during the 1998 World Cup would be orchestrated from there by Abu Hamza.

Jérôme had set himself up as the linkman fighting the terror activities emanating from London. I was the man in the line of fire tasked with attending the Mosque and reporting back on significant developments – particularly the Friday sermons that Hamza would use to issue Fatwas. I would quickly become familiar with the newsletter of the GIA in the UK, produced by those attending the mosque and responsible for publicising its communiqués to its activists and supporters beyond Algeria.

I had, of course, kept my cards close to my chest with Jérôme. I hadn't told him all that I knew. I simply wasn't sure how safe it was. It was important that I kept my head when I was around him and that I hid my anger at escalating horrors in Algeria.

* * *

I was well aware that the responsibility for all the massacres had been claimed by the GIA and, importantly, it was Finsbury Park Mosque where the information was always freshest. It helped me conclude early on that the links between Hamza and the Algerian terrorist network were regular, organised and solid. It seemed to me it was no coincidence that the massacres were publicised in a GIA press release issued in London. Abu Hamza and his band of eager young Islamists were using their St Thomas' Road base to gloat to the world about their successful jihad. I think people call it basking in the glorious reflection of others.

It was easy to hang out at the Mosque, because they were grateful to see more eager followers. I'd spend a lot of time listening to people, reading notice boards, and picking up names of people passing through. I would go home every night and write up my notes so I kept a log of the comings and goings.

The more time I spent at Finsbury Park the more sickened I became by what I was hearing. I witnessed Abu Hamza over and over again claiming responsibility for all these atrocities from the pulpit inside the Mosque and outside the Mosque in his increasingly public campaign to promote jihad. He exuded a deluded pride. I promised myself if anyone from my close family was to be murdered and he celebrated it, I would gun him down. I should have realised then that my double life would inevitably take its toll on my own health. I was never one for learning from my mistakes. My obsession took precedence.

Jérôme was only too aware of the dangers presented by the GIA. He and his superiors were focused entirely on the threat emanating from Finsbury Park. They took every opportunity they could to pass information about Abu Hamza's illicit activities on to the British security services. Although the British would argue that their system of justice always requires evidence to be translateable into a prosecution before they can act on it, the French believed dealing with them was like sowing seed on stony ground.

Jérôme was keen to up the ante. We met just before Easter at the Bouvier restaurant in Knightsbridge. I could tell he had a plan up his sleeve because he was extremely excited and as soon as we had taken our seats he started to talk about creating a newspaper supporting the jihadists. I was taken aback by such a suggestion as he could tell from my reaction. He reassured me that the reason was one of control. Jérôme was convinced that if I controlled the newspaper's editorial inputs and it was to be used as a first port of call to publicise jihadi atrocities then I would become privy to even more sensitive information about potential terrorists who could cause serious harm to France.

The journalist in me wanted to do this as an exercise in misinformation but I also worried that it would flatter the ego of Abu Hamza too much and I was getting into dangerous territory with this man. But Jérôme was a very persuasive man. He was naturally charming and good company and the more the wine flowed the more I felt it was a good idea. To seal the deal he used flattery, telling me how much better a contact I had proven to be than his Algerian counterpart 'Le Moustachu'. The proposition was sold.

Jérôme always knew when to stray into sensitive territory. He asked me if I had known 'le Moustachu's' predecessor in London, the Algerian Colonel. I told him that, in fact, even when he had left London for Algiers the Colonel had maintained contact with me. I was actually meeting him later that day as he was paying a flying visit to London. At the time (alcohol consumption usually deadened my critical faculties) I failed to ask the obvious question – how did Jérôme know the Colonel?

Jérôme became very serious and asked if I minded him following me to my meeting with the Colonel so that he could see him with his own eyes. I thought it was a strange request but I felt it could do no harm so agreed. At that meeting with the new Algerian Colonel in charge of gathering intelligence in London in a bar off the Edgware Road in central London I noticed Jérôme at a discreet distance. I cannot be sure that the Colonel didn't see him too because I never saw or heard from him again after that meeting. But at least from that point on Jérôme knew that I had sound sources of intelligence on my own terms.

Within a few days Jérôme was on the phone to me again. This time there was a sense of urgency in his voice when he asked if I could meet him at the Bangkok Brasserie, a basement restaurant in Piccadilly, the following day. That meeting showed me just how far the French were prepared to go to neutralise the threat they believed Abu Hamza posed. He asked me how realistic I thought it was to kidnap Abu Hamza from Finsbury Park Mosque to bring him to face justice in France. Even though I was as upset as Jérôme was that the British seemed to be doing nothing to curtail Abu Hamza's stream of hate, I thought it was a crazy idea. I felt sure that the British were watching the Mosque too and that any such attempt at kidnap would lead to an almighty row with the British.

Jérôme wasn't persuaded by my reluctant stance and instead moved the topic of conversation onto Abu Qatada and his preaching at his makeshift mosque at the Fourth Feathers club on Fridays. He was already familiar with

Qatada's vitriolic preaching and he asked me to see if what he said publicly was as bad as his sermons that people could buy on tape cassettes.

The Fourth Feathers community centre was about as far from a mosque experience as one could imagine at first sight. The building was more used to seeing mothers and toddler groups, I would imagine, than hardcore radical preachers and their wide-eyed followers. The proceedings were all in Arabic in stark contrast to other centre users whose broad cockney accents seemed more associated with *My Fair Lady* and Lisson Grove.

My first personal exposure to Qatada made it obvious to me he was not running a drop-in centre for delinquents – these were hardcore followers of the pathway to jihad. Killing infidels for the glory of Islam seemed to dominate their discussions in Arabic. They talked of bombing the London Underground, car bombs and murdering innocent people to provoke an all-out war. I was overwhelmed by how brazen these men were and particularly Qatada's sway over the young men who came to listen to him talk. Of course if one didn't speak Arabic there was no obvious sign of the nature of these discussions. It was like a little terrorist bubble in a sea of London calm.

Qatada was as firm as Hamza was in telling his followers that the Gates to Paradise are sealed by two swords – only by picking up one of those swords and striking down the infidel could the true believer be sure that the gates would be unlocked for him to pass through.

Many people in Islamist circles viewed Abu Qatada as the spiritual leader of the GIA. One particular sermon stuck in my mind because he displayed a perverted logic in explaining the deaths of young babies who, it had been claimed, were burned alive in ovens. I was struck by how he quickly used scripture to defend the indefensible. He made it clear that in his view these 'innocents', as the babies were, had gone to paradise. This was far better than allowing them to live with apostate parents whom in the end they would have surely followed to hell. By roasting them alive, their murderers had done them a favour.

Just thinking of his words now still nauseates me. But in the hysteria that he whipped up in the mosque, violence was not seen as an end in itself, it was a means of transformation and if you encountered martyrdom gloriously on the way it would be your entry to paradise. Like Hamza, Qatada proved adept at encouraging in his sermons, both in person and circulated by videotape, hundreds if not thousands of young men to go to training camps in Afghanistan to prepare for the war that was only just the beginning of securing the demise of the infidels.

His followers were mesmerised by him. The feeling of elation after his sermons was tangible. I firmly believe if he had preached in English and not Arabic, people would have picked up on his poisonous ideology much earlier. Qatada gave his blessing to the killing of Jews, and urged that Americans should be attacked 'wherever they were found.' It was easy enough to disguise this vitriol in a land where there were so few Arabic speakers.

The next time we met, even Jérôme was visibly shocked when I gave him my written report and explained exactly what I had heard. It justified his fear of Algerian terrorists. As far as he was concerned it made the wave of arrests now taking place in the European Union even more necessary. He was becoming increasingly incensed that there appeared to be no movement on the British side.

It quickly became clear that I couldn't be at Abu Hamza's and Abu Qatada's mosques at the same time. I suggested to Jérôme in a phone call that I should recruit someone to work for me to attend mosque on Fridays. He was pensive but could see the merit in the idea. We arranged to meet the following Friday to settle it.

I was a little late getting to my rendezvous with Jérôme and he was not happy. As I walked into the Bouvier restaurant with the Arabic-speaking journalist I had recruited to help, the maître-d warned me he was in a foul mood. Approaching the table I could see the scowl on his face. As well as my unpunctuality, bringing a stranger inside our closed circle had seriously upset him.

He took me to one side. 'Are you crazy? You are becoming a dangerous maverick. You cannot work freelance with the DGSE. It could compromise everything we are trying to do. Get rid of this guy now. I don't want to meet him.'

It was a warning that I had to be careful and not get too comfortable with these spooks. I left with my journalist recruit telling him that the boss had double-booked and we would meet him the following week.

It was already mid-April and I was seeing precious little progress in getting the two radical preachers shut up or locked up. My patience was wearing thin and this accounted for my risk taking. Sailing close to the wind seemed to be the only way to force the issue.

* * *

When we next met a few days later at the Bangkok Brasserie everything was more chilled. The entire afternoon was spent swapping stories and from the first glass of wine Jérôme told me with great glee that Paris had indicated their approval of the information flow I was able to send them first hand from Abu Hamza's pulpit. So keen were they, in fact, that they backed my idea to take on a new recruit. He also had news that the idea to publish a newspaper as a way to gather more sensitive information was seen as either a stroke of genius or a massive folly. They were considering the political implications before deciding how to proceed. It was obviously a big risk to fund the organ of a terrorist organisation, whatever the benefits.

The French were still focused intensely on the World Cup and my continuing contact with the Algerian Colonel Ali – by now back in Algiers – - meant that information I received from him could be passed on to Jérôme. I felt seven feet tall. I was now a player, bridging the gap with the old enemy. Jérôme and the Colonel had both been great Professors of the craft of spying.

Jérôme may not have looked the part of a spy but he certainly had the imagination for it. Some of his ideas not only seemed unorthodox but seriously flawed. First of all he suggested that we should consider an arson attack on the Fourth Feathers community centre and make it seem like an attack by Qatada's rivals. Even I had heard of the Rainbow Warrior and the debacle and international row that had followed its sinking by French security agents in New Zealand. I was certain if we set fire to the Fourth Feathers I would never hear the end of it, especially if someone died. I wasn't keen to make martyrs in London. I was keen to get them behind bars using the rule of law.

I had been a good student and already I had in the back of my mind the idea that I might have to link with the British security services to finally get Hamza and Qatada off of their respective jihadist pedestals. Being involved in arson on behalf of the French was not going to make that possible I was sure.

The next few months were the most intense of times for me and Jérôme, as the French grew increasingly frantic to have daily updates on what Abu Hamza was saying and thinking. Now I had both mosques covered I was working flat out to provide the material the French believed was critical to knowing how to keep the World Cup matches safe from terrorist attack.

Our meetings at the Bangkok Brasserie became ever more surreal in that summer of 1998. Jérôme was always in a state of high stress. His boss, the French Interior Minister Jean-Pierre Chevènement was having sleepless nights. Jérôme made a joke of it saying that my notes had become as addictive as sleeping tablets to get the minister to sleep.

His schemes to overcome what he saw as the laissez faire approach of the British seemed to grow more and more outlandish. Abu Hamza he reasoned could be kidnapped, drugged and bundled into a car and driven at speed through the Eurotunnel to French soil where he would be promptly arrested and imprisoned. Jérôme was like some relic from the Cold War but I couldn't see a French judge accepting the idea that Abu Hamza had suddenly arrived unannounced without a passport on French soil. Jérôme was disappointed when I picked holes in his fanciful schemes.

When he came up with the idea of assassinating Abu Hamza outside his West London home and blaming it on far right British nationalists, I prayed for the weeks to hurry past to the end of the World Cup because I knew that by then Jérôme would no longer be so desperate. It was as if the two sides were as crazy as each other. The chaos that would be unleashed by such an assassination would not only potentially harm Franco-British relations but it could make a bigger martyr of Abu Hamza or, even worse, start a race war. I certainly hadn't come to Londonistan to start that.

Jérôme never stopped pushing either the kidnapping idea or the arson attack on the Fourth Feathers. He was getting more desperate to think of unconventional ways to stop the jihadists as we were frustrated by MI5's seeming lack of interest to intervene. Unlike me, he seemed unperturbed by the consequences of being found out – the big difference being that he had a passport diplomatic immunity and I had neither to stay in the UK.

Needless to say neither came off. I'm sure neither would have been fully sanctioned by the top brass in any case. I always felt it was a great irony that the success of the World Cup and the fact that no attacks were carried out by Algerian terrorists strangely helped to make Zinedine Zidane an even greater national French hero. Far from ruining the World Cup, a French-Algerian had actually delivered the Jules Rimet trophy to France at a time of great uncertainty. It was perhaps France's greatest multicultural moment. It was soon to pass.

Then Jérôme provided the money and I delivered the Jihadist publication he had suggested. I used one of my African contacts whose newspaper was in trouble – so it was easy for me pay for the use of his working facilities and materials in order to publish the organ of the GIA abroad. He wanted the money – no questions asked. For me, although I was playing for the wrong side, it was for the right reasons. I had inherited the mantle of my grandfather in using my pen to match the swords of the enemy.

It took me and one other person to get this publication ready and so we were able to do it in great secrecy. I used the services of an old colleague from Algeria, now living in Paris, and the printer had no idea what the content was because it was all in French or Arabic.

* * *

For a few months it felt like old times in the nascent democracy that had been my country. It reminded me of why I had become a journalist and how much I was actually missing my trade. Despite the bile we were about to publish it had already helped me become privy to sensitive talk of bigger and better triumphs against the West to come. Jérôme was very happy. He got ten thousand copies for a snip at three thousand pounds and a whole new library of information.

During the production run of *le Journal du Francophone* he was on the phone incessantly. He was very conscious that the whole thing could backfire on him. He wanted to know what I was writing and how it would be published. Over and over again he asked if I was sure I could keep the whole thing a secret. 'Because if you don't it will be the biggest disaster ever in the history of modern espionage.'

As soon as the Newspaper came off the printing presses I sent a bundle of copies to Jérôme. It was uncompromising in its style and content. When Abu Hamza and his cronies were delighted with it, I was confident that I had hit the spot – I was also confident that copies would find their way to MI5. Jérôme and I celebrated a successful operation in style with a bottle or two of champagne. He told me he had been called back to Paris to meet his bosses about the newspaper. I assumed that success would breed success and that now it was a question of establishing the costs of running a regular monthly newspaper with DGSE cash. It took six months to get a response – the world of espionage is fickle. One small change can necessitate an overhaul. When I met Jérôme in November at our usual haunt, the Bangkok Brasserie, I could tell by his long face that something was wrong.

Over lunch he told me that a new man had taken over at the security machinery at the Algerian Embassy, yet another Algerian Colonel.

The French knew and feared this new intelligence gatherer. He was recognised to be good at his job. In particular they feared that he would get wind of the fact that the DGSE was funding the main external newspaper of the GIA. This would clearly send out all the wrong signals in the Middle East. Looking back they were probably right. At the time I was sick to the stomach at having such a promising operation brought to a crunching halt.

Jérôme was clear about one thing – only I had the knowledge to point the finger at the DGSE and the service wanted to pay me a sum of two thousand pounds to buy my silence on the matter. I could tell Jérôme didn't agree with the decision. It had proved such an easy way to gather valuable intelligence and he had tried to convince his bosses that it was the wrong decision, or so he told me. He reminded me that if I did talk then in all likelihood I would suffer anyway. French Intelligence would deny it and tell the British I was a turncoat working for the GIA all along.

Jérôme and I did agree on one thing. These madmen still needed stopping in Londonistan. In my mind I only really had one option, to finish the job I would have to go to the British. Although the British didn't know it, I convinced myself that I had to teach them that only they now had the incentive to intervene. Jérôme was relieved. He had played his role in protecting France from a potentially disastrous World Cup and this newspaper was now a sideshow for him. We spent six hours commiserating with each other.

I walked home alone on yet another dark drizzly November evening in London. Once again I felt alone against the jihadists. But this time I had conquered my fear and I knew my next move.

CHAPTER 7

Scotland Yard's Special Branch: Information Broker

OMING TO LONDON had been a tough transition. It had changed a lot since I had been there in my early twenties as a waiter. I had seen a lot of pain and that had changed me, and of course I had a different purpose. I had tried hard with the French security services to work my way into a position where what I learned from the jihadist groups could be helpful to stop the carnage both back home or spreading to Europe.

After my final meeting with Jérôme, I found myself kicking my heels at home. My family that might have given me some distraction were now living apart from me and, although I tried to see them as much as I could, my unpredictability had made my wife anxious to maintain the children's equilibrium by limiting the contact. She was right of course, she had to make sure they had the least disruption possible and even on my good days my mood swings could be trying.

Despite the fact that I had enough money to survive for a while, I found myself constantly thinking about the lost time, time that I knew my enemies were busy exploiting. Sitting at home was getting me nowhere and still these networks of exiles and returning jihadists seemed to grow exponentially. The words of my French handler kept going around in my head. 'The British know a lot but they do nothing.' Doing nothing, as I well knew, was not an option with these militants. Give them an inch, as the British say, and they'll take as much as they can to get to paradise.

In spite of a shaky start I was becoming more confident with my English and I felt it was now good enough to be able to explain my mission and myself. I decided to make direct contact with the British security services. But if I'm honest, I still needed some Dutch courage.

So, on Tuesday 10th November 1998, I went to a pub near Victoria Station in the heart of London and downed a few shots of whisky; fortification against my natural disposition towards nervousness. As Big Ben on the Thames chimed 4 o'clock I marched out of the door and headed straight for the reception desk at the Headquarters of the Metropolitan Police at Scotland Yard.

Goodness knows what the receptionist made of me with my fiery breath when I asked to speak to any officer in the anti-terrorism squad. She reacted as if I'd asked her the state of the weather – she was completely unruffled. 'May I ask the reason you would like to see an anti-terrorism officer, Sir?' I told her that it was of a very sensitive nature and I would rather discuss what I had to in confidence with an officer.

She asked me to take a seat. I preferred to stand to let out some the nervous energy that was making me shiver. Eventually I saw two officers heading straight towards me. They asked me to follow them to an office just nearby on the ground floor and as soon we sat in the office, one of the officers gave me his business card. On it his name was given as Steven X. The second officer introduced himself as Richard.

I initially explained my frustration that I had been waiting for a call back from a Special Branch officer, Vernon X, for six months. I reiterated that I had met him at a police station near Liverpool Street having been introduced by the *Sunday Times* journalist David Leppard who supervised my entry into that meeting.

I felt like I was going over old territory, tedious but necessary in the circumstances. It was important Steven X understood that my conversation with that officer from Special Branch was about my involvement with the French security services. At the root of that relationship was the DGSE's well-founded fear of the dangers posed by Abu Hamza and Abu Qatada, allied, as they were, with those at the heart of the terrorist organisation the GIA (Algerian Islamic Group).

It seemed that Vernon X had in fact paid close attention to what I had to tell him. He had written copious notes, all the while intimating my relationship with the French was a good thing, but none of the nice talk had ended up with any action. No one called. David Leppard had warned me that the fact he came to the meeting as a journalist had possibly compromised the potential relationship. No intelligence agent can have his cover compromised by having a third party know about the connection with the security services. It was a roundabout way of saying why I had come alone this time.

I obviously sold my position well. Steven X was interested in the story I was telling him about the North African Al Qaeda connection in London. He too promised to get back to me within a month. This was no normal job application or interview. I assumed they needed this time to run background checks on me to see I was who I said I was.

This time Scotland Yard kept their promise. In fact it only took them three weeks to come back to me. On Thursday 3rd December 1998 Steve called me at 9am. I confess mornings have never been my best time to do business but I soon learned that this life was entirely unpredictable. Others rule an intelligence asset's life.

I was to go to the Burger King restaurant just next to Waterloo station and look out for Richard. 'Don't approach him and don't talk to him. He will not acknowledge you in any way. If you try to approach him he will ignore you and the meeting arrangements will be cancelled. You are just to follow him. Is that understood'? I could hardly contradict him so I learned quickly a new way of working. This did not, unfortunately, involve the same addiction to fine Gallic cuisine and wine as the French agents I had encountered.

Remember, this was England. So following Richard in the freezing cold with a light November drizzle chilling me to the bones was not my idea of fun. After thirty minutes of following him around the streets of Waterloo, in what felt like aimless meanderings, the thought did cross my mind I should just get on a red London bus and go home.

It was surreal. I felt like a character in one of those films I used to watch back in the 60s on an old cinema screen in Algiers – only the dark and mysterious music was missing. Eventually we arrived at the reception of a non-descript Holiday Inn. At that point Richard turned on his heels and introduced himself as if we'd walked through some invisible mirror into another dimension.

Richard was a picture of civility. He shook my hand and invited me to go to a suite where Steven X was waiting for us. Over coffee we discussed my work with the DGSE and the concerns that they had had about a potential bombing campaign during the 1998 World Cup. The meeting was brief, just an hour long. It was clear his superiors had not yet given him the clearance to take me under his wing. As we parted Steve – we at least dropped the X and became more informal – again promised he would be back in touch within the month.

Whilst I waited I spent a large part of Christmas 1998 camped at Finsbury Park Mosque making sure the relationships I had already built were nurtured and extended. After setting up the newsletter I had become like one of them. And although I had made my excuses why I could no longer be available to produce the newsletter, I said my diabetes was taking its toll, I had clearly bought myself enough credit to rise above the suspicions of the Mosque leadership – at least for the time being. There was plenty happening for me to get my head around. The plots for international action in the Middle East and Afghanistan were coming thick and fast.

* * *

The next call came from Steve in late January. The usual clandestine meeting arrangements followed. A meeting at the exit of Green Park station, a stone's throw from Buckingham Palace at 11.15, just as the Queen's guard was getting ready to change. We had different business but in my own way I felt I was doing my duty to the English Queen.

It became clear to me during this next conversation that the message of our previous encounters was getting through because Steve was increasingly interested in pinpointing my exact knowledge of Abu Hamza's circle. They were not leaving any detail to chance either. As well as explaining the comings and goings at his mosque in Finsbury Park he wanted detailed sketches of the layout of the Mosque. This raised my hopes that they were planning an intervention that would halt Hamza's murderous sermons and links with the jihadists in my own country, Algeria.

He was clearly satisfied with the quality of information that I was providing as towards the end of our lunch he told me his bosses wanted me to be their 'eyes and ears' at Finsbury Park Mosque. As far as I was concerned the risk I had taken in going to Scotland Yard on my own the previous November was starting to pay dividends.

The downside was that the British didn't want to talk money. It was as if the talk of payment was a dirty distraction and not a commercial transaction. My labour and intelligence, for enough to survive on, was the way I looked at it. I had come to England to do a job and this remained my top priority. No one writes a contract for this kind of intelligence work, it is done on a bond of trust. I trusted that once the work was done I would be paid. So day in day out for the next month I spent as much time in Abu Hamza's mosque as I could. I gathered information and wrote up details of what I found. I would deal with the money issue next time we met.

Six weeks passed and eventually Steve made contact, which was just as well because I was down to the last handful of coins in my pocket with virtually no credit at all on my mobile phone. These were desperate days. I was getting progressively lonelier and more isolated, with my wife and children living away from me. I would spend hours staring at the four walls of my flat and the longer I had to wait the more frustrated and anxious I became. I called Steve from a public phone box to ask for an advance on what the agency would be paying me. A few days later he called me to arrange a meeting with Richard.

Goodge Street was the tube stop for the rendezvous this time. I was convinced I would soon become an expert on the London Underground the way these intelligence agents used it. I was tiring of being strung along but at this point I was in deep and there was little option for me to pull back. So when Richard took me to a nearby pub on Tottenham Court Road and over a glass of wine handed me £100 and a promise of a better pay cheque a little further down the line, I was not in a position to refuse.

Richard had brought along a senior officer from Scotland Yard, a man calling himself Mark. I had begun not to take any of these names too seriously in any case. Mark was like the proverbial cat on a hot tin roof – his nervousness was visible and his skills as an undercover operative were hopeless. He was looking around so much I began to think he must be frightened of his own shadow. It was a good job the meeting was short because he was beginning to attract attention to himself by his antics. He was clearly scared of meeting me in such a public place, to the point that he leant forward to tell me that if anyone asked me who he was just to let them know he was a journalist.

I thought that was the most bizarre of encounters. What kind of fool did he think I was? I wasn't all that keen for people to know I was with police officers either. Then the strangest thing of all happened. Mark asked to see the notes I had been compiling about the illegal activities going on at Finsbury Park and then proceeded to hand me a piece of paper which he said he required me to sign in exchange for the £100 I was receiving from Scotland Yard. This seemed unnecessarily bureaucratic – they would never get me to court to verify the transaction. It made me doubt their focus.

One thing was certain, though. They were homing in on Abu Hamza and his activities at the Mosque. It was clear to the local Algerian community that the types of people flocking to the Mosque were experienced fighters from overseas wars and increasing numbers of young British Muslims keen to rub shoulders with real warriors.

Some of the British Muslims were only boys of thirteen or fourteen. It was not a suitable place for them but I could see the Hamza logic in catching young minds and brainwashing them into becoming sleeper cells that would one day wage jihad anywhere it was necessary, even in Britain or the US.

I was to learn later that television documentary crews (including Kurt Barling) were already beginning to sniff around the Mosque to see what Hamza was really up to. Meanwhile the existing Mosque trustees were trying to warn people of the dangerous turn of events at the Mosque. They had realised too late that the imam Hamza they had invited to help run their Mosque had in fact hijacked it for political ends. This was the most important message I had to get across to Special Branch.

The following day, Steve called me to confirm that 'jumpy' Mark saw the Hamza story as a top priority and they wanted me to continue my intelligence-gathering exercise at Finsbury Park. What he called intelligence I was starting to see as evidence. I reminded Steve how dangerous this whole exercise was for me and that I wasn't proposing to risk my skin for nothing. He said they would call me by the end of the month of March.

By now it was obvious to me they were off the pace. Things were moving fast at Hamza HQ. Hamza himself was confident for some reason that the authorities would not touch him. That certainly struck me as odd. He was brazen and despite warnings from the Chair of the Trustees, a highly respectable man Mufti Abdul Barkatullah, Hamza continued to use his sermons as a political platform to incite a call to arms for young mosque-goers.

Hamza also decided to branch out and make alliances with other exiled jihadists. On Friday 12th March 1999, just after Friday prayers, he joined forces with the man dubbed by the British media as the Tottenham Ayatollah for his fiery sermons. Omar Bakri Muhammed was the leader of Al Muhajiroun (The Emigrants), a political group intent on uniting all Muslims under a revived caliphate governed by Sharia law. Between the two men they organised a vocal and visible demonstration opposite the home of the British Prime Minister Tony Blair, 10 Downing Street. The target of their demonstration was the British justice system. One of their jihadist comrades, Rachid Ramda, had been locked up in a British maximum-security jail after the French had requested his extradition. I knew of Ramda and had warned the French and British about him.

In court it was alleged that Rachid Ramda had been the quartermaster and chief fundraiser for the Algerian terrorists who had bombed the Paris Metro in 1995. The evidential trail had led British investigators to a series of money transactions at a branch of the Western Union money transfer business in Wembley North London. From there the trail had led to Rachid Ramda. He denied the charges and told the British courts that he feared torture by the French and therefore should not be extradited. He was eventually extradited after a tortuous process some 10 years later and remains in prison in France. It infuriated me that these people were busy killing people and yet at the first opportunity they turned into cowards, unwilling to face justice. For me it was a demented mentality, void of all reason.

On that day, I was in the thick of the throng of protesters who just wanted Ramda out of jail and made lots of noise to get their point across. I suggested to them that they should make sure they delivered a letter to the Prime Minister and a letter was duly handed to one of the policemen on duty in front of the gates to Downing Street. I'm sure Whitehall had never quite seen such a jihadist ensemble, with their mixture of Islamic dress and the khaki veterans' uniform.

On the surface the focus of the protest seemed to be on the GIA's London accountant Rachid Ramda. In reality the motive for the protest was a series of arrests of Egyptian nationals by the British law enforcement agencies for terror-related activities. The layers of intrigue in this whole Londonistan affair were becoming ever more complex.

As I sat there watching this demonstration against the British government in the heart of Whitehall – the centre of British political and administrative power – just 200 yards from the British Parliament, I marvelled at this British way of doing things. There was no way the émigré jihadists would have lasted an hour in any government district in their own countries of origin. For the young British contingent, they seemed to be using this vehicle to give voice to their many frustrations with their lives in Britain.

Sitting on the pavement on Whitehall, I was snapped out of my contemplative mood by a phone call from David Leppard. 'Hi Réda, I have big news. Abu Hamza is going to be arrested within a couple of hours.' I looked across at Hamza and then at Downing Street. 'Actually, David,' I said with a certain amount of surprise, 'there is a good chance I will be arrested with him.' David sounded puzzled, 'Why?' 'Well, because I'm outside Downing Street, standing a few yards from him, right now.' Now David was excited. 'If he gets arrested during this demo, call me right away. I am sitting on a scoop and I want to be first with it.'

With every call I was beginning to understand the complex layers surrounding the British security services operations also. I was beginning to understand why I had been asked to stick to Hamza like glue. I was beginning to understand the intensity of the relationships between some of my journalist contacts and the security services, but on this story their 'whiteness' neutralised their efficiency and made me indispensable.

I felt a surge of relief and told myself I had just engineered a significant victory for my countrymen by putting the spiritual head of the GIA out of the jihadi picture. Hamza's time was up.

But there was a vital question here that I could not answer. I was at the heart of a demonstration with the number one target, talking to a journalist who knew about the impending arrest – something didn't quite add up. I called my security service contact Steve. I wanted him to explain how a journalist could know about such a big arrest before it had even happened. I knew the target, Abu Hamza, was still very much at liberty because he was within spitting distance of me.

By now my heart was racing, as I started to think about the far-reaching consequences of rounding up all the people at the demonstration: Omar Bakri Muhammed, Abu Qatada and Abu Hamza. I could see Qatada – the spiritual leader of the GIA at the time of Paris bombing – was busy giving an interview to a journalist (Camil Tawil) from the Arabic newspaper *Al Hayat*. What a prospect to make the world a safer place in one fell swoop I told myself.

Then out of the corner of my eye I saw Mark, one of my Scotland Yard contacts. I had to shake my head to make sure I wasn't dreaming. As our eyes met I saw him panic. He looked away abruptly and literally turned on his heel and marched away. I made my excuses to the others at the demonstration and went in hot pursuit of Mark, following him all the way down White-hall, across Parliament Square and then towards St James' Park underground station. I managed to catch up with him. 'Excuse me sir, I think you dropped this piece of paper,' I said handing him a note from my pocket (there was nothing on it – it was just a ruse in case somebody saw us).

I thought he was going to faint as all the blood drained from his cheeks. I realised I probably should have been a little more discreet in approaching him but my mind was racing with the possibilities that came with arresting Abu Hamza and his jihadists comrades. He was physically shaking and he grabbed the piece of paper, thanked me through gritted teeth, and disap-peared into the bowels of Scotland Yard HQ.

I was left no wiser about Abu Hamza and more than perplexed about how on earth Mark could function undercover with such a nervous disposition. Within the hour, Steve, who had been ignoring my calls all afternoon was on the phone to me. 'What the hell do you think that was all about? Do you realise how dangerous that manoeuvre was? You could have compromised the whole operation. Not to mention your cover. Don't do that again. If you do, all contact will be broken. Do you get me?'

Steve was furious. He let me know if in future I recognised an agent in the field then under no circumstances should I engage them. I pointed out to him if he had communicated with me more effectively there would have been no need for me to approach Mark. 'I've been trying to get through to you all day. My brain has been racing since I heard from a source that Abu Hamza was about to be arrested. I was standing next to Abu Hamza when I took the call. Obviously it would have been nice to have some warning that something like that was going to happen. I've been risking my neck to give you the evidence you need to take this dangerous jihadist off the streets.'

I knew telling him I had inside track would provoke a reaction. He came straight to the point. 'Who the hell have you been talking to? How did you get that information? That's restricted. You had better keep your mouth shut or we are dead meat.' I told him my source was one Vernon X.

'I'm going to call you in exactly one hour. Keep your mouth shut until then. Here's my pager number. This means you'll get through to me quickly if you need me urgently. For God's sake, don't breathe a word of this arrest to anyone or I know who to blame if anything goes wrong.'

I knew this was a threat but he also now knew that I knew that our connection went all the way back to the journalist who first connected me with Vernon X. The penny had dropped that David Leppard must be very well connected to the security services.

I made my way back to the demonstration which had pretty much fizzled out by 4.30pm, so I returned home with a thousand questions swimming around in my head. But I had the sense of satisfaction knowing that this was the end of Abu Hamza. That at least was what logic told me.

The weekend passed with no news. Then early on the following Monday I received a phone call from David Leppard. 'Réda, I told you, didn't I? I was spot on. Abu Hamza has been arrested just a couple of hours ago.' So it took a weekend to confirm what I had already deduced. It was less a matter of being a good journalist and more a matter of being on the inside track. Steve knew that I knew. I left it at that.

Within an hour of that conversation Steve was on the line. Could I go to Finsbury Park to check the temperature of the militants and see what plans they were making about reacting to the arrest of their leader? I thought it odd to be asking to know what his comrades were feeling and thinking. Why the hell should he care now that he'd got a dangerous man off the streets and he had the evidence to get him taken out of circulation? I had given them tapes of his rabid sermons, notes of his speeches and countless examples of illegal activities at the Mosque including child protection issues with young boys watching violent jihadi videos.

By midday I had called Steve back to let him know that a sit-in at Charing Cross station, where Abu Hamza was being held, was planned for two hours' time. In fact I went with the militants to the sit-in and remained with them until the demonstration petered out as one by one they left.

The following day Abu Hamza was released. He took great pains to thank all his supporters in his Friday sermon. He stressed the support everyone had given him was welcome, particularly that of the British authorities. He told his congregation, 'They respected me and I was treated well in the police station. They made sure that everything I asked for was made available. It was clear to me that they did not want to make me a hero by taking me to Court.'

I was dumbfounded. Why would the police release a man spreading poison in the way Hamza was? Surely they had enough evidence to convince the Crown Prosecutors that he had a case to answer. Or had this smooth transition from arrest to release been facilitated by some kind of deal? Was he more useful out and about to the security services, I asked myself, rather than locked up where he could limit the damage to people in other parts of the world?

Perhaps the French were right. Jérôme would speak incessantly about how the British security services would often provide them with useful information but that no one could rely on British law to tackle these murderous jihadists if the target of their schemes wasn't in Britain itself. Jérôme would spread his hands and say 'These British don't understand there is a difference between freedom of speech and incitement to murder.'

* * *

Sometimes we are driven by deep instincts. My fear and certainly paranoia for my family, my friends and my country couldn't be switched off like a tap. Out of a sense of duty I continued to go to Finsbury Park Mosque. By the Easter of 1999 it was clear that this place had become a satellite base for Al Qaeda in London. My relations were beginning to cool with most of the key activists in the Mosque because they sensed that my radical fervour (bolstered by the French inspired newsletter) had subsided. They only had time for true believers. I kept up the conversations with as many people as I could and still the information came about their political and criminal machinations. Abu Hamza was becoming it seems more brazen and untouchable.

Eventually I got another call from a calmer Steve. He wanted to meet me again in Central London outside Green Park tube station on the following Wednesday. I thought perhaps my reward would be a trip to the Ritz just a few yards from the meeting point. Surprisingly, he actually suggested we go to a much more upmarket hotel. Once there I was introduced to yet another Scotland Yard officer. He called himself Dick. Dick was extremely pleased with himself, telling me he had personally arrested Abu Hamza and that he had directed the questioning at Charing Cross police station.

'I've heard a lot about the work you have done with us,' he said. 'It has been really useful and for that reason I suggested it would be good to meet you, to get to know you better.' It seemed an odd introduction. After having worked with them for the past three months, after risking my neck to get inside information for them, it seemed a little late to be asking to get to know me! I'm sure he could tell I was piqued although he seemed relatively unconcerned by that. I reminded him I had had plenty of experience as an investigative journalist getting tough stories, so I knew what I was doing. At that point I was on the point of losing my temper and it took all of my self-control to stay calm.

'You want to get to know me,' I said, 'after I have been risking my life with these bastards for three months. And for what, I ask myself every night? It seems to me nothing. I don't get paid enough to do the work and my results are wasted because you don't lock the people up despite having plenty of evidence supplied to you by me. And why are you stopping my asylum application at the Home Office? I tell you why. You are taking advantage of me, because of my status.'

I may have said too much but at least I felt I had said everything I needed to say. Of course money wasn't my principle motive but I did need money to live and my handlers knew this. In my mind by constantly dragging their feet on payments, they were showing me how little they valued the information I was giving them – very little. My expertise was getting inside these jihadists' heads sufficiently for me to get a sense of what motivated them. I could get closer to them than any Englishman without the need for probes or wiretaps. It was a simple but effective way of getting information but somehow it was if my handlers didn't fully trust me.

Dick remained unmoved. 'I tell you what, let's see how much more you get and meet again in two weeks. Then we'll talk about what your value is to us.' On Wednesday 28th April we returned to the same hotel and Dick was sitting in exactly the same place as I'd left him two weeks before. I continued where I had left off. If they were going to mess around with Abu Hamza I didn't have much to lose in speaking my mind. 'Instead of only having Islamist informers, it might be an idea to recruit people who can actually help you really understand the people you seem to want to protect.'

Dick could see my frustration was growing and knew what was unsettling me, 'Look we will sort out your administrative problem. It's just a matter of timing.'

Leaving that meeting I was unsure of what situation I had really let myself in for. Walking down Piccadilly a little voice was telling me these people are all abusing me. They were having their cake and eating it whilst I was living alone in a one-bedroom flat. If I was fighting a war, I felt like I was doing it on my own.

I walked through Leicester Square and decided to go to see one of my Algerian friends, Ali, at the Bar du Marche in Berwick Street. I cracked open a bottle of wine and then another. I was drowning my sorrows at a predicament I felt increasingly powerless to extricate myself from. Here I was in London, I had no job, I was beginning to feel that I was making enemies in my own community and my marriage was pretty much over. I felt that these Special Branch people were treating me as though I was worthless. On the other hand, now that I had spoken my mind, I figured they would have to find something soon or create the new risk of a man who knew too much.

It took Special Branch three months to come back to me. Eventually Steve called me. 'We may have a development,' he said, 'Let's meet the day after tomorrow outside Victoria Station.'

The news was quite ironic given I was being told on 14th July, Bastille Day – or the day which commemorates the revolution in France. After meeting Richard outside the station, we walked to the Holiday Inn nearby to meet Steve and Dick. It felt like a high-powered delegation. As usual Dick came straight to the point. 'Look, mate, we have taken this as far as we can. In two weeks we'll introduce you to an MI5 agent who will basically recruit you as an undercover agent. How does that sound?'

'It sounds promising, but I can't live on thin air.' One of the men pulled out an envelope and gave it to me. 'This is for your trouble.' I opened it and counted three hundred pounds – a pittance for putting myself in danger for six months.

If it hadn't been for my freelancing on the side, feeding stories to David Leppard at the *Sunday Times*, I would have been destitute. At least, I kept telling myself, his newspaper was a real weapon in my fight against terrorism. Leppard could say what I couldn't.

The three men shook my hand and thanked me for what I had done to help them and explained that now I was going to be working for MI5 our contact would cease. In some way I was relieved. I felt I had got very little so far from that relationship. They were busy playing games with fire and it wouldn't be long before they were burned.

Despite all the information they had, the Metropolitan Police were clearly demonstrating they did not have the appetite to enter a real fight against individual terrorists like Hamza. They were busy doing deals with the devil. But it was, they thought, a devil they at least knew. I knew they were wrong. They were underestimating the power of this man to turn the heads of young people and radicalise them. His incitements to harm Americans, Brits and Jews would have been a cause of alarm and indignation had they been articulated anywhere else in British society. So I was starting to think that either the police were as racist as everyone claimed and didn't believe people like Hamza were capable of causing serious damage or – in my view more likely – he was on their informants list and he was feeding them information (or for all we knew misinformation).

The French had given me plenty of warnings and all they had promised me was turning out to be an accurate assessment of the British police service's dealings with the Islamists. I now had one more chance to deliver these jihadists to justice. Whether MI5 would do any better was still open to question. But now Abu Hamza was about to put himself centre-stage internationally and transform himself and his reputation as a jihadist supremo in the British and American press?

CHAPTER 8

Trouble in Yemen

MEANWHILE ONE THING was absolutely for sure; Abu Hamza was growing increasingly contemptuous of British authority and even bolder in his willingness to foster international links to promote jihad. In this Al Qaeda network it seemed he was growing increasingly important.

The most outrageous of his attempts to increase his profile and foster a global movement from Finsbury Park Mosque came in his links to an international incident in the Yemen. The way this unfolded opened my eyes to the operational objectives of the GIA and the influence it had begun to have on Al Qaeda strategic thinking. It was the start of the 'big spectacular' event on a global stage designed for nothing else but its shock value and impact.

Abu Hamza himself was an incredibly charismatic figure. He appealed to young men who felt marginalised in their own communities. He would sit for hours cross-legged on the floor talking to youths from Britain's young Asian Muslim communities, second-generation Bangladeshis, Pakistanis, and Somalis and among them some Afro-Caribbean boys who'd converted to Islam, many of them whilst in prison.

They would watch videos together of battles in war-torn territories and Hamza would implore the youngsters, some only in their mid- teens, to see that their Muslim brothers needed support against the forces of the West ranged against them. These videos were brutal, showing decapitations and body parts, completely uncensored and used purely to shock and radicalise the viewer.

Finsbury Park Mosque was an ideal place for young men without jobs or purpose to come for camaraderie. Most didn't smoke, drink or do drugs – such was their religious commitment. They didn't have girlfriends or go to all-night parties. The levels of testosterone were palpably high and the basement gym was well used. Kick-boxing and other martial arts competitions were a regular feature of Mosque life.

They were given money when they needed it and slowly pulled into the orbit of the other battle-hardened veterans who then worked out when a recruit was ready for a trip overseas to a training camp. Not only was the Mosque secure in the sense that no white man could afford to step inside the place unless he was a known convert, it helped provide a contact point for people in Pakistan and onwards to Afghanistan. I saw it increasingly as an Al Qaeda guesthouse in London. When combatants returned from foreign wars they would exchange stories with wide-eyed kick-boxers and they would eventually be ready for Abu Hamza to step in and finish the job of brainwashing them.

I understood why many people beyond the Mosque saw Hamza as a buffoon. He was always ranting, he misquoted scriptures often, he said things that were simply seen as so outrageous they were laughable, but within the Mosque it was no laughing matter to see young men come under his influence. They were dicing with their lives.

At first my focus on Algerian terror attacks had distracted me from the growing clamour to internationalise the methods used by the GIA. The objective was not only to bring terror to Europe but also to attack European and particularly US targets in places where the jihadists thought they were most exposed and vulnerable. There was also a point at which the only legitimacy needed to select a target was that the victims were Western, with the highest prize value being placed on American lives. It didn't necessarily matter if the targets were military; holidaymakers could be fair game too if they were in the wrong place in 'Muslim lands'.

Abu Hamza was among those spiritual leaders who stoked the fires of hatred against what he called the 'United Snakes of America'. The bombing of the US embassies in Kenya and Sudan was celebrated at Finsbury Park Mosque as an example of how to escalate the war of terror against the Americans.

Throughout 1998 Abu Hamza had been raising the battle standard of his own group, the Supporters of Sharia (SOS). Hamza could count his own sons as members of SOS. Those who chose to become SOS members were expected to be willing to put themselves in the service of jihad. Of course the opportunities to get involved in jihad in London were limited mostly to tough talk, war games and the occasional outward-bound course in Kent or Wales.

Nevertheless through his international contacts made both in Afghanistan when he operated with the mujahideen there and through the numerous exiles passing through Finsbury Park, Hamza's ambitions to get his SOS members real training and action were beginning to take shape. It was obvious to me that men were leaving London to go abroad under the strict directions of Abu Hamza, although it wasn't always clear where to.

I remember thinking that London was looking very festive. It made me feel even more depressed than usual because I was not sure if any of this growing jihadi network was of any interest to the Security Services for which I had been working so hard. It seemed to me that the more the jihadists' ambitions grew the less valued was my intelligence; perhaps they thought it was too outlandish. Floating hot air balloons above the Sahara with bombs attached was one of Hamza's stranger ideas delivered in a public discussion of taking the war to the West. If a man could say that publicly and get away with it, it was abundantly clear to me nothing was being done to actively stop this escalation in activity.

* * *

Ramadan that year started on 20th December. The Mosque was even fuller than normal whilst everyone was fasting. These people were nothing if not conscientious and they even held Tawarih prayers after the final prayers of the day beyond sunset. Sometimes the Mosque was so full you couldn't move for prone bodies sleeping in every spare place possible. At times walking off the streets of North London into Hamza's lair was like passing through the looking glass into a parallel universe.

Sometimes it was difficult to know exactly what was going on and I had to be very careful to listen more than I talked in case I compromised myself in some way. Whilst I was pretty well known at the Mosque, I went out of my way to be as inconspicuous as possible. Finsbury Park Mosque had become a truly international forum with worshippers from every Muslim country you could imagine. But one group wasn't there. Under the banner of SOS they had been dispatched to Yemen to train in mountain camps to carry out terror attacks on Christmas Day on British targets. Malik Nasser, Mohsen Ghailan, Shahid Butt, Hamza's stepson and real son Mohammed Mostafa Kamal were the amateurish adventurers. They were soon to find out that training in Yemen was a whole lot harsher than being on an outward-bound course in the green valleys of rural Wales.

A former Afghanistan veteran, Abu Hassan, who had befriended Abu Hamza during their Afghan excursions, had arranged to use these men to mount a spectacular assault on the British consulate in Aden. Yemeni investigators were to later uncover evidence that Abu Hamza had supplied a state-of-the-art satellite phone and thousands of pounds sterling to Abu Hassan's 'Army of Aden' in return for the SOS members' training in weapons and warfare. It remains unclear if these British men were on a mission to return as a British terror cell lying low until the right moment to launch an attack in the UK.

At Finsbury Park Mosque I was slowly learning more about the tactics these men were deploying to recruit more young men to the jihadi cause. There was also a constant chatter around important prayer times about the need to constantly raise money. Talking to some of the young men themselves it was clear they were filled with a mixture of exhilaration and trepidation as they left to travel overseas. It was really difficult, however, to prove definitively that a cash pile was being used for jihadist adventures abroad. The absence of this type of proof hindered me as much as it hindered journalists trying to report the story. It went to the heart of why the security services in Britain failed to deal with the issue earlier. They needed to treat these people in the same way they treated the Irish Republican Army but at that point the resources weren't made available.

Of course my initial concern had been with Algeria, but with the range of nationalities coming and going I could see that Abu Hamza was getting more and more ambitious. It was no surprise to me that some of this money ended up in Yemen. That is no doubt why he encouraged the boys from Finsbury Park – including two of his own sons – to go to Yemen in the first place. He had schemes to get involved in all sorts of other international venues.

It's hardly surprising that Hamza entertained fantasies of escalating scale about strikes all over the Middle East. Finsbury Park had been turned from a sleepy backwater place of worship into an international hub of jihadists. There was no one around to challenge him and the place was looking more and more like a Middle Eastern enclave with robed men throughout the Mosque. He was living a self-fulfilling prophecy – the authorities were blissfully ignorant of, or blissfully ignoring, what was really going on inside the Mosque.

More and more worshippers came to use the place as a homeless hostel drawn by Hamza's radical reputation and the fact that there was good business to be done in the basement. At the end of prayers there continued an active market in selling false passports and ID cards for multiple European nationalities. Stolen credit cards were a top priority because they could be used to buy lots of goods which could then be converted into cash to be sent to their jihadist collaborators in the GIA. Whatever you needed was there – the latest videotapes (including jihadi ones), jeans, and trainers. Just like a traditional *souk* back home (a goods market).

It was in my mind a travesty that this place was still called a mosque with so much criminality. But that misses the point. Abu Hamza would expressly tell his followers during his sermons that this was not criminal activity but legitimate work in pursuit of jihad.

In his warped perspective he could issue a fatwa (holy ruling) that his followers were entitled to steal from the 'kaffir' society – even to peddle hard drugs – as long as the targets of their salesmanship weren't Muslims themselves. It was a corrupting and corrosive message which had even affected close friends of mine who had attended the Mosque since long before Abu Hamza arrived there as the imam.

Take Halim the brother of a friend of mine from Algiers. He had set up shop just across the road from the Mosque and would serve those worshippers breaking the fast. From what I could tell the bulk of the proceeds to set up the business came from selling his ill-gotten gains at the Mosque *souk*. He and the jihadists justified what they did because their imam Abu Hamza said it was fine to rob and cheat as long as it was from kaffir society. Sometimes I felt bad that I had used my friend's brother to get close to Hamza. My friend had been like a personal referee. I used to work with his sister on the same newspaper back in Algiers. But whenever I felt torn I reminded myself exactly what they were up to and how they were in effect abusing the freedoms they were enjoying in London.

Halim not only ran a restaurant but because of his connections passing through he was well connected to the terrorists in Algeria I was interested in. The GIA exiles who hijacked Finsbury Park were his friends and associates. I didn't even have to pretend who I was because they already knew I was a journalist back home. On 28ᵗʰ December, after breaking the Ramadan fast, I sat down to have a digestive of mint tea with Halim before going back to the Mosque together. The atmosphere in the Mosque that evening was electric. It had turned into a special evening for the jihadists as there was news filtering through that the mujahideen in Yemen had kidnapped Western tourists including Americans and Britons.

At times like these I would sit as close as I felt was safe to Abu Hamza and his 'council of war'. They were in constant conversation, taking telephone calls and feverishly discussing the serious events as they unfolded. You could almost feel the euphoria passing through the Mosque now that they were at the heart of a major international incident. It was a time when I also sensed a degree of paranoia creeping into the way they conducted themselves. They were less self-assured and there was certain information they didn't want to share. Serious trouble would inevitably bring serious interest from the authorities and they knew this.

Of course there was a good deal of uncertainty surrounding exactly what had happened on the ground. I remember the irony of the news reports on British television talking about concern over the kidnapping of tourists, whilst the jihadists were busy praying all night long for the kidnappers. 'They showed the world that they are true mujahideen'. That was the prevailing wisdom inside Finsbury Park Mosque.

Halim, who was secretly filmed by British television journalists a few months later selling stolen passports, was well aware that Abu Hamza had close links with Abu Hassan Al Yamani, the mastermind of the Yemen kidnappings. His indiscretions helped to fill many gaps in my understanding of what Hamza was up to. Halim has now returned home.

* * *

It was becoming perfectly clear to me that the climate and culture emerging at Finsbury Park was one that was helping foster close links with the leaders of many Islamic terrorist organisations. From the sanctuary of the Mosque

Hamza was able to recruit and brainwash vulnerable young men. He was able to raise huge amounts of cash to supply to his contacts overseas, including Abu Hassan in Yemen. He was fast developing a reputation in the British press as the mouthpiece of radical Islam in London.

Given Hamza's position as a landlord for a jihadi guesthouse and immigration centre in London, it seemed obvious to me that Al Qaeda chiefs would be thinking about exploiting this man's position at the heart of the enemy. There were simply too many ex-fighters from Al Qaeda units in foreign wars, particularly Algerians passing through, for there not to be some solid connection. This might have looked like a ragtag army but they had the crucial advantage of coming together at the start of the internet and mobile phone age. It cost them virtually nothing to maintain a credible network – even if further down the line this would undo many of their operatives as the authorities caught up with their methods.

It was in my view no accident that Abu Hamza used his Newsletter for SOS to sing the praises of the Islamic Army of Aden. The tools I had given them were now turning not just into mouthpieces for the GIA but a global front against the 'Great Satan'. He'd even issued a communiqué warning the US military and other 'kaffir' forces to leave Yemen or suffer the consequences of their occupation of Muslim lands. For months the Newsletter spread a poisonous invective against the authorities in Yemen and backed it up by sending a succession of SOS followers with thousands of pounds of 'souk' cash to be trained by the Army of Aden.

The euphoria was short-lived. The day after he released the so-called communiqué, all hell broke loose as the unthinkable happened. The Yemeni Army took a stand – it tried to rescue the American, British and other hostages. It was a fiasco that ended in the death of several of the hostages.

Ruth Williamson a thirty-four-year-old health worker from Edinburgh was shot at point blank range and bled to death. Peter Rowe a lecturer at Durham University was similarly hit, so too Margaret Thompson an American tourist and Margaret Whitehouse from Hook in Hampshire. All except Margaret Thompson died instantly from their wounds. Mrs Whitehouse died trying to help Australian backpacker Andrew Thirsk whose wounds would also prove fatal.

Laurence Whitehouse, who saw his wife die that day, later said he believed that Abu Hamza was instrumental in the kidnappings as a way of forcing the release of his stepson who'd been despatched as part of the Supporters of Sharia (SOS) group. It is also clear that Hamza enjoyed the attention that came with his association with the event.

In the gunfight, alongside several hostages, a number of the kidnappers were killed. Abu Hamza was full of praise for them. He declared to his jihadist supporters, 'They are in heaven now. That is their reward. We should pray for them and be jealous of their action. They died as a martyrs.'

The fact that the Yemeni authorities were accused of bungling the rescue, and that it was this that led to the deaths of the hostages, cut little ice in the international media. Abu Hassan in Yemen aided by Abu Hamza in the UK tried to play on these initial criticisms of Yemeni government forces by propagating a message that the authorities in Yemen were on a mission to kill Abu Hassan even at the expense of killing the hostages he'd taken. This version of events was vehemently denied by the Yemeni authorities and was also not supported in the event's aftermath by survivors like Laurence Whitehouse.

Hamza was never one to lose an opportunity to propagandise as he insisted to his followers that, 'Our brothers in Yemen are heroes. It is our duty to help all our brothers who are engaged in jihad, wherever they may be in the world. We should destroy the United Snakes of America and all its allies.'

I think Abu Hamza believed that he was heading down a pathway that would bring him into conflict with the authorities. In fact I think he positively relished the idea. From a position of virtual anonymity in Britain he was propelled into the national spotlight by blanket media coverage of his alleged involvement in the trouble in Yemen. He appeared not to care that the headlines were uniformly negative and that he was notorious rather than famous. From that moment on he was able to command news headlines for his ever more outlandish public utterances.

In his view he had become a true leader. Watching him at close quarters during the Yemen episode he was like a man who felt he had found his metier. His peers admired him and his ego was growing with every news headline. With no one to keep him in check he was at a point within his band of followers where he had enormous convening power. I think he probably felt untouchable.

For his followers his boasting was more like a rallying cry for the jihad that they believed was now unstoppable. Finsbury Park Mosque had suddenly been elevated in jihadi circles to a place where recruiters could continue to attract young passionate men – sometimes disillusioned with life in Britain – and dispatch them for weapons and terror training in Afghanistan. Now the prize was not just the war in Algeria but a spreading conflict that they hoped would end at the doors of the Great Satan – the United States of America.

* * *

Despite the notoriety and the obvious influx of many more worshippers and now spies from other intelligence agencies (I was never under the illusion I was alone) the collections of money continued apace. At the heart of it all was Abu Hamza. He was emboldened and to my ever-growing frustration the British authorities were taking little notice, it seemed to me, of my warnings. He now called himself Sheikh Abu Hamza (although it's unclear why or how he was elevated to this status) but from where I was sitting he was looking more and more like the terrorist-in-chief, more respected by his followers and operating with impunity from the police authorities I was informing.

New faces still came from abroad to Finsbury Park Mosque but increasingly young disaffected men from Britain also arrived. The Mosque was becoming a transit point for international terrorists stopping off in London but also, more worryingly for Britain, home-grown converts and would-be terrorists. Radicalisation was in full flow. Now on my weekly visits around the key prayer times on a Friday it was more difficult to keep up to date. There were so many new faces and more and more people were going to Afghanistan. Abu Hamza revelled in his role as the best radicaliser in the business.

It is perhaps unfair to say that the security services were paying no attention. They were taking a keener interest in the comings and goings from Finsbury Park, but they seemed incapable of putting it in its proper Al Qaeda context. They continued to view it as a little local skirmish by a clown.

I made it clear that what happened in Yemen could be traced right back to the Mosque. I even sketched a map to show them precisely where they could find all sorts of contraband from the Mosque 'souk'. I wasn't able to give them documentation to support my claims but then I doubted at the time that the cash economy in the Mosque would allow for much tracing of information – for that you would need access to bank accounts and the like. I could only describe what was going on, not unravel the organisation. The authorities would need to act for that, but they believed they needed real evidence – they couldn't stop people going abroad, they couldn't stop people coming in.

I'd done my best in my first official meeting with the police officers at Scotland Yard in 1998 to explain the seriousness of what I was alleging had taken place at the Mosque. They seemed content to wait and allow Abu Hamza to act as a magnet for all the jihadists in London so they could monitor them more effectively. Although they were interested in what I was telling them, perhaps they had their own suspicions about me. I now believe they viewed me as a 'snitch' and a snitch is rarely trusted in criminal circles. What they didn't understand, because of their own ignorance, was the politics behind all this – but it must have been plain for them to see that I was on friendly enough terms with Abu Hamza and his circle to continue to gather information without arousing undue suspicion.

They asked me to be their 'eyes and ears' in 'Jihadi Central Station' at Finsbury Park Mosque. But with my congenital optimism, even if they didn't have full confidence in what I was telling them and how reliable I was, it gave me the opportunity to continue my war against the man who was helping kill my countrymen and women. His network and ambition was broadening by the day and I felt sure I could expose his criminal organisation in time. I felt at last the Yemen disaster might force the British police to move against him

Abu Hamza's Yemeni misadventure would eventually return to haunt him. Despite crudely trying to shift the blame onto the Yemeni authorities for a botched rescue attempt it was clear he was deeply involved in the whole affair. The enquiries of the US law enforcement agencies led eventually to his indictment on April 19th 2004. Prosecutors in New York laid out their grounds for instigating proceedings to extradite him to the US to face charges for conspiracy to take hostages in Yemen, in which American lives were lost. If they could ever get him to America then he would face American justice. When Hamza finally ended up at the Old Bailey on trial for terror-related offences in 2006, the American authorities made it clear they were prepared to wait for him to serve his British sentence before seeking to make him face justice in America.

Meanwhile there were still battles to be waged in Londonistan and new people to help fight them. I was developing a strong network of journalists who were taking a keen interest in the developing Al Qaeda story. I also felt I was on my way to achieving my aim of working with all three security services – Algerian, French and British – who I thought could undermine

Abu Hamza and Abu Qatada in their attempts to build an Al Qaeda outpost in London.

In chapter 15 we will see that when Abu Hamza was finally extradited to America in October 2012 he still refused to plead guilty to his full involvement in the Yemeni incident. He left it to the jury to consider his guilt. The evidence would also be heard in his 2014 trial that he sent Haroon Aswat and Oussama Kassir to Oregon to set up a training camp for terrorists. I am glad he faced justice in America, because he hated that country even more than Britain. The 'United Snakes of America' got to hear in that trial his pathetic defence for his violent words used against them. He released me from the burden of having to be a public witness to his crimes. He finally told them from his own mouth why he hated them so much.

I was a witness to what he said from the pulpit so I know he offered Heaven to those supporters who committed themselves to killing unbelievers. 'Paradise is held by swords', he would say, 'win your place in it by killing anyone from the United Snakes of America.' On this matter too his memory would fail him again in his 2014 New York trial.

Beyond Yemen I will never forget the thousands of Algerians who lost their lives whilst he revelled in their deaths. I was there to hear with my own ears and see with my own eyes when he claimed the deaths of those who died in the Bentalha massacre from his platform at Finsbury Park Mosque. The truth about the Yemen debacle though was that it showed that the focus for Abu Hamza was no longer the GIA and the conflict in Algeria. That conflict was beginning to run out of steam. Now Al Qaeda provided an opportunity for him to be involved in mayhem, murder and jihad on a much bigger global stage, and he had seized it.

CHAPTER 9

A Tripartite Arrangement

AT THE START of 1999 my contacts at the Algerian Embassy in London who had changed their approach and demeanour significantly since I had first arrived in 1994 (as a result of the changes in government and the end in sight of the civil war) now confirmed that the Algerian security services needed a big man in post in London in the wake of the Yemen affair.

The new government was busy trying to restore a democratic dispensation there and they believed jihadi operations from London were escalating and continued to pose a real threat to the security of Algeria. London had in this sense become a more sensitive and important posting than the US capital of Washington. The new Colonel Benali (also known as Allili) was a man of considerable repute.

In his last meeting with me before heading back to Paris, Jérôme made it clear that with this Colonel's relatively youthful energy and detailed knowledge of terrorism, the DGSE assumed that it wouldn't be long before I was sucked into his orbit. Jérôme concluded, Algerian security service interest was convincing evidence that Londonistan was taking root in the British capital and that things would start to get very hot indeed once he had gone. I detected an air of regret in his voice when he described what he believed lay ahead.

I mentioned the French concerns to my Special Branch contact. They seemed to take that as a cue that this was a good enough reason to foster a good relationship with the new Algerian Colonel – not exactly with their blessing but certainly in their interest. In any case anything to get one over on the French seemed to be a good motivator for the British security services.

I finally met the Colonel the day after Valentine's Day in 1999 in a small coffee shop in Holland Park not far from the Embassy. He was initially quite matter of fact, an opportunity for him to establish contact and look me up and down, and invited me to join him for dinner three days later at a local Notting Hill pub.

Dinner was a chance to introduce him to the culinary delights of London, so I recommended two portions of fish and chips, washed down with a decent bottle of French white. It was incredible how easily we settled into a friendly banter. It clearly helped that we were of a similar age and background. I found that we were both singing from the same song sheet so to speak. We were able to talk competitively about our knowledge of the Algerian terror networks and the tragedy that had unfolded in our country.

At those first meetings I was more inclined to listen than to talk. I had become so embroiled in Londonistan that it was good to talk to someone who could create the big picture of how what was happening in London linked to Al Qaeda terror training camps in Afghanistan and the associated recruits from North Africa and London. It was clear the Colonel was privy to information coming from informants inside the Al Qaeda networks. I could tell from his manner and confidence that he knew a lot about terrorism. He was plugged into a confidential network within the Algerian security services that had access to the highest quality of intelligence from the DDSE (Direction de la Documentation de la Sécurité Exterieure) the Algerian equivalent of the CIA or MI6. And although his knowledge was patchy on what was currrently happening in London it was clear he had informants based at Abu Hamza's Finsbury Park Mosque as well as within Abu Qatada's network.

One thing that did surprise him was how wide a network I had with journalists in the British media. He seemed to be taken aback that he had not heard of me in more detail, because he had been looking for someone with my profile while he was based in Washington. 'You would be very useful to us here,' he told me. 'I think we should make a regular arrangement to meet each other. Our country needs all the help it can get to bring an end to the troubles we are facing.'

We began to meet often. The more we discussed the problems we faced in dealing with the jihadi networks being rapidly built in London the more a sense of comradeship developed. Although it would be fair to say that the

Colonel was something of a closed book; he kept his cards close to his chest but always gave me the impression of being entirely sincere in his desire to protect innocent people back home from the consequences of the rhetoric spewed out by Abu Hamza and Abu Qatada in London.

Within a month he had become sufficiently relaxed with me to draw me into the Algerian understanding of what Londonistan really meant. 'Réda, this has been for the past few years mainly a problem for us Algerians. The carnage at home has been painful to experience and none of the Western governments have really understood the nature of the beast we are dealing with. All they seem to worry about and force on us is elections, elections, elections.'

What he was driving at was the fact that in government-to-government relations fair and free elections had become a form of Western dogma without understanding that the Islamist opponents of the government only wanted elections to carry on their carnage in a different way. They were not demo-crats and the fundamentalists amongst them wanted a return to some kind of medieval system of government underpinned by Sharia law.

Colonel Benali was quite sanguine about the prospects of changing Western governments' attitudes. 'When they are hit by the kind of terrorism we have had to face these past few years then they will fully understand the situation we are confronting. When someone is prepared to kill themselves just to kill others and go to Paradise it makes them a very difficult foe. They will find out soon enough.'

I couldn't argue with the logic of what he was saying and certainly it was my impression from my dealings with the French and British that what was happening in our country was treated as an internal problem. Why else would they allow jihadists to settle in London and carry on propagating their message of destruction if that were not the case?

The Colonel then explained to me the significance, in the Algerian view, of Londonistan. 'Why do you think that so many thousands of people from all over the world are going to military training camps in Afghanistan? Is it just to fight wars in their countries? Is it likely? Osama Bin Laden is planning a big thing against the West. We don't know exactly what, nor exactly when, but something that will justify all this expense on training people. They are training fighters to take the war to the West.'

Finally I was able to place my efforts in the broadest Al Qaeda context.

I had watched with dismay and disgust as the Londonistan networks had grown. I had witnessed and tried to help foreign agencies slow down these developments but London had effectively become an international logistics hub for brainwashing new recruits and dispatching them to training camps in Afghanistan. Furthermore, London had also become a location where by legal or illegal means finances could be raised to support these terrorist activities and the propaganda wars could be fought without the censorship they would encounter in the countries worst affected by current terror activities.

$$* * *$$

The Colonel was an expert in forming relationships. Of all the people I had to deal with in my time as a spy he was the one who took most care to show he valued my information. He also needed me to bring him up to speed quickly on what was happening in Londonistan. He was flattered that Jérôme seemed to know so much about him and even held him in high regard compared to his rather surly predecessor. My contact with the French gave me a distinct advantage in building a trusting relationship with him almost instantaneously. The Colonel made it clear that if he felt he had important intelligence for me to pass on he would let me have it.

For my part I knew that such a reliable source at the heart of the Algerian spy network would give me valuable information which could help me connect with my journalism contacts to help expose the jihadists. This was particularly important now that the British press were starting to take an interest in the activities of Abu Hamza. His 'one eye and no hands' persona made him a gift villain for the newspapers and his increasingly high-profile stunts were getting him attention but not always the positive exposure he craved.

Shortly after Abu Hamza was arrested and then released in March 1999, the Colonel and I met in our usual meeting place. He was furious. 'What are these crazy British up to? They have enough evidence surely to take him to Court. What does he have to do, kill someone to go to jail? I can't imagine the French putting up with his shit for five minutes. He would have been in jail years ago.' I confirmed that Jérôme had formed the same conclusion so both French and Algerians saw eye to eye on this matter.

I knew I needed to tread carefully here because I didn't want the Colonel to know that I had been instrumental in getting Abu Hamza arrested. I did tell him how strange I found it that a national newspaper journalist seemed to know about the imminent arrest before it happened. The Colonel hardly missed a beat before suggesting that if I knew any newspaper journalists who could be helpful in exposing Abu Hamza then as long as I maintained a good relationship with him he would happily use me as a conduit for information to them.

At long last I felt I was on my way to achieving my aim of working with all three security services, Algerian, French and British. Their combined resources I knew – used wisely – could undermine Abu Hamza and Abu Qatada in their attempts to build an Al Qaeda outpost in London.

By now however, the British had proved they were schizophrenic when it came to dealing with informants with links like mine. Even though on the one hand they wanted me to foster certain relationships (because they clearly weren't allowed to) they also became increasingly suspicious of all my connections. It was obvious to me that I had been put under some kind of surveillance, so I held off meeting the Colonel in public places although we did maintain contact by mobile phone. I took the Machiavellian view that if they saw me with such an important contact they would at least know I was serious.

Such was my own concern – and often confusion – over all these overlapping relationship that I thought hard about becoming a telephone spy only. But the reality was that although the Algerians and French no longer needed me to gather detailed reports from the mosques for them, the British had suddenly cottoned on in a big way to the need to keep a close eye on what Hamza and Qatada were saying to their congregations.

The only way to be credible in this new relationship with MI5 was to be on the ground and risk my neck to gather first-hand information (in French and Arabic), but I nevertheless felt instinctively that by dealing with all these different agencies at some point my good fortune at remaining undetected would run out.

* * *

A good few months passed before I had another meaningful exchange with Colonel Benali. We met in the basement of the Algerian Embassy. We talked about my on-going surveillance work for MI5 and I decided it was time to push the boat out in cementing my triangular objective (Algeria–France–Britain). 'Do you have any intelligence which you think might be useful to help the British make up their minds to act against Hamza or Qatada?'

He gave me a rather knowing smile, as if to say, there is no point in me giving you something if I get nothing back. He made a joke of it, saying God himself must have chosen Réda Hassaïne to navigate the messy relationships I found myself in. 'Look I will give you good solid information if I think it is useful but to be frank I am not going to waste my time if I make the effort and nothing happens as a result. The British like to do things in their own idiosyncratic way.' That was code for saying the British security services liked to keep an eye on people but without intervening. It was a style of engagement which security services in a war zone like Algeria were unaccustomed to. There the ends (stopping wholesale killing) inevitably justified the means (eliminating alleged terrorists).

The Colonel wasn't slow to articulate his frustration and deep irritation that despite sharing sensitive information with me about Hamza and Qatada the British had not thus far appeared any nearer to putting them on trial. His frustration boiled over into outright fury after the March 1999 arrest debacle. 'I'm not giving them information for nothing. Our boys are risking their lives to gather this intelligence. For what? It's bullshit.'

By this time MI5 had no real idea how plugged in they were to the heart of the Algerian security service machinery. I could hardly tell them, and perhaps their own surveillance was not up to scratch if it failed to identify this. (The MI5 connection is described in greater detail in the following chapter).

As Arabic speakers and having dealt with the GIA and its mercenaries for over a decade the Algerians, and – as a result of the huge Algerian community in France – the French, had very effectively identified and penetrated the heart of Al Qaeda in Afghanistan. It pained them to see so many young men being sent from and returning to London from the Afghan front line without any intervention from the British from what they could determine. The British kept a tactical silence with their spy counterparts.

In reality I found myself one step away from General Attafi who was the overall Head of the DDSE back in Algiers. He had clearly decided Londonistan was an important theatre of operations and when I heard the Colonel on the phone to him during some of our meetings I realised I had secured a privileged position in trying to put the jihadists in London on the run. It was ironic that given I now found myself trusting the Algerian agents more (remember I had essentially fled from them in 1994), the weak link in the chain I had tried to create was now the British with their reluctance to intervene. These fluctuating fortunes meant I simply couldn't quite synchronise my work across the different services to make a greater impact.

The final straw for Colonel Benali in his attitude towards the British was the arrival of a group of Algerian terrorists via the Yemen into London and the persistent links between Hamza and Algeria. A known activist Abu Ibrahim was amongst them and knowing the atrocities these men had been involved in pushed him over the edge of rage. It was the Colonel who tipped me off about the group settling in Birmingham and when he realised the British were going to sit on their hands he was speechless. His conclusion, 'These British are jokers. Now will you believe me when I tell you that they sleep with Islamists?'

So whilst my British handler, Simon, was incandescent with fury when the story of Abu Ibrahim appeared in the British tabloid *The Sun*, the Colonel was falling over himself with satisfaction. He called me immediately he saw it and put me in touch with a Captain Touhami Sebti, who he assured me had the full story on Abu Ibrahim. 'I mean if we are going to expose this character let's make sure people know the full horror.'

* * *

Captain Sebti was a real life James Bond (except for the fact that he was Algerian). He had seen active service for Algerian intelligence in Afghanistan. This man was as hard as nails. If I were about to be confronted by Abu Hamza's henchmen there was no one I would rather have by my side than Captain Sebti. He was teetotal, multilingual, had a lively mind and was completely willing to explain what he knew about Abu Ibrahim in full graphic detail. He even provided me with a document he'd written in Arabic. All that was left for me to do was to translate it and sell the story to a rival tabloid newspaper *The Daily Mirror*.

I couldn't fail to be impressed with Sebti and his information and I made a deal with him that if I sold the piece for a handsome profit I would invite him to dinner in any restaurant he liked. That would serve as an excuse for an even longer exchange – the next instalment to add to the information I had been gathering for the past four and a bit years.

I suddenly found myself in serious demand from journalists interested in the complexity of the story of these Algerian–Yemeni–Afghan veterans. It also wasn't just the security services but the tabloid newspapers who now couldn't get enough dirt on Abu Hamza, ever since he had been implicated in his Yemeni adventure. It was unfortunate that the Captain had to return to Algeria – his Al Qaeda expertise could have made me a small fortune.

It was a great pity Sebti left so quickly because a few days after his departure was exactly the moment when the usually inscrutable Colonel Benali unwisely decided to go to Finsbury Park Mosque with a camera crew to film people coming and going from the building. It was obvious to me at the time that the fracas that ensued between Benali and Abu Hamza's key enforcer Boualem Jolie Vue on the street in broad daylight could be reported by a local resident and then the police would be called and all hell would break lose. That's why I recommended a reluctant Hamza who was enjoying the spectacle should take his man inside the Mosque to avoid police intervention. It was at that point that I realised that the complicated alliances I had built might now be in danger of alerting people's attention to my divided loyalties.

CHAPTER 10

MI5 – Information Broker

TO MAKE SENSE of all the tensions in my life resulting from my multiple security service allegiances – and how they were beginning to collide by mid-1999 – I need to explain a little of the complexity of my world once my Special Branch handler organised my 'handover' to be handled primarily by MI5 (although I remained in regular contact with both organisations).

On the one hand I was enormously gratified that I had established enough credibility for a third security service to want to recruit me. On the other I was beginning to worry about whether I was any longer in control of my life. I also detected in myself a sense of rising panic. The more occasions on which my different priorities with security services collided the more I became anxious about what might happen to me if I tripped up in the wrong company.

I was also really struggling financially and I felt the small amount of pay I received didn't reflect the value I believed the information I was passing over was worth. The fact was, I saw the whole picture from mosque to conflict zones but the spy agencies made me feel I was only giving them local gossip. I had been neglecting my family and the money I was earning was not enough to feed us so my wife had to try and earn some cash too. My focus on Hamza had taken its toll on my marriage and I had become a closed book, unwilling to share information with my wife in case I sucked her into the messy world I was now immersed in.

What was giving me more cause for concern though was the fact that after putting my neck on the line for six months with Scotland Yard and managing to provide enough evidence for Abu Hamza to be arrested on 15th March 1999, he was promptly released 24 hours later. I figured that there was a good chance that Hamza was himself now on the books of the British security services and it wasn't at all clear what this meant for my own security. The UK, as well as my own country, Algeria, would be safer if he wasn't able to spout his message of hate and organise the jihadist fraternity so freely. He needed to be in jail. But from what I could see, this clearly wasn't on the agenda of Scotland Yard. I could only laugh at their stupidity. To dwell on it would have sent me certifiably mad.

Abu Hamza's arrival in the Mosque coincided with the burgeoning number of Halal butcher shops, coffee shops and barbers in the Finsbury Park area. I was amazed at how so many countrymen of mine were able to raise the money to launch such businesses. I'm afraid to say I had long suspected some of them were able to draw on the proceeds of credit card fraud and other illegal money-making ventures carried out at the Mosque.

As crazy as it may sound, Abu Hamza proclaimed a fatwa 'authorising' his supporters to commit crime in Britain because, he argued, it is a country of unbelievers. It's no exaggeration to say that many of his supporters had one foot in the piety of the Mosque whilst the other one was in the practices of the mafia. It seemed to me the police either didn't believe my reports to them or they thought it was too fanciful to be true. Eventually at the end of July, I was put out of my misery.

On 29th July 1999 Steve called me and arranged an early morning meeting at Green Park station for the following day. I was sick of the follow-me game – it seemed so pointless – but at 11.45 I saw him and followed him as usual to the same Holiday Inn I had been to before. In a private room I was introduced to an MI5 officer who called himself Steve. But because there was another Steve involved in his team I should call him Simon. As far as I was concerned Simon could call me Ali Baba, they made too much fuss over these damn names. In the end they settled on Kevin as my codename. I'm sure Kevin was not an effective disguise with my heavy French accent and Berber looks but why should I object if it got the job done. They all seemed to like it because from then on Special Branch contacts stopped calling me Réda and starting referring to me as Kevin too. Simon, the MI5 officer told me that from now on he would be my linkman for the service. He gave me a pager and arranged that when we needed to be in touch he would page me and I should call a telephone number that he would give me at the time straightaway.

Simon seemed genuine. He was already acquainted with the issues with my immigration status and he promised to sort the matter out as soon as he could. That was a good start. He was also better informed than his Special Branch counterparts. He asked after a certain Abdelaziz who worked for the Algerian security services out of the Holland Park premises of the Algerian Embassy. I knew the man and told Simon that Abdelaziz was busy trying to appease all of Algeria's opponents living in the UK.

Simon had brought a whole exam with him. He asked me about a number of people to test my knowledge and showed me a picture of someone I was unfamiliar with. He was trying to probe how deep my knowledge was and therefore how useful I would be. Then he got serious. He asked if I knew Qamar Eddine Kherban. Kherban was a fighter pilot in the Algerian Air Force before he joined Bin Laden's jihad in Afghanistan. Simon delved into my understanding of the peace process that was beginning to get underway in Algeria. He was interested to know if I had come across Ramdane Zouabri who was the brother of one of the leaders of the most notorious of the GIA's killing squads in Algeria. Zouabri was now a big figure in 'Londonistan' (Benramdane, 1999).

'You need to befriend this guy. We need you to take him under your wing and help him get a flat and any benefits he might be entitled to.' I thought to myself I really don't want to be a social worker for such nasty killers. It was obvious they were planning to recruit him as an MI5 informant and I was reluctant to be the man to bring him in.

It was an easy exam for me to pass because no one knew the Algerian community better than me after years of working for the Algerian, French and British security services. I was in, and Simon made it clear that I was on probation for six months. I would be paid three hundred pounds a month and eighty pounds for my expenses. Not a king's ransom but money, which made me a little bit more financially, secure, for six months at least. I could barely believe my luck. I had a free hand to tell them what I knew about Abu Hamza, Abu Qatada and an encyclopaedia of information I had learned from the French. I pinched myself and said, 'Let us wait and see. The British do things differently.' At least it was a good start. Simon promised to get in touch with me in mid-September.

* * *

Catching the tube back to North London I kept catching myself in the reflection of the underground window. It was the first time I had seen a smile on my face for a long time. I had no idea of knowing that day that I was entering the end game of my underground role in the tragic story of 'Londonistan'. As far as I was concerned at that point I had just entered the world of privileged information in which I would eventually be able to tell the story to the world at large.

I reflected on what I had achieved. Whilst working for the French I had gained real insights into the way things had developed in the English capital. I had an impeccable source of intelligence from the highly competent Colonel who led the Algerian counter-espionage unit in London.

Finally, I had now developed strong contacts with British journalists and was working for British intelligence. It may have been a long way from my idea of helping the various security services to pool their information but I was suddenly sure I could make a big difference in bringing Abu Hamza and Abu Qatada to justice.

I set about finding and befriending Ramdane Zouabri. It didn't take long; it's difficult to hide in London if you are part of a small migrant community. In Algeria he may have been a tough guy but here in London he was more vulnerable. He had a cold look and I suspect he had seen an awful lot of bloodshed back home but here he was pretty lost and needed some friendly advice.

He spoke very little English and like most of us he hated the cold English weather. Courtesy of MI5 I was able to help facilitate his benefit entitlement, getting him registered with a doctor and getting him some accommodation, I made sure he made the right connections. I pretty much organised his life. I don't think he suspected anything, which just goes to show how vulnerable migrants are in a strange country even if they are troublemakers. It didn't take long for the bond of trust to develop and he started to confide in me. Of course he realised that all Algerians were eager to have news from home, so I was pushing on an open door when I asked him about the troubles within the GIA and what the real story was within the group in Algeria. I was particularly interested to hear whether there was any truth in the talk of a strong relationship between his brother in Algeria and Abu Hamza. He seemed almost casual in telling me that of course it was true. Hamza had become a respected figure for his fatwas in the Algerian GIA.

I had to work hard to conceal my mixture of disgust and excitement at getting this confirmation about Abu Hamza. The day Zouabri told me I could barely wait to get out of his company to get this information to Simon. I called Richard in Special Branch and ask him to arrange an urgent meeting with Simon my MI5 handler. The information I had couldn't wait. Richard made quick progress and called me to arrange a rendezvous at his favourite spot. We met at Green Park tube station.

It was 26th August 1999. The ritual began of Simon paging me with a specific number and me calling him back on that first occasion. He was certainly eager to hear what I had to say but made it abundantly clear he didn't want a wasted trip because he had other things he could be doing. I told Simon that something big was going to happen. These people, I told him, are hatching plans to use bombs in the underground and there is a lot of chatter about something bigger the terrorists have in their plans that the world will remember forever. I had no idea where it would happen or when but it was clear that whatever was being planned the whole objective was to create as many casualties as possible.

Simon was naturally keen to know where I got this information. I told him Ramdane Zouabri was extraordinarily well plugged into the jihadist circles both in Algeria and London. Although I couldn't document it, it seemed clear to me that his relationship was like that of a broker between Hamza as a spiritual leader of the GIA and those on the ground in Algeria. I didn't tell Simon I had checked out the information that Zouabri had given me to verify its credibility with Colonel Benali of Algerian intelligence in London.

What I needed Simon to understand was that it was clear from all my daily dealings in Finsbury Park Mosque that people were arriving in London on a weekly basis. They were using the Mosque facilities like a transit point before going off to military training in Al Qaeda bases in Afghanistan. I was utterly convinced that Finsbury Park had become a terrorist forwarding base for jihadists. Finsbury Park had established an infrastructure through which Abu Hamza was raising funds and organising to send material to Afghanistan using these international travellers as mules to bases in Pakistan. It was why so many young Pakistani men were the targets for recruiters. Many had dual nationality and could come and go without proper detection by the security services. Hamza himself spent hours trying to brainwash these young men.

I explained that inside the Mosque Abu Hamza was telling every young Muslim from the pulpit, as well as in private conversations, some of which I was occasionally privy to, that it was a duty for them to go to train overseas in order to come back and fight and take on the 'kaffir' or the unbelievers. Abu Hamza was no longer just an imam but a principal organiser of terrorist-related activity. Worse still he was increasingly credible to his congregation because they respected his strident anti-American and anti-Israeli political views, expressed during his regular inflammatory sermons.

Whilst all this was going on I witnessed the hopeless attempts, by the original Mosque Committee that had brought in Abu Hamza, to smooth over a domestic rift led by Mufti Abdul Barkatullah to reign in Hamza's excesses. Barkatullah was the chair of the trustees of the Mosque who deeply resented the direction the Mosque was heading in. He had approached the Metropolitan Police at Scotland Yard for help and they had told him it was an internal matter that the trustees would need to deal with. Barkatullah also wisely approached the regulator of British charities (the Mosque was a registered charity) for advice on how to deal with the mayhem he was witnessing. He had strong evidence of the political subversion of the Mosque's objectives. He had been personally assaulted and most of the other trustees were too terrified to attend the Mosque any longer.

The British Charity Commission (the regulator of charities) was very polite but utterly ineffectual. They, like Special Branch, were ignorant of the realities of what was going on inside Finsbury Park and they didn't want to listen to those of us who knew. They kept saying they needed evidence to act, but with no one inside the Mosque to challenge Abu Hamza they were reliant on whistle-blowers. I increasingly realised that they were very bad at trusting those who are not like themselves. I am sorry to say I felt that until they overcame their own prejudices we would never deal effectively with Hamza and his henchmen.

Meanwhile, MI5 remained my only real hope. Simon and I met up again at the end of September. He insisted I needed to drill down deep into what was happening at the Mosque. Through my conversations at the Mosque, the increase in the numbers and type of worshippers in jihadist style 'uniform' I could see things were hotting up and Hamza was becoming more brazen in what he said and how he went about his business. Simon seemed distracted and said he needed a break, 'I just hope that nothing kicks off before I get back', were his parting words.

But things were happening all right. I'd made that clear before my hand-over to MI5. I had already called Richard, my old Special Branch handler, to tell him that an individual shown to me by Simon in a photograph on our first meeting, who I hadn't recognised then, I had now actually bumped into at the Mosque. Richard arranged to meet me in a Mayfair pub to show me the picture again. Clearly they were getting more relaxed with me so I didn't have to go through a whole cloak and dagger follow-me routine any more, but the pictures he brought along were not of Simon's mystery man. Instead he showed me a picture of a man I knew as Rachid Dilmi and another jihadist I didn't recognise.

Before we had a chance to get into any detailed discussion, Richard's pager went off and he had to disappear. When he returned it was with a senior MI5 officer called Mark, who had the air of a man who knew this Islamist terrorist underworld very well. He also had a problem with me. I could feel the aggression before he even opened his mouth. He was clearly distrustful of me. Perhaps he thought I was a double agent or even a bona fide jihadist. 'If you mess with me matey, I swear I'll have you deported quicker than you can say Jack Shit. We are watching your every move and you had better deliver because we don't take piss takers lightly.'

I was a little confused. Was it bravado because actually he was pretty scared of terrorists or was it his way of acknowledging he knew how dangerous these people were and he was just showing how ruthless he could be? Part of me was relieved to meet someone with real balls. I was pleased someone finally had the power to make decisions and deport people from the UK.

Mark raised the issue of a GIA communiqué just published in a free news-letter widely distributed in mosques all around Britain but particularly in London. He wanted to know precisely who had prepared and published the newsletter. I told him that the two people concerned were in all likelihood his own informers, alluding to Abu Hamza himself. He could barely conceal his anger at my response, 'I don't know if you are joking? But I hope your information is accurate. I've no time for time-wasters and you'd better know I meant what I said about deportation.' He left the pub barely having calmed down.

Richard advised me that my aggressive tone was probably not all that helpful given that Mark was actually the team leader. He rarely ventured out to meet informants and he really wasn't yet convinced I was the real deal. 'Richard, I don't care. I know as much as he does about these terror networks, if not more, and he is telling me he will deport me. What is he talking about? Without me you lose your contact with these people.' Richard backed off. I was MI5's man now and he didn't need the aggravation that would come if I got into a tricky patch with my new handler.

* * *

Simon had been right to be worried before he went off on his holidays. Despite my official handover I only had Richard to contact in an emergency and issues were coming thick and fast. Two days later, I had to call Richard again to tell him a new group of terrorists had just arrived in London. These men were associated with the Algerian terrorist group the GSPC (The Salafist Group for Preaching and Combat). This group now looked to Abu Qatada as a spiritual leader. Their job was to reorganise the group now some of their militants had pledged their allegiance to Al Qaeda.

We agreed that 'aggressive' Mark, who himself was due to go on holiday, would need to be informed. I found it faintly amusing to think that people were hindering the fight against terrorism by taking their annual holidays.

'He had better not be so aggressive with me this time because he's likely to get the same response.' 'Calm down Kevin. You actually quite impressed him. He recognised you go about your business professionally so don't go getting all funny on me. I'll call you as soon as I get hold of him.' I was beginning to find it difficult to keep track of who I had talked to and on whose behalf and to whom I should be reporting.

On Friday 10th September 1999 it nearly backfired on me. The Algerian Embassy had decided to hold a meeting about the Algerian peace process in the Town Hall in Kensington and Chelsea. The new President Bouteflika had decided to put the broad principles to a referendum. I attended as much out of hope as expectation. What I didn't bank on was bumping two of my contacts, Jérôme my old French DGSE contact and Simon from MI5. He was busy taking notes on what the Algerian Colonel was saying, accompanied on the stage by the Algerian Ambassador. For all I knew there were Special Branch people in the room too.

I admit to being a trifle paranoid at being in the same room as two of my contacts from different security services. When I told Simon about the collision he had a clear idea of what he wanted me to do. Break all contact with the French but cultivate Colonel Benali because Algeria was becoming interesting. On this occasion the Colonel and I discreetly made contact as we departed and agreed that if we saw each other again in public like this we should walk in the opposite direction.

MI5's Simon seemed to hold back from the contact after that encounter but there was more activity on the arrivals front. Richard from Special Branch still warned me to watch out for any another potential arrivals from the Salafist group. This time it was a veteran who had lost an arm in Afghanistan and had just arrived at Heathrow; the feeling was he was a key member of the GSPC. My network was beginning to prove its worth because, armed with his description and details, I was able to track him down very quickly. The exile's world is a small one.

Eventually at the end of September Richard managed to organise a meeting with MI5 Simon, fresh from his summer holiday. He looked relaxed and much tanned – the break had done him good because he was full of energy and raring to go. I brought him up to speed with the flurry of activity at Finsbury Park Mosque in the two weeks he had been away. I set out my stall. 'I'm more convinced than ever that this is no ordinary mosque. Of course it does still fulfil some of the spiritual functions but more and more it is becoming a terrorist transit point. Just one example: there is a small Asian guy of Indian descent who was with Bin Laden in Afghanistan. His name is Haroon Aswat* and it looks to me like he is establishing himself as a key adviser to Abu Hamza. He is perfectly placed with his experience and jihadist pedigree to recruit British-born jihadists. It is his main play.'

I continued to remind them that of course at the mobile shop in the Mosque as well as the usual condiments like tea, rice and other staples, there was important contraband on sale: fake passports, stolen credit cards, stolen goods (jeans and expensive trainers) as well as jihadist videos and books.

---

* Haroon Aswat has been detained under treatment for paranoid schizophrenia in Broadmoor since 2008. He was subject to an extradition hearing from the United States until the European Court of Human Rights blocked this in September 2013. He was named in the 2014 New York trial of Abu Hamza as a key intermediary in the Oregon jihadist camp venture.

'In fact the toilets are so busy with the trade in fake identity papers that it is sometimes difficult to do your business in peace! You can put in orders for most things and get a half-price deal on it. Stolen to order.'

They had wanted me to drill down deeper into what was going on and I had tried to do just that, but I was forever explaining that it was essentially a cash business and almost impossible for me to get access to paperwork without drawing attention to myself. The assembly of terrorists were using stolen and cloned credit cards to finance their activities. They had recruited a whole network of people working in petrol stations, hotels, and restaurants who had been given smart boxes to collect the details from customers' credit cards before cloning them.

'With this simple technique they are able to create whole new identities equipped with new credit card details and passports. They then set up false electricity, gas or telephone accounts using a temporary address. With that done they are opening dozens of bank accounts through which they can launder money.'

By now I was in full flow, but Simon was not making any notes. Richard was just there to observe so I wondered how all my detailed information could be helpful to them. I was rather surprised when Simon stood up. He thanked me for the information and handed me an envelope with three hundred and eighty pounds in it, my income for a month's work.

I was getting the taxi driver feeling again. I roll up, give information and they pay the bill on the meter. But I was not confident that I was doing any more than running errands simply because I could blend in, whereas they would have been immediately spotted as out of place. Every time they called I seemed to be gathering information that took me away from my core concern of Abu Hamza. They wanted me to get better information on who had stabbed a jihadist in their sights named as Mohamed X, as well as other people I didn't know. Perhaps I was expecting too much as an informant, but I had hoped for more. I had hoped I would be able to neutralise Hamza.

* * *

MI5 seemed increasingly frantic without any obvious purpose. At the beginning of October Simon's secretary called me, saying he wanted an urgent meeting and I was to go to Victoria Street and then call the number Simon had given me when we first met. 'He'll be there in ten minutes. So you'd better get your skates on,' she said, 'If you're not there on time you'll have to call me back in an hour.'

I was seriously angry with all the running around I was being made to do. It made me feel I was being used. I felt they were always putting me on the back foot and pressurising me only to find no one at the rendezvous point when I got there. Then from around a corner they appeared.

'Hey Kevin, don't stress out, why are you running', Simon said smiling. 'Because your secretary told me I only had ten minutes that's why,' I said angrily. 'No need to draw attention to yourself running,' he said, 'I'd rather you were late than followed by a dozen pairs of eyes.'

The British culinary reputation was sinking to new depths as they brought sandwiches with them to the meeting. Simon wanted to make sure I was not playing with his officers. I soon realised he wanted privacy and real hard-core detail of how I managed to survive detection in the Mosque. He clearly had difficulty in accepting that I had operated there so long without being rumbled as an informant.

'For a start,' I explained, 'I have made it clear that I have a huge admiration for Abu Hamza's style. I don't make a big play of it but I make enough noise for people to see me as a loyal supporter. My disappointment when he is not there is obvious! Simple things work too. I have a complete change of clothing every day I go there, even my trainers. People remember what you were wearing the last time they saw you but not last week. It's not the most effective disguise but it seems to work.'

I made it clear to Simon that I was always on my guard in the Mosque. I had repeatedly seen the physical harassment of the trustees including Mufti Barkatullah being beaten quite badly and I didn't want to get such close attention. I was well aware that a lot of these guys had a tenuous hold on their status in the UK. This made many of them extremely short-tempered.

'In my mind I operate as if I'm inside a terrorist base. The English say, birds of feather flock together, so I stick with some of the Algerians who know me from way back. I feel a bit more secure that way.'

Simon was showing a real interest in what I was explaining. He was making the odd note and neither of the men interrupted me.

'I always make a point of sitting on the left side of the Sheikh because it is his dodgy left eye. That way he can't keep up with my body language.'

The truth of the matter was this. Abu Hamza may have appeared a fool to outsiders but he was utterly convinced of his righteousness and committed to getting young men to believe in him. This made him an excellent recruitment sergeant for Al Qaeda. Imagine a young boy in his presence being flattered by the attention of this 'great' imam who all the adults and veterans revered. It didn't take much to persuade them that what he said should be followed. It was intense and could only be described as brainwashing.

In another context it would be seen as grooming. Paedophiles are well practised in the art of seducing a young person with extravagant promises. Abu Hamza was no different. He would tell them incessantly that Islam is all about jihad and that jihad would bring out the good man in them. He would tell them that swords of truth protected the gates to Paradise and they would need to use legitimate violence to find favour with Allah to enter paradise as a martyr.

'He holds court on the first floor of the Mosque most days. Most of the young boys are of Pakistani origin so he talks to them in English. But he's no fool. He is like a chameleon. When he is with the Algerians he adopts a different stance, offering them coffee, mint tea and dates. He'll hang around whilst the jihadi videos are playing in the corner of the hall on an old television and say to them, 'Look at your brothers. Look at what they are doing. They are heroes. They are martyrs.' Feed someone on that diet for long enough and they will want more!'

In all my time dealing with the British security services, I had never commanded this much attention. I was into my full stride and it was clear they wanted to understand exactly where I was coming from.

'Hamza is one of those people who will just push it on a little further if people are eager to listen. 'Look, imagine being a martyr just like them. Once you enter Paradise you too will have seventy-two virgins to care for your needs. The life you have now is not a patch on what is waiting for you in eternity. London is a toilet.'

Simon was struggling to keep up with my explanations of Abu Hamza's obsession with Osama Bin Laden and his warmongering in Afghanistan to liberate Muslim lands from the oppression of the 'kaffir'. As far as I was concerned his principal objective seemed to be to recruit people to train in the art of guerrilla warfare in war zones and then return to the Western world to perpetrate acts of carnage. I really couldn't have made my feelings clearer to Simon. I sarcastically asked if MI5 would offer me protection if I tried to pass through Heathrow with a fake passport on my way to training in Afghanistan.

'Yes, and we'd make sure you went there in first class! Do me a favour. That is not the business we are in,' he said.

'Can I ask, then, why it is you don't arrest people who are going to Afghanistan for one reason only – to train and come back and kill people here?'

Simon was starting to get agitated as I was moving on to sensitive territory. 'Listen, Kevin, we give the orders and you follow them. It's not for you to worry about how we go about our business. I sincerely doubt Britain's minority communities would thank us if we started picking up people left, right and centre on suspicion of going to train as terrorists on your say so.'

This infuriated me, 'What? Am I risking my neck for nothing? We are just observing to make up nice stories or what? Meanwhile you are taking no action. What kind of rubbish is this?'

Simon then told me something I had not fully understood up until that point. It was the organising principle around which the security services seemed to want to operate with these fanatics. It was either utter cowardice or utter madness. For me it amounted to the same thing – more unnecessary deaths.

'Look we have freedom of speech in this country Kevin, so what they want to organise here, as long as it's destined for somewhere else on the planet, our instructions are to operate a "covenant of security" – which means we watch them but they keep carnage off the streets of the UK.'

If they thought this would last they were pathetic but then few of them had lived through the kind of civil war we had had in Algeria. I tried one final time.

'There is a guy in the Mosque who is enormous, long hair, beard, thick neck and he has been boasting about being a hit man for Bin Laden. His name is Oussama Kassir*. He is never out of a combat suit and when the jihadi videos are playing he is entirely unpredictable. Sometimes he cries out with joy when he sees a mujahideen being killed, "Praise be, they are now in heaven." Do you think this kind of attitude has no impact on the young men

---

* At time of writing, Kassir remains in prison in the United States for involvement in the Oregon jihadist camp venture. Abu Hamza also faced charges for the Oregon offence in his New York trial in spring of 2014.

attending the Mosque? I'm sure if it was in one of your churches you would have something to say about it!'

I had all but used up my time slot with them. They had said hardly anything the whole time, just taking the odd note down and seemingly engrossed in what I was recounting. They always seemed to run out of steam so easily. Simon waited until he got up to leave to give me some good news. Finally, after working with the British for nearly eighteen months, they were confident that my immigration status was going to be sorted out. Despite my concerns, they wanted me to continue monitoring Ramdane Zouabri.

So although frustrated, I left them that day on a high. I had got so much off my chest I felt a huge relief and now I finally felt I might be able to stop worrying about whether I would be allowed to stay in the UK.

* * *

I was developing a good relationship with Ramdane Zouabri. He was quite personable and we were able to exchange stories of places in Algeria that we both knew. But I was always on my guard talking about home because the talk would eventually get to politics and then people inevitably took sides. Zouabri was actually great company inside the Mosque. Everyone had a healthy respect for him as a result of his brother's leadership status in the GIA. This made him a go-to person in the minds of those who wanted to ingratiate themselves with Abu Hamza in order to in turn curry favour with the man in Algeria with a fearsome reputation.

His presence had even attracted the attention of one of the leading Arabic newspapers based in London, *Al Hayat*. The paper ran a sizeable report on his arrival in the capital and how he was seemingly finding it easy to settle in and secure his asylum-seeking status. It wasn't something I wanted to take the credit for even though some people were showing an interest in how I managed to get things moving so easily. My excuse was always the same. Journalists have contacts otherwise they are useless journalists.

The occasions on which my multiple allegiances collided were becoming more frequent. It was putting me in increasingly stress-inducing situations. What if my contact greeted me in a way that was deemed too friendly by their enemies? I always felt most vulnerable when this happened. I knew there was always a chance of exposure.

* * *

Without warning my contact the Algerian Colonel Benali turned up at Finsbury Park Mosque with the Algerian TV journalist. Unfortunately one of Abu Hamza's security guards turned on him and was giving him a sound beating outside the Mosque in full view of everyone. Boualem Jolie Vue (aka Attalah Mohammed) was well known for his short temper in the Mosque and had a reputation for having been a combatant of extreme violence back in Algeria.

In the presence of Hamza he was like a naughty teenager but turned into an attack dog if he thought his master was compromised. With his long hair and ginger beard he had the air of a madman when he flew into a rage. I have no idea why I intervened but I managed, with help from others, to separate them and restrained Jolie Vue by getting his comrades to haul him red faced back up the small flight of steps into the Mosque.

Abu Hamza was applauding him for his vigilance and said anyone who was against us was also against the jihad and deserved whatever they got. That got a whole lot more cheers. The Colonel had been unwise to stray without security into this place. It showed that even he underestimated the type of people who were now running the Mosque, and their protectors. They were as battle hardened as he was. It showed me how dangerous they had become and convinced me further that the British were clueless.

Now I had a new problem. Perhaps out of jealousy, some individuals were beginning to get agitated about Zouabri's influence with Hamza. One of them, Mohamed Sekkoum, had a healthy reputation for standing his ground with most people at the Mosque. He started to spread rumours about Zouabri and cast doubt on the reasons why he had come to the Mosque.

This of course put me in a very difficult position again, because I had to take sides. MI5 wanted Zouabri protected until he was recruited and I had been given that responsibility. I was beginning to worry about my cover being blown. If anyone at the Mosque got an inkling of my relationship with the security services I was confident they would hunt me down and cause me serious harm as they had done to the Colonel. But I had no choice but to take Zouabri's side.

I admit I felt a complete hypocrite in this situation. Here I was trying to fight terrorists and now trying to protect one of the worst. I felt I was allowing myself to be used now that the carrot of residency was being dangled in front of me. Deep down I realised I was getting sick of this underworld existence, living a double or even a triple life. My status in Britain was all that was preventing me now from getting out of this. I was no longer convinced that the British would help me if things turned against me.

I was even less sure that they were 100% focused on taking Abu Hamza off the streets. I was becoming worried that I was going to trip myself up. I was torn between nailing Hamza and these people and also having a safe life. My children were getting older and suddenly I felt my responsibilities as a father were changing my focus. My wife and I were getting more estranged the more remote I became because of this crazy world I was operating in.

The second close shave with the Colonel (remember we had agreed to walk in opposite directions the next time we met) and the growing aggravation with Zouabri was an uncomfortable reminder for me that everything the French had told me about the British was probably true. I felt I was getting in deeper with little reward or outcome. After these two incidents I decided that as soon as I had my immigration papers I would end my life as an informant and instead start working with the contacts I had made in newspapers to help them as an undercover journalist. It was certainly a better way for me to earn a living and potentially an easier way to unsettle Abu Hamza if the security services weren't interested in arresting him any more.

When I next reached out to Colonel Benali it was clear his ego had been badly bruised but his position as intelligence chief in London had also been potentially compromised. He had let his irritation over the release of Hamza get the better of him; he'd stepped too far into the field for a head of intelligence. I arranged to meet him in a pub near Holland Park.

We drank white wine together and spoke about the improving situation in Algeria. He asked me if I would act as a middleman to give some important intelligence to MI5 because there were no official relations between Algeria and Britain and he would soon be leaving London. The piece of intelligence he passed on would ultimately end my relationship with the British (see next chapter). He told me that Abu Walid – a well-known Al Qaeda operative – would attend Abu Qatada's mosque before flying back to Afghanistan to meet directly with Osama Bin Laden. The fact that such a high-level Taliban veteran was passing through London was clearly of significant interest to the British. I thought hard about what I should do with this information.

Leaving the bar, perhaps unwisely given the state I was in, I decided to call Simon. He said it was impossible to see me for a few days. But I told him I had nothing to live on so he would have to get me some pay. I also said that I had a vital piece of intelligence that I wanted to pass on and it couldn't wait because it was soon Ramadan and there was no way I could meet him for two weeks. He reluctantly agreed to meet me the following day at 3.30pm at Warren Street tube station.

At 3.30pm sharp the following day, Simon appeared at Warren Street tube station and went straight away to a public phone box to fake a phone call. I knew I had to follow him and saw him place a cigarette packet just on top of the telephone casing. After he walked out of the box I quickly slipped in and picked it up. To my relief I counted out six hundred pounds. He had understood my hint about Ramadan and left two months wages. He either completely forgot about the vital bit of intelligence I had to pass or didn't want to be seen in public with me, so I held on to it and decided I'd probably be best to verify it first in any case.

✳ ✳ ✳

Over the Christmas period I kept up my daily checks on Finsbury Park. I would go for prayers, press the flesh with a few people I knew, ask after their families and buy just enough halal meat and cakes to last me a day so that I had an excuse to come back the following day to restock my provisions. Eventually on 19th January 2000, Simon called me again and arranged for me to meet Richard at Hyde Park tube station.

This time I was going to meet yet another new face. He told me his name was Tom and he and Richard began to interrogate me about an unnamed bearded man who had arrived in London just a few days previously. They seemed quite agitated about him. As it was abundantly clear I didn't know who they were talking about, Simon said that he would make contact with me at Warren Street the following morning at 8. He said we would use the same phone box as the money drop location a few weeks earlier. He would fake making a phone call from the public phone and leave a cigarette packet with a picture of the bearded man inside.

'We need you to get to Finsbury Park as quickly as you can after that because he is due there some time this morning. If you see him we need you to contact us immediately. By the way, it might well be Tom in the box doing the drop and not me.'

Simon asked me about the situation in Algeria and the deadline given to the terrorists by the President to give up their weapons. I was not impressed. Suddenly they had an air of panic about them. 'Look as far as I know the Salafist GSPC and GIA leaders are probably well ahead in making plans to come to England to apply for asylum. As you are making an army of terrorists here already why not just finish the job! Yes, you are making an army of terrorists in London, why not them?'

The faces of all three men changed. Simon did not like my sarcasm one bit. But I was becoming sick of their games. Before we parted he said that I had one more month before my trial period ended. What they wanted to do now was forget about Abu Hamza and concentrate instead on Abu Qatada. Simon's reasoning was simple, 'We need to forget that harmless clown Hamza and start focusing on a guy who is a real menace. Qatada is in need of some of your close attention. You can leave Hamza to us.'

This was news to me. I had been at the Fourth Feathers youth club just behind Marylebone Station in a quiet part of central London several times and Abu Qatada's congregation was like a university compared to the brawlers' gym at Finsbury Park. For me Qatada was not the problem. But now things were moving back in Algeria, Abu Hamza appeared less of an issue to the British. If they really believed this they clearly had not understood everything I had told them about Finsbury Park being an Al Qaeda guesthouse in London. But their approach also aroused my suspicions about Hamza's links to the security services. If Hamza was one of MI5's men, then of course that would be the perfect explanation for why he could be left to them.

Once again I felt I was being manipulated and outmanoeuvred. I was utterly enraged. 'So, whilst Abu Hamza is busy recruiting hundreds of people to send them to Afghanistan to train in Al Qaeda Camps, and then to come back to the West to prepare terrorist attacks, you are telling me that he is only a clown? Are you crazy? Are you not seeing what it is going to happen to you all here? If I concentrate on Qatada, everything I have gained at Finsbury Park will be lost.'

I had no idea what was going on and my paranoia was starting to set in. I was pretty sure sending me off to Abu Qatada's Fourth Feathers meeting place was a game MI5 wanted to play with me. So the following morning, assuming they were now putting me under surveillance for whatever reason, I went to all my usual haunts – the coffee shops and both mosques at Finsbury Park. I wanted to take the opportunity to show them that I knew everybody in the area. I even stopped to buy a newspaper and photocopied a report as well as the picture and the date on the paper.

By now I was finding it hard to contain my frustration. It was making me unwell. It made me start to see that perhaps they had not valued my information after all. It also made me realise I'd never entirely left my journalistic instincts and values behind. I needed to see my work leading to results. I was not just an information broker; I wanted to make an impact with what I was doing. I wanted to avenge the thousands of dead brothers and sisters back home. That was why I had come to Britain in the first place and the business was most definitely unfinished. No arrests and no let-up in Hamza's activities, was like bringing a cracking story to an editor that he continues to refuse to publish. It could give me a heart attack if it carried on much longer like that.

I was beginning to feel I had taken the relationship with MI5 as far as I could. Qatada was a menace but most of my evidence was enough, I was convinced, to convict Abu Hamza of something illegal to take him out of circulation. I had as much information as I needed to step away knowing I had done my best to bring Abu Hamza to justice. I did not want to start on another wild goose chase with Qatada and end up just passing on information with no results. I was not in this for the money; I was in it for justice.

I vowed that at my next meeting I would tell them my time with them was up. The only thing that was really stopping me was the reality that I still had not secured my immigration papers to start the new life I felt I had earned.

* * *

Now the time seemed to drag. I had made up my mind and I wanted to get on and make a decision. It was a full month though before I could arrange a meeting with Simon. We arranged to meet at Victoria Street and then made our way to the Stakis Hotel in Caxton Street.

Over a lunch of coffee and cheap salmon sandwiches Simon apologised for the delay in setting up the meeting but there had been some issues with my immigration papers and he hadn't wanted to come empty handed. 'But the good news is your papers are now sorted and on the way to your lawyer.'

I could not contain my excitement and banged the table so hard I thought the glass top might shatter. I was thinking (but could not say), 'My God I can see the big bright light at the end of the tunnel.'

Simon pressed on, "Kevin we actually hoped you would continue to go to Finsbury Park as a kind of test. The service needed to know how capable you were of conducted surveillance, how much you really knew.'

I stopped him mid-flow and pulled out the photocopy of the paper article I'd made on the day with the date. 'Simon, you guys really do underestimate me. I've been a journalist for fifteen years, people tried to blow me up in Algiers, I had to change country, you think I survived by being an idiot?'

Now Simon had a wide smile. 'Well you'll be pleased to know you passed the test with flying colours. I sent a report to my boss praising you and they have said you are good enough to keep on. They have approved a twenty per cent increase in wage and in six months' time they will increase it again. But you need to think about things first and you will want to see those papers first before you make any decisions. You've two weeks to think about it and give us an answer yes or no. All right Kevin? You've done a good job.'

Something filled me with ambivalence about the offer. It would give me some financial security, but it would definitely not make my life my own. I would still be part of their game. With the immigration papers game still hanging over me. As I saw it all these slights were only speeding up the moment when I would need to turn back to journalism and away from spy craft.

On 25th February just before Friday prayers Richard called me to check some intelligence he had received that Abu Hamza was going to attend a sit-in outside the German Embassy in Belgravia. But the message was confused? If I was at Finsbury Park and I saw him I should just ignore him. If they had a strategy I couldn't understand what it was.

Prayers were a bad-tempered affair that day, mostly because Abu Hamza was in a rage. He had discovered that Germany had already deported two Egyptian Islamists back to Egypt so any protest would have been futile. The protest was called off. Reports had filtered through that the Egyptian authorities had already killed both men. Abu Hamza was livid and that day he made me feel truly uncomfortable. He told the believers that this proved it was open warfare between the West and 'Us.' 'They hate Islam and those who are against us deserve whatever comes their way.' I have never seen an angry 'clown' before and Hamza's words of vengeance and hate could not have been a clearer indication that this assessment by the British security services was fundamentally flawed.

As promised, I called Richard to fill him in with the latest news. I was able to confirm the names of the two Egyptian 'martyrs' the Germans had deported. All he could say was 'Excellent, Kevin. Good work mate.' I no longer had any confidence that my insight and intelligence would do much good beyond being fed into the MI5 intelligence sausage machine.

It was with an almighty sense of relief that on Monday 13th March 2000 I took an early morning call from my lawyer. 'You need to come in Réda. Your papers are through; it's not quite what we were expecting. But I'd rather not talk about it over the phone.'

I made my way into Central London as soon as I could. I could tell by my lawyer's demeanour that it was not wholly good news. He handed me the letter from the Home Office.

I read the words and didn't quite believe what I was seeing. I looked up at my lawyer and down again at the words. I stopped myself, just, from ripping the paper to shreds. I was bitterly disappointed with how MI5 processed my immigration papers. I felt this confirmed their propensity for duplicitous behaviour as I had felt they had behaved all along. It was an extension of their game with me; like giving themselves extra time in a football match. As far as I was concerned they had badly let me down.

I had anticipated that, with the amount I had sacrificed and risked, I would have been given 'indefinite leave to remain', the right to remain in Britain with my family indefinitely. All they gave me, in the words of the letter, was a four-year visa. They had left the option open to get rid of me back to Algeria if it suited them.

Perhaps I was paranoid, I felt they were trying to have a hold on me, whilst I was desperate to be free of their control. Despite the praise Simon had heaped on me I felt they were still treating me with contempt.

CHAPTER 11

The Man Who Knew Too Much

THE PREVIOUS YEAR had been a difficult year all round. Terrorist activity was mushrooming. Sometimes it was difficult to keep track of all the comings and goings from London to Pakistan and other places. I had multiple growing conflicts in my work with the agencies and as a result a re-emergence of the conflicts and stress in my head. And now I knew I only had a four-year visa.

The war at home in Algeria was edging towards a resolution. A newly elected Algerian President Abdelaziz Bouteflika had secured popular support for a policy of reconciliation through a referendum. Although the civil war had effectively been declared over, small bands of GIA diehard fighters would remain involved in skirmishes with the state for years to come.

My relationship with Special Branch had also developed. Richard was still my main contact and on a dark and damp November evening I had news I had arranged to pass on to him. He had come to recognise that I was reliable. He and the others were in a state of constant high agitation at that point so as soon as I'd rung them he arranged a meeting. We met beside Westminster Bridge and he suggested we walked to a nearby hotel in Charing Cross. I always found it so odd that this secret world was carried out under the full gaze of an unsuspecting public.

As soon as we entered the reception of the ornate building that was built at the height of the railway boom in Britain, I noticed a tall man watching us. He wasn't the slightest bit inconspicuous. To me he looked like a police officer operating undercover, which was exactly what he was. This special branch officer introduced himself to me as Bob. Bob and Richard had a slightly tetchy relationship and it was clear that Bob was the more senior of them. He tried to pump me for information on a jihadist with known terrorist connections. This highly suspect character had arrived with his two wives and fifteen children, along with four other Algerian veterans. They had all found their way to Yemen after being kicked out of Pakistan and now planned to stay in England. Over a couple of drinks I explained that at that point I didn't know much about these new arrivals, but I made it clear that within a week I would make it my business to know as much about all five of them as possible.

The following Wednesday, 24th November, Simon from MI5 called me to tell me he and his colleague Steve needed an urgent meeting with me the next day. That suited me because for the entire previous week I had been running from one part of London to another trying to gather information and confirm it with my contacts. I was keen to get a lot of it off my chest. Somehow you feel contaminated when you learn certain things and cannot share them. They were the sort of people who were so focused on killing in the name of jihad and showed so little pity for their victims that I worried I might lose my mind trying to not to be brainwashed by their constant scheming.

As usual there was a rigmarole to go through to meet up with Steve. He was the ultra-secretive type. So, on Thursday 25th November I took the Victoria line south from close to my flat. When I got there I was to ring a number he had given me.

A woman answered, 'When you get to the traffic lights on the corner of the road, you need to turn left and then take the first turn on the right.' Suddenly she stopped. 'Are you listening, or am I wasting my time?' she asked. Perhaps she could sense I was distracted. 'You will then be on Caxton Road. There is a hotel directly opposite Scotland Yard. You know where the revolving sign is. They'll be waiting for you in reception.' I made it clear I had indeed understood.

Shortly after I left the red payphone box I realised two men were following me. From a distance, I assumed they were Steve and Richard. I had seen their reflections in the window of the office block we had passed on the way. Once I reached the concierge they approached me and shook hands formally. They had come to do business but this time it was not to be done in the open. They had booked a room in the name of Abbey. We entered the lift in silence and went to the third floor. They were clearly agitated about something.

We sat around a small coffee table and Simon immediately handed over eighty pounds in cash. He told me this was a reimbursement for my expenses for the month and confirmed they had already seen to it that Richard had given me my pay of three hundred pounds the previous week. It was clear the money issue was what was agitating them.

For my part I wanted Special Branch and MI5 to realise who these terrorists were so they could take them out of circulation. As far as I was concerned, one person arrested here in London meant dozens of lives, possibly hundreds, saved in Algeria. But of course as it was my only way of making a living I could not ignore issues of finance.

To the point of the meeting. Out of my pocket I pulled a long hand-written list of veterans from the Afghanistan war against the Russians. I had spent months compiling it from dozens of conversations I had had inside Finsbury Park Mosque and elsewhere. I was absolutely confident I had identified clear links that put these men directly into Osama Bin Laden's orbit.

It would be an understatement to say they were taken aback by the list I had prepared for them. I had laid out very carefully the real names of the men and as many of their aliases as I had been able to identify. I also went one step further and provided the identification number on each of their fake passports.

Simon held the list in his hand. It was shaking. Richard was stretching to see the list too. They studied the list carefully, very carefully, and then looked up at me and back at the list. I was obviously waiting for a response. One of them piped up, 'Where the hell did you get all this information from?' 'Let's just call him Agent XI', I said. They both had a confused look on their faces. I'm sure they felt I knew more than they thought I should. It was difficult to tell.

What I had given then was clearly of interest. But they gave me no indication of how interesting it might be. Steve called an abrupt end to the meeting. 'Perhaps we should go and get a bite of lunch downstairs in the restaurant.' I wasn't particularly hungry.

Then I could no longer resist the temptation to press my advantage to make sure I was properly recompensed for the information I was handing over.

'Look,' I said, 'these people are really dangerous. All they want to do is kill, kill, and kill. They tell others who they are preparing to go and kill. It is their ticket to paradise. I don't see you moving so fast and I want you to use my information to get these people off the streets.' 'Kevin, it's not as easy as that. It's complex. We have to be careful not to lose track of these people and their contacts; sometimes it's better to keep these really dangerous types under close surveillance.'

I looked them over. Silence. 'I need these people exposed not tracked. David Leppard over at *The Sunday Times* would pay good money to get hold of this story.' They looked at me. I really couldn't tell what they were thinking. That quickly changed. Simon came straight to the point, 'That would not be very helpful. We are on the case and will do what we can.'

✳ ✳ ✳

A couple of weeks passed. No one from Special Branch called me. I was getting restless. News had filtered down to me that the Algerian Afghan veterans had moved to England's second city Birmingham, all the way from Yemen. With its large émigré community from Pakistan, Birmingham was one of those places large enough to be fairly anonymous and where the local faith community could provide reasonable camouflage for their activities even if the communities they lived in were unaware of their real purposes.

I was chomping at the bit to find out what they were up to. I called my MI5 handler and asked if they would pay for my expenses to take the train up to Birmingham to investigate which mosque they were using. I was expecting a friendly response – I only needed a couple of hundred pounds. But they didn't want me to go to Birmingham but to stay in London. To do what, I asked myself. Sit back and watch these people infiltrate another community and get more sons of British Muslims to sign up for jihad? Their response puzzled and angered me.

I may not have been in an army but I was fighting a war. All my journalistic instincts were surfacing again. This was too good a story to lose to some bumbling idiots. I picked up the telephone to David Leppard at *The Sunday Times* Insight team. They agreed to pay my expenses. Why wouldn't they?

Algerian jihadists, ejected from Pakistan, then Yemen, ending up in Birmingham. It was a cracking story and no one else was anywhere near it.

No one else even knew what was going on behind the scenes. We were ahead of the pack, just like I had always been back in Algiers before the war killed journalists and free journalism.

* * *

On Friday 4th February 2000, I turned up at London's Euston station and took the first fast train to Birmingham. It took me less than three hours to track down the Afghan veterans to the Al Amana Mosque, in the Sparkbrook area. Typically their base was in a poor rundown area of the city with a large migrant population. It was a natural 'social camouflage'. Years later these communities would pay heavily for this.

As soon as I found these particular countrymen of mine, I called Richard from a public pay phone. I basically wanted him to know that I was in Birmingham from the number that came up on his telephone screen. He was livid that I had tracked down these so-called warriors. MI5 was hopping mad at what they considered to be my freelance intelligence gathering operation. But why?

I think I realised on that day that they must have known where these Afghan veterans were. It made me take more seriously what my Algerian Security services contact had already hinted at last time I had seen him. He claimed it was MI6 themselves who organised the Afghan veterans passage to England. Richard's reaction gave that explanation more credibility and he probably worked out that I was suspicious.

Logically it made sense. It was surely impossible for five Afghan veterans of Algerian origin, all with strong links to Osama Bin Laden, to arrive at the same time and on the same plane, with false passports, and get out of Gatwick Airport without the full knowledge of MI6 and MI5. What defies belief is that the security services could be that stupid or naïve to believe there was some advantage to having these murderers in Britain.

Whatever doubts I had been harbouring about the people I was dealing with, they were now turning into more paranoid observations about who I could trust in the situation I now found myself in. I needed to be careful that the hunter didn't become the hunted.

It seemed to me if they had the same cavalier attitude to these Afghan veterans as they showed to me, it meant they fundamentally misunderstood the power of the jihadist propaganda. This was a recipe for creating an army of terrorists in England after turning them into informers and paying them for the privilege. These jihadists would take your money and slit your throat, because that is their way to paradise. They don't care about the consequences on earth. It was like giving a flock of sheep a wolf as a bodyguard.

A few weeks later when I met up with Simon, his face turned red, with rage (or embarrassment I couldn't tell), but they knew I had the measure of them.

* * *

Three weeks later I got an angry early morning call from Simon. 'Why the hell did you sell the story on Abu Ibrahim to the papers?' The tabloid *Daily Mail* and *Sun* newspapers had splashed a front page story about the Yemeni 'refugee' who'd arrived with two wives and fifteen kids and now had two houses all paid for by British taxpayers.

I told him I was as surprised as he was about the Abu Ibrahim story because the information had not come from me. In fact I was pretty fed up myself losing good money on a story like that given I had been sitting on the information from Colonel Benali for months. I began to put myself on guard and think of my own safety and that of my family, on whom my work acting as an informant had taken its toll.

What the newspaper scoop should have told my handler and the security services was that what these men were up to was now attracting the attention of many more journalists, not just me. Clearly MI5 didn't believe my explanation. They were now worried about my loyalty to them.

As far as I was concerned my travels to Birmingham had shown me a way out. I had reminded myself my journalistic instincts were still very much alive. I had spent the first day sitting outside a branch of the Halifax where most Algerians banked their money. As soon as an Algerian appeared I asked them where I could find the mosque that most veterans went to. Being an Algerian they showed me the way. Once there I picked up a copy of the Koran and read some parts of it very conspicuously. Eventually someone approached me and we began a conversation that ended up giving me all the details I needed on these Afghanistan veterans.

This convinced me that if I now took the story to the media I might be able to put pressure on the security services to act. At the same time I might be able to feed my family and repair some of the damage I had done in my wife's eyes to the welfare of our children. Given my family situation I couldn't really see a downside.

So, on 4ᵗʰ April, 2000, I sold the full Abu Ibrahim story to the *Daily Mirror* for several thousand pounds. It made a full front-page splash. It felt just like the old days. I felt liberated re-engaging all my journalism skills to speak the truth.

A week later I met up with Simon. This time I told him I was the source of the story. I argued there was no point holding back now that it was in the public domain. I bluntly told him I felt travelling down the path where I knew I could make an impact with the story made more sense to me than passing information on when nothing would get done.

Steve wanted to know exactly how much money I had made, so I told them a year's worth of money from them. But more to the point working with them I was putting my neck on the line and not achieving my objectives, whereas with the press I could stay out of the way of any troublemakers and guarantee trouble for the likes of Abu Hamza.

* * *

I had been keeping my ear to the ground to verify the tip-off from Colonel Benali that the 'respected' Al Qaeda terrorist, Abu Walid, would be attending Abu Qatada's mosque. I got a call from a contact amongst Qatada's growing following to confirm it would happen the following Friday and I felt it was time to pass on this information to my MI5 handler.

The Fourth Feathers Community Centre, in Lisson Grove, was a few hundred yards walk from the central mosque; a kind of breakaway gathering in a community centre that backed onto the train line coming into the old train station at Marylebone. The prayers were intentionally radical and more political. Qatada's sermons were like a university lecture, compared with the soapbox politics of Hamza.

Prayers were in one sense more informal because it wasn't a proper mosque but more intense because the sermons were in Arabic and the worshippers were somehow more fervent in their attitudes towards explaining the need for engagement in foreign wars.

I finally organised a meeting with Richard and Simon to pass on the information Benali had given me some time before. When I told them Abu Walid was going to his final prayers before heading to Afghanistan – passing first through Pakistan – to meet Bin Laden himself, Simon nearly fell off his chair. MI5 had asked me to follow Abu Qatada's activities. Here I was delivering again.

'Who the hell is your source this time?' Simon asked. Of course I knew this information was rock solid because it had come from Colonel Benali and I had verified it – he of course was the same guy who had passed me information about the Birmingham-based Afghanistan veterans. How could Simon not be impressed? I detected a visible excitement at the prospect of such a nugget of information. This link to the Algerian security service with its long experience of jihadists was a real gold mine and I hinted as much.

Simon insisted that I cultivate my relationship with my Algerian source. He also made it plain that he wanted to make sure that I had broken all the vestiges of my links to the French Security services. He insisted on that permanent break because as he told me the DGSE were giving them 'nothing but shit' over what the French were increasingly and openly deriding as 'Londonistan'. I sensed a clashing of institutional egos. There was something in Simon's manner, however, that put me on my guard. I was starting to think that perhaps I knew more than my handlers about the big picture of what was happening in Londonistan. Perhaps even, that I knew too much?

We parted company, with Simon telling me I should wait for his call. I thought to myself with a sense of bitterness, 'Always waiting, never doing!'

Finally after a few days of silence, always on tenterhooks, thinking about the time we were losing, Steve called to tell me everyone in his team and Simon's were agreed that it would be a good idea for me to attend Abu Qatada's mosque for Abu Walid's special prayers.

* * *

Friday 21st April 2000, I rose early. It had been a night of fitful sleep. I had a sense of nervous anticipation at what I would find and hear at the Fourth Feathers.

Little did we realise at the time how tragic would be the results of seeds sown at this place. It was just a few hundred yards from the devastating bomb at Edgware Road underground station on 7th July 2005 that killed six tube travellers. Homemade organic-peroxide-based devices packed into rucksacks caused the explosions. In my view utterly predictable, but missed.

The Fourth Feathers was unusually busy when I got there. It wasn't an ideal space for prayers but people made do. Inside the prayer room I sat cross-legged in the middle of several lines of mostly young men listening to the fiery Islamic cleric Abu Qatada. He would intersperse his sermon with sharp bangs of his stick on the wooden floor for effect as he preached a hate-filled speech against the British, American and Jewish people.

I estimated there were at least sixty men and some teenage boys listening attentively to the inflammatory words of the man who would later be dubbed by a Spanish judge as Osama Bin Laden's right-hand man in Europe. Once he had raised the temperature then it was time to call those present into their words of devotion to Allah.

It was then that I noticed Abu Hamza's Algerian bodyguard whom I knew from Finsbury Park Mosque. I was taken aback to see Boualem Jolie Vue at the Fourth Feathers. He never under normal circumstances came here. Something unusual was happening. The two men – Qatada and Hamza – had fallen out after the Algerian Islamists had split into two separate groups. Of course I had last encountered Jolie Vue when I had helped drag him off my friend Colonel Benali whilst he was assaulting him outside Finsbury Park Mosque.

Given the internecine warfare amongst London Islamists Boualem Jolie Vue wouldn't attend Abu Qatada's prayers because he was still a part of the GIA and Abu Qatada had become a spiritual leader of the Salafist GSPC, a rival Islamic faction in the increasingly brutal civil war in Algeria. That was probably why he was an Abu Hamza enforcer – working for him as a heavy and making sure all the illegal activities at Finsbury Park ran smoothly to raise money for Hamza's – rather than Qatada's – growing terror network.

I saw the bodyguard stand up nonchalantly and walk over to Abu Qatada. I could see that he was making a gesture in my direction and I felt a cold shiver down my back. I had no idea what they were saying. But I figured if it was about me, I might be in real danger. I probably realised at that moment that this was the last time I would be able to come to Qatada's prayers.

I could feel a cold sweat come over me. I was determined not to panic, but I felt I was in big trouble. I figured I had a stark choice – leave straight away once prayers started or wait until the end. I couldn't decide which would arouse most suspicion. With hindsight I probably made the wrong choice.

I walked out of the prayer room slowly, conscious I was drawing attention to myself by being the first to leave as soon as prayers had ended. I entered the hallway to retrieve my shoes and sensed a rising panic in my anxiousness to find my shoes, put them on and get out of that place as fast as possible. As I was bending down to put my shoes on, I had my foot halfway in one shoe when I felt a warm sock hit my face on the bridge of my nose. It had a foot inside it. I could taste blood in my mouth. More panic. Then I felt another blow to the head and suddenly I was being kicked all over, whilst the pious were praying next door. I looked up and recognised the men as part of the team of men who were the self-appointed bodyguards to Abu Hamza including Boualem Jolie Vue. I could see his long hair, red beard and mad eyes and I had a feeling he didn't intend just to scare me.

I had enough presence of mind to cover my head but the kicks to my stomach and groin area were well placed. To this day I am convinced that I was only saved from greater injury because Muslims have to take their shoes off when they enter a mosque. With their army boots on these thugs would have pulverised my brain. These thugs were experts, aiming for my kidneys, thighs and genitals.

There was not a flicker of doubt in my mind that Jolie Vue would be sure to try and seriously injure me, even fatally. There were no witnesses around as the call to prayer had ended and everyone was getting ready to pray next door. I knew I had to get out and with my mouth starting to fill with blood I fought my way through the swinging legs and feet. I managed to get out in to the street stumbling as I tried to pull on my second shoe and run across the railway bridge towards the Central Mosque. I thought there might be safety in numbers there. I was relieved to find no one was following me but I was choking and trying to feel a cut on my head. Islam's rituals had saved me for a worse mauling. The fact that those thugs couldn't get their boots on quickly enough gave me time to get away.

As I was running I was dialling Simon's number. He picked up straight away. 'I don't know what happened but someone from Abu Hamza's mosque recognised me at Qatada's place. Next thing he is speaking to Qatada and this group of thugs sets upon me. I managed to get away but I think I am in real danger. I need to get to a police station. These guys are psychos.'

His reply was emphatic and stern. 'Whatever you do don't go to a police station. Keep them out of it. You shouldn't report any attack.' I was in a state of shock, 'What the hell are you talking about you know the people we are dealing with just want an excuse to go to paradise.' 'Just go straight home and let me know when you get there,' he replied.

I must have looked a complete mess on the tube. Mid-afternoon travellers kept moving away from me. When I arrived home, I realised why. My face looked like I'd gone a few rounds with Mike Tyson; it was bloodied and severe bruising had already started to appear.

At about 5pm, Richard called me. 'Can you get down to a hotel in Victoria for 7pm?' 'Are you bloody joking?' I was extremely reluctant given the circumstances. But I agreed and felt much better after a quick shower and placing a bag of frozen prawns on my face to calm the swelling.

When I arrived at the hotel Richard was with a female colleague, Mary. Over dinner and several glasses of wine – which I needed to calm my nerves – they probed me about my attackers. Obviously I knew the prime suspect so I gave them all his details. Name, address, description, how he hung around at Finsbury Park Mosque and often slept there. Boualem Jolie Vue. Mr good-looking. There's an irony in this name for a killing machine. 'You are going to arrest them aren't you?' I insisted. Call me naïve but they were the police and that was their job. Well, nothing happened to him, nor any of those other murderous thugs.

Piecing together the circumstances of the beating, I concluded from their rather nonchalant responses that Attalah Mohamed was a police and MI5 informer. Worse still perhaps it was Abu Hamza himself who was given the information by MI5 and he dispatched his red-bearded bodyguard to teach me a lesson? Within a few months this became a matter of fact for me. It had practically become an open secret in the Finsbury Park area. The Algerian émigré community always closely monitored these men. They had their measure even if MI5 didn't.

The more I knew the more I began to feel I had been set up for a fall. Either Jolie Vue or Hamza knew I was at the Fourth Feathers because his handler told him I'd be there and they should go and teach me a good lesson for being a freelance operator. It's a small blessing that they only kicked me with their socks on. Despite the bruising there were no serious fractures.

For me the message was clear. MI5 wanted me under control or completely out of Londonistan. This meant blowing my cover so I could no longer gather information from Abu Hamza's and Abu Qatada's mosques. I had become an uncontrollable asset. 'He's a man with a big mouth and contacts in the press who are beginning to crawl over this story and make our lives even more difficult than they already are.'

Looking back, I believe that after the stories of the Afghan veterans and Abu Ibrahim appeared, MI5 took the decision to put me in harm's way so as not to disturb their relationships with Abu Hamza and Abu Qatada. They were big fish informants and I was getting in the way of their big fish fishing expeditions.

Of course if I had gone to the police on Friday 21st April 2000, covered in blood and reported a violent attack at a Community centre in Lisson Grove, the local police would have raided the place with me in tow. I would have pointed out who had done it and the investigation would have led straight to Hamza and Qatada. More significantly it would have put the police cat amongst the security service pigeons and led them directly to Special Branch and MI5 too. I was learning to my cost that the world of espionage protects its own and I was no longer one of them.

To this day I remain convinced my handlers blew my cover to shut me up so that I wouldn't use the press to expose the men they were playing their dangerous games with. Perhaps they thought that a warning would be enough. Again it showed they under-estimated the ruthlessness of the people I had been spying on for them.

The logic of this, of course, is that not only did the British security services order a criminal attack on me; they also made these two evil men feel even more secure than before. Slowly you could sense Hamza and Qatada felt untouchable. Given what happened just a year later, the security services should now hang their heads in shame. It was one of many missed opportunities to deal with these terror organisers before their megalomania ran out of control.

* * *

It was perhaps no coincidence that Colonel Benali left London shortly afterwards. I was actually sorry to see him go. Abu Hamza was no longer the principal GIA organiser (the improving situation in Algeria saw to that) but a significant global Al Qaeda one. With Benali gone and Jérôme's claim that the British would never intervene as long as they were untouched by jihadi terrorism playing on my conscience, I exited the world of intelligence and espionage. My hopes for bringing together the Algerian, French and British security services lay in tatters.

After being physically assaulted by the same Abu Hamza enforcer who had beaten up Colonel Benali it became clear to me that my luck had finally run out. I could no longer continue to work for any intelligence agency. I realised that I would have to turn to the newspapers permanently to try and get the truth. What would help me on this course was the fact that Hamza's global notoriety would I was sure bring with it global attention. The US authorities in particular were already plotting their moves to put him on trial in the United States of America.

Benali's last words of advice to me were prophetic. He said the only way to prevent myself being killed by the jihadists was ironically to make as much noise in public as I could. He believed with a media profile I would now be in a good position to warn of the perils to come. He added that the West needed to know that now they would have to prepare for the inevitable big event that Bin Laden and his supporters were planning to shake them out of their innocent slumber. He even suggested that I consider making the effort to approach a fourth security service, the American Central Intelligence Agency (not something I ever seriously considered – I'd had my fingers and toes burned enough already).

In any case the political debate was changing fast and I could see that my decision to place all my eggs back in the journalism basket might happily coincide with growing interest in radical Islam. This would put me in a position to expose these men on the stage of public opinion. Where the newspapers in Britain hadn't cared about the murder, massacre and brutality of the civil war in my homeland, they sure as hell would want to know about these men who were turning parts of London into the terror capital of the West.

It remains a source of great regret that I never managed to convince MI5 of the seriousness of the threat. In effect I believe they either didn't want to see or they didn't believe these men had the capabilities to do serious harm. I believe they were hampered by their own prejudices that in my view blinded them to the obvious.

CHAPTER 12

Journalist Unmasked

THE FOURTH FEATHERS experience was not only terrifying, but also chastening. It didn't take too long to patch myself up – bruised lips, eyes and a sore head passed quite quickly. After all I had done and risked it was profoundly depressing. I had worn the mask of a terror sympathiser for so long that I was now isolated. The fact that I had no protection either was slowly sinking in.

I was now fully estranged from my wife and my children were fast growing up. Now I had finally been unmasked I decided that one positive thing to come of this was that I would be able to rebuild a relationship with my children at least. I wanted my son to play football so I made it my business to work out how I might get him playing at the weekend for a club. In that way I would give myself an alternative focus whilst at the same time trying to earn a living as a journalist. The story was still the same just a different destination for the information.

I think it had already been clear to me for a long time that I was better 'plugged in' to this London Al Qaeda network and knew more about its links with the Algerian GIA than anybody else. At that point I was in all likelihood the best-informed person about the nature and extent of Londonistan. That's what made the Abu Qatada episode so stupid in the fight against terror. I had stepped on too many egos and I had been exposed to save more ego bruising.

I also figured, more disturbingly, if I was killed by one of these psychopaths no one would even notice. I would be rubbed out like a footnote in the war on terror. I was not going to allow that to happen so I needed to find a solution. Here again I suddenly faced huge hurdles. My uncertain immigration status meant that I didn't have freedom of movement in Europe so I couldn't just go to another country. Even if I could get a visa to leave England it would be for no longer than three months and leaving would jeopardise my status in the UK. The irony was not lost on me that whilst I had risked my neck to expose the London based jihadists and was now, as the English say, 'up the creek without a paddle', the security services had provided immigration papers for the five Algerian jihadists who had arrived from Yemen. It was wrong – they use me to provide information and keep me in immigration limbo whilst giving murderers the right to stay. There is little loyalty in espionage.

My choices were limited so I applied for a visa for the country I least wanted to go to – France. I went to Paris and then on to Brussels in Belgium to stay with some old friends who showed me great hospitality and soothed some of my fears.

To this day it still seems extraordinary to me that the security services did a deal with the men of terror. Abu Hamza claimed he assisted MI5 during his trial in New York. They thought they had a deal with Abu Qatada, Abu Hamza and the man known as the Tottenham Ayatollah, Omar Bakri Muhammed. How and why they thought they could manage these firebrands is beyond me. These men lived in a fundamentally separate moral universe and the security services hadn't figured that out.

The naïvety of the British security services was colossal. The notion that you could have a sort of 'gentleman's agreement' handshake with these jihadists bent on wreaking havoc at the heart of the democracies now protecting them was utterly laughable. Only I didn't see it as a joke. As far as I was concerned they threw me in the fire for the sake of a deal which would certainly be broken, the only question was when and how much time had the jihadists bought themselves. MI5 used my intelligence to neutralise the threat, but in my view betrayed the just cause they were supposedly fighting for. They brokered a form of appeasement.

For my part I had left Britain to spend three months in the relative safety of Europe fretting about what I should do next whilst I let the dust settle after the attack. I decided I would have to take my chances in London, return to my journalistic roots and expose as much as possible in the British and

American press. I had no idea what would happen, but I had believed Colonel Benali when he told me something was on the cards, it would be big and it would prove that I was right. At least then, I told myself, if I die doing the right thing then, my kids, my family, my friends and anyone else who cared about the rise of these terrorists would know why I had been killed.

As soon as I arrived back in London I got on the phone to David Leppard at *The Sunday Times* and offered him a big story. He invited me to lunch the next day at his members-only club in London. It was, to be fair, a little like the world of espionage only these journalists had contacts not informants. They were less worried about compromising a contact than about their competitors getting the story first. I had re-entered the world of pleasant surroundings, coiffured women, friendly waiters, and gentle manners. The boats were glistening on the river, the food was delicious, if a little rich, and the wine was a step up from the local supermarket plonk that I had to rely on now.

Once I started to relax and begin to tell the story all I could see was David's eyes getting bigger. At one point I thought he would fall off his seat he was leaning so far forward. 'I bloody well knew it; I knew that you were hiding things from me. Every time I checked out one of your stories I could find no flaw in it. You were either a bloody good liar or what you were telling me was well sourced and printable.'

When I told him I had been associated with the Algerian security services, and working for the French DGSE (Direction General de Securité Exterieure – the equivalent of the CIA), Special Branch at Scotland Yard and MI5, he showed absolutely no emotion. In fact, I suspect that he had wondered all along how I had such good information.

Of course it had been David who back in 1998 had introduced me to a Scotland Yard officer called Vernon X. I'd gone to a police station near Liverpool Street station to meet this fellow who had quizzed me about my work for the French spying on Qatada and Hamza and their burgeoning terror network in London. We had a long conversation about whether I should continue to work with the DGSE. We agreed he would follow up on our conversation. 'Yes. Continue. Within a month, I will call you.' Vernon never did call, but David must have had his suspicions ever since.

After ordering another bottle of a fine wine, David suggested that we should adopt a strategic approach to the story. 'First we'll do the story about the French and then we'll move on to the British. It has a certain chronological relevance,' he reasoned.

It was a typically English gentleman's deal, like the one MI5 had done with the jihadists. Only I would honour my handshake because, from that point on I had reinvented myself as a journalist in England with a major newspaper and finally someone else knew my story. At least part of the burden on my shoulders was lifted.

David Leppard was far too experienced just to take my word as gospel. He needed some corroboration of my French story. So we decided to take a trip to Knightsbridge to the restaurant where I used to be treated to sumptuous French cuisine by Jérôme.

No sooner had we taken a seat at the usual table by the window than the waiter came up, a big smile across his face. 'Hello sir. How is your friend? I've not seen either of you here for a while. I thought we had perhaps offended you in some way.' The waiter was a little puzzled when David asked him directly what this friend looked like. 'Well, I suppose that is easy. Typical French. Very coiffured. I thought he always looked like a spy,' said the waiter laughing. The description was almost identical to the way I had described Jérôme to David. It was one more little piece of the jigsaw to convince him he was on the right track for his big *Sunday Times* splash.

Finally, I was getting some traction. If this couldn't put pressure on the idiots in the security services, then nothing would. No one likes to be embarrassed. *The Sunday Times* took an entirely different approach to my personal security worries. David felt he couldn't predict the reaction to the story from the spooks so he convinced the paper to send me to the Sheraton Hotel in Brussels for a week so I was out of the way. I suspect he wanted to keep me away from the prying eyes of his main rivals at the London *Observer* too. The fact that he had found a mole inside the whole developing Londonistan story was a coup for his paper. He knew it. So did I.

Having been away from the fully functioning newspaper world for so long, I had perhaps forgotten just how quickly news could travel. When a reporter wants to maximise the impact of his scoop he will plunder his contacts to make sure they are fully aware of the story and follow up on it.

Whilst I was enjoying room service in Brussels, David was on the telephone every half an hour with a different request for me to fulfil. First an interview with the French cable channel Canal Plus. He next arranged an in-depth interview chat with the Arabic newspaper *Al Shark Al Awsat*. He had even set up a lengthy interview with one of the largest circulation French dailies, *Le Parisien.*

Now I understood David's strategy. It was a master-class in maximising the impact of his scoop. Having me in Brussels meant that I was captive to his audience. He knew where I was and exactly how to get hold of me without compromising my details. The hotel was a set-up, my office for *Sunday Times* unofficial business.

✳ ✳ ✳

As far as I was concerned, for the sake of a wave of international headlines about the Al Qaeda terrorism base in England, neglected by MI5, I seized each opportunity like it was the first time I had ever spoken to a journalist. I had a story to tell and each of these stories would be me being a public witness to what I had tried to do and how the British were failing to get a grip on the pedlars of murder and mayhem in the shape of Abu Qatada and Abu Hamza. For too long I considered these men had got away with inciting hatred and murder and now it was time to expose them and put communities providing camouflage for their activities on alert. The security services were failing to protect innocent citizens from this evil climate that was brewing in London.

I started to spread the word as widely as I could, being careful to make sure that I kept to the story David and I had discussed. There was more to tell but it had to be told selectively so there could be more headlines the following week, and the week after that. I took the view that I needed to cause as much damage to this network as I could, as quickly as I could. I talked for England…and France…and Algeria…and America. I talked until my throat was sore and my head swimming with the detail of all the murderous intent of the jihadists. I could barely sleep that night.

Being in Brussels I had taken the precaution of turning my English mobile phone off to avoid incurring charges that I could ill afford. By the time I listened to my voicemails when I switched the phone back on the following Thursday, I realised the wisdom of dispatching me to Brussels. There was a stream of angry messages from my MI5 handler. He was so mad he was screaming down the phone. I imagined him at the other end sweating profusely, red in the face, trying to figure out where I had gone. One thing

I learned about espionage. It is not like the movies. If you want no one to find you it is easy to do for a while. For the next five days I listened to the messages over and over. Each time I got more pleasure knowing that I had angered them. I reminded myself that if they had been better at their jobs this wouldn't have been necessary. Eventually I called them.

'Hi Simon, yes I've been out of the country. I thought it wise to keep under the radar for a while. How are you? I've been meaning to call you.' I spoke calmly but with a deep sense of satisfaction knowing I'd got my own back for their betrayal. It was also obvious the story had been more impactful than David and I had anticipated.

Simon was still angry. He practically exploded down the telephone line. 'Is this what you call staying under the radar – splashing the story of your collaboration with the French all over the national newspapers? What kind of moron are you? We are dealing with psychopath terrorists and you want to tell the world you are some superhero. Oh, and by the way, the French security services couldn't organise a piss up in a brewery. Anyway when the hell are you coming back to London? Look Kevin, you have dropped us in the shit from a glorious height and we have every boss in Christendom wanting to know who this mad Arab is who has plastered the French all over the world's press. What the hell does he know about us? When will you be back?' I could hear Simon was beginning to run out of steam.

'Simon we both know we want the same thing. Your enemy is my enemy too. Just now I am more his enemy than you are and they want to kill me personally. Anyway, I'm not an Arab. I'm a Berber and proud of it. I'm due back in to Waterloo on Sunday around 5pm.'

'Great – three more days with no more explanation – you really meant to drop us in it didn't you? Richard will be there to meet you. Just follow him and wear some disguise because someone is bound to want to get your picture at some point. And for God's sake don't talk to any other journalists until then. We've enough French shit to shovel for the moment.' There wasn't much for me to say, so I just agreed to be there at the appointed hour.

* * *

On the Eurostar train on the way back I felt I needed to fortify myself for the battle I knew I was going to have with Simon and his colleagues. Although he didn't know I suspected them of organising the beating, he must have been worrying about what else I might reveal. To calm my nerves I drank a whole bottle of red wine, so by the time I had followed Richard to the police station, not only was I blind drunk but exhausted.

Simon was waiting and pacing the room when I walked in. I didn't trust them and I realised that someone else should know where I am. So I told them, 'I'm supposed to be meeting David Leppard tomorrow. I told him I had to meet you tonight so that if I don't turn up he should look in the Thames for a mutilated body.' It was a defensive lie.

'Oh, that's just great. What is your problem? Why do you suddenly want to sing like a canary to a *Sunday Times* journalist? What has he ever done for you? He's hardly going to fight these jihadists on your behalf. Aren't you forgetting that?' Simon looked at Richard and raised his eyebrows.

I was as blunt and honest as I could focus on being. 'From when I was a young boy I wanted to be a journalist. Then I became a very good one and these GIA bastards tried to kill me for it. I told you from the beginning that I was a journalist investigating Londonistan. I told you this enemy wants to kill my people and I don't use the gun, I use my pen and my contacts to fight them. I told you I am not a mini-cab driving snitch.'

I could feel my blood pressure rising and the suppressed rage of having been so close to the truth of Londonistan and then being betrayed. 'One day you will understand what these people are capable of. One day it won't be just my people who are suffering and being slaughtered. One day it will be your people too!'

Then without a hint of irony, Simon, informed me that my relationship with MI5 was being terminated immediately. He explained it was because my cover had been blown and that I was too much of a liability with such a big mouth. Perhaps he had forgotten what Abu Hamza's cronies had done to me. Probably he didn't really care. He was just a cynical cog in a wheel following instructions. Simon took out a white envelope from his pocket and handed it to me. 'It is £500 for services rendered,' he said. 'Please don't publicise your relationship with us.'

With that I left Richard and Simon inside the police station and I walked out of MI5's strange and convoluted world. 15th October 2000 was the last time I saw them. Just 11 months later, 9/11 changed the course of history.

* * *

There was one unforeseen consequence that I hadn't quite anticipated. The interviews I had given about my relationship with the French Security services, had made headlines in many parts of the francophone world, including Algeria.

The history between our two countries is fraught and painful. My parents were scared for me, for themselves and also embarrassed about their son seeming to collaborate with the old enemy. Particularly bad, as far as they were concerned, was dealing with the people who had murdered so many innocent people during the War of Independence in the early 1960s.

My father was part of that revolution and he felt shame that I was betraying that legacy. I didn't see it that way, of course, but all I could tell them was that it was impossible to explain the whole story over the phone (I was sure the Algerian security services were bugging their lines in Algiers). I told them that soon they would know the full story. Then they would understand my motives. At least, I hoped they would.

As far as I was concerned this made it all the more important to get the story about the British Security services out in the national papers as quickly as possible, despite Simon's anxieties. In that way my parents would see that I was working against a common enemy, the jihadists that had dragged our country into the mire. I reasoned that back home in Algeria this would firstly restore a measure of pride and more importantly protect them somewhat from the attentions of a paranoid Algerian State.

I also believed that the jihadists were close to the spectacular event they had been whispering about for years. Once the security services started to clamp down on their activities it would make acts of terror more difficult to carry through. I had shaken the terrorists' big tree and the apples were beginning to fall. Now we all had to be vigilant.

I called David Leppard and told him I was anxious to get on and publish the second part of the story. He was a little taken aback. 'Why are you in such a hurry to publish?' he kept asking. He reckoned we had made a huge splash with the French story and we needed the waves we started with that one to stop, before creating waves with a new story. I told him we had always agreed that a good story shouldn't wait because someone else might get it.

In fact, David had, through his own security service contacts, confirmed that I had been working on behalf of MI5, but he was extremely reluctant to make that information public. No matter how much I pressed him it seemed obvious to me that he had been leaned on by those contacts not to publish the story.

I was angry with him. I had given him a scoop on the French but now publishing a follow-up story was making him, it seemed, deeply uncomfortable. Like all journalists he was probably having to juggle with the sensitivities of his sources if he went ahead and published anything about MI5. He told me later that he had a meeting with one of his senior contacts on the morning we had had lunch together to discuss the French story. In the world of espionage you can trust no one. You never know who is spying on whom. Once again I felt badly let down.

There was nothing for it but to use the power of competition to get the story out. I went to see Jason Burke of the *Observer* who used to work with David and now plied his trade at the rival Sunday paper. In February 2001 I got to tell the world how I believed the British security services had betrayed me and fatally damaged their cause of fighting the jihadists already planning chaos in Europe (Burke, 2001).

For the first time I was able to say publicly (I knew my family would be reading this) that I had risked my life infiltrating militant Islamic groups for Scotland Yard and MI5. Jason laid out in black and white how two years of pain and separation from my wife and kids had taken its toll (in fact my marriage had by then broken down irretrievably). He explained the people who needed Réda Hassaïne most had betrayed me.

I told Jason to attend an international gathering in the Quakers meeting hall in Euston in Central London where Abu Hamza and his friends would address 400 committed Muslim militants. By no means were all of them violent jihadists, but there were enough supporters for the violent ones to embolden them. Looking back, the whole 9/11 scenario was encapsulated here where these foreigners huddled in the freezing English winter, in a building dedicated to peace, talked about unimaginable violence and carnage.

I later learned that the BBC's Kurt Barling had also been at that meeting. Other journalists filmed it covertly. That footage would be shown in his documentary *Trouble at the Mosque* in 2002, but even then the graphic description that Abu Hamza gave of floating bombs tethered to balloons over the Sahara – so that the prevailing winds would take them over Europe where eventually they would drop randomly and cause chaos in the flight lanes – did not merit police intervention. We were all eyewitnesses to a kind of madness.

Jason was able to see from this one meeting how terrifying the whole propaganda assault had become. The only talk was of victories and defeats, of holy wars and martyrs, of betrayal and dire consequences for traitors to the cause. The room was packed with people wearing the guerrilla uniform adopted by Afghan and Algerian fighters. Many in the room were battle hardened from combat in countries across the Middle East.

This was turning into more of a disaster than even I had imagined. I was watching Abu Hamza puffed up by his own sense of invulnerability. Jason was able to see the way I worked, engaging with those present in a mixture of French, Arabic and English.

This event more than any other persuaded me of the urgency of the task at hand and the need for me to force the security services to intervene more robustly, in my view by exposing their inadequacies. Here is an extract from that Burke report and my version of how I believed then that MI5 had mishandled these men of terror.

> When the talk and the prayers were over, Réda Hassaïne did not join the others in drinking coffee late into the night. He went home and began to write up what he had seen. Though a journalist by profession, his dispatch was not for any newspaper. It was for his handlers in Scotland Yard's Special Branch, the élite police squad dedicated to monitoring Britain's terrorists. Hassaïne was a spy.

> Hassaïne has now agreed to tell The Observer his story. In a series of lengthy interviews last week – and in an 11-page statement – he gave one of the most detailed descriptions of the shadowy world of the security services and their operations in Britain. His is a tale of duplicity, crime and violence. More than anything it reveals the breathtaking cynicism with which the vulnerable are ruthlessly exploited in the name of state security.

> Until the spring of 1999 few people had heard of Finsbury Park Mosque. It sits on a grim traffic-choked corner in north London surrounded by clouds of exhaust and long terraces of Edwardian houses. On Fridays the pavements outside are full of young Muslim men heading for Friday prayers and the sermon of the fiery and controversial preacher Abu Hamza.

> Hassaïne had lived nearby since fleeing to the UK in 1994. He was well

integrated into the local community and was a popular figure. His wife and children were known and liked.

But Hassaïne was living a double, or indeed treble, life. In order to get his family out of civil war-racked Algeria, where left-leaning journalists were dying by the dozen, he had been forced to make a terrible pact with the Algerian security services. In return for safe passage to the UK he agreed to help them as they struggled to put down the Islamic insurgency devastating their country. Once trapped into the world of espionage there was no way he could turn back.

His first assignment was commissioned nearly two months later. It was no surprise. He was to infiltrate the Finsbury Park Mosque and gather as much information as he could on Abu Hamza.

After years in relative obscurity the fiery preacher had suddenly sprung into the news. Just before New Year a group of tourists in Yemen had been taken hostage by Islamic extremists. They were freed after a bloody shoot-out and Yemeni police claimed to have traced the plot back to Britain. They accused Abu Hamza, a veteran of the war against the Russians in Afghanistan, of inspiring the attack. Abu Hamza denied it and hard evidence was thin on the ground.

Over the next weeks Hassaïne spent almost every day at the mosque. Each night he would write up a report for his handlers detailing Abu Hamza's associates, his speeches and the attitudes of those around him. The Observer has seen these reports. He was asked to provide the police with a sketch map of the mosque showing all the possible escape routes and detailing the hard line preacher's security arrangements.' (Burke, 2001)

Within days of this article appearing in the *Observer*, my former collaborator David Leppard was on the phone. He invited me to lunch. I may have been angry with him but the war was hotting up and I wasn't going to lose allies unnecessarily. He wanted to know how much of what I had told Jason was true. I reminded him I was an experienced journalist. I told stories but I didn't make them up.

He told me 'Réda, this is unbelievable. You have made a lot of people unhappy. If I were in your shoes I'd be bloody nervous. But I can see how, from your point of view, you would see that they have let the genie out of the bottle and have no idea how to get it back in.'

I had warned them. They didn't listen. I realised I had made enemies and I could no longer be certain of my safety from any side. The climate had become murderous and the security services were lagging so far behind they would never prevent the atrocity that I felt was bound to happen.

In July of 2001 I talked to Kurt Barling about his film for Channel Four *Dispatches* on the unregulated nature of British mosques and the way in which Abu Hamza had been given a licence to promote murder by the British Intelligence services. We agreed that when he returned from his trip to New York we would collaborate on some television reports to follow up my work with the newspapers. Other than that I felt there was nothing more I could do so once again I decided to dip beneath the radar. As far as I was concerned it was time for me to lie low and keep myself safe.

Whenever and wherever the jihadists were planning something spectacular I could no longer stop that. Events would have to take their course. I felt at least that I had done what I could to give the world fair warning to be vigilant, because these fanatics would stop at nothing to get to Paradise.

CHAPTER 13

From Secret Agent
to Journalist

I KNEW THE ISLAMISTS would be looking for me to seek revenge. The few weeks after the first big story came out in the *Observer* in February 2001, I kept my head down. The reality was I knew even some of my friends would find the whole spying thing distasteful so I avoided situations where I might have to explain myself. For me the crucial point was that the story was out and I felt a huge relief in no longer having to live a life accompanied by three secret ones. But I knew there was also no turning back; the future required a complete re-engagement with my journalistic roots.

One good thing to come out of my openness was the fact that as soon as the Algerian press picked up the *Observer* story my family was able to make sense of my secretive life and my long periods of silence. They also understood why I was always so broke. For the first time in years my father was able to puff out his chest and say, 'My son has been busy trying to protect freedom.' I was no longer a traitor or collaborator with the French but an operator in the service of justice for all the carnage during the Algerian Civil War.

Months passed by with me trying to keep myself occupied. I was almost crushed by boredom when a close friend called me, asking me to do some translation work. Easy money I thought, no craziness, no jihadists – just the tonic I needed. His offices were in South London, near Clapham Common and the change of atmosphere, not to mention the fresh air on my face, made me feel a whole lot better.

For London it was a pleasant July. The grass was still green, the flowers were out, and the sun was shining (occasionally). Waking up with a fresh purpose and brushing shoulders with strangers on the Underground was all beginning to connect me with real life once more. Clapham is a lovely part of London, with pleasant shops and cafes. It was refreshing to walk around watching young families just biding their time with seemingly few cares in the world. It was a world away from where I was living near Dalston, a suburb in North East London. People there always seemed so much more frantic. Even supermarket sandwiches tasted better in Clapham.

Two months passed without any stress or any real anxieties, just watching my back in case some extreme jihadists decided to stab me in it. It was a couple of the most carefree months of my life in England. I had re-established a relationship with my ex-wife; my children were settled and now I was translating texts from Arabic to English. I can't say it was interesting work but it was absorbing. Once my head was a whirl of Arabic and English I was lost to anything else.

My peaceful interlude aside, the West didn't have to wait long to see that they had completely missed the writing that had been on the wall for everyone to plainly see. Within months of me deciding to lie low, two jumbo jets flew into the Twin Towers. None of us who knew what these suicide bombers were capable of were surprised it happened. But even my friend the Algerian Colonel who'd been based in Washington and knew the lengths the jihadists would go to must have been surprised at the scale of the attack

✳ ✳ ✳

September 2001 had arrived lazily. I had fewer cares than ever before. On the evening of 11th September I was still trying to work out how this Arabic idiom might be translated into English without becoming gibberish when I realised my friend was shaking my shoulders. I looked up and was shocked by how ill he looked.

'Réda, why are you still working? Have you not heard what has happened today?' I looked at him and shook my head. 'What happened? The sun came out in September. The British are always talking about the weather.'

'This is serious, Réda, someone flew two planes into the Twin Towers in New York.' I felt a sudden overwhelming feeling of nausea. It was all I could do to stop myself from vomiting. 'I assumed you would have been on the internet looking at it all day. It was the most shocking thing you could imagine. Even Hollywood couldn't have dreamed it up.' I was dazed and just said, 'No I was trying to find a way of translating this Arabic so it made sense in English.'

I stopped working straight away and left the office without saying anything to anyone. I was speechless through utter bewilderment. I had waited so long for the big event that the Colonel had told me about, and now it seemed it had happened. I walked from Clapham back to North London just to clear my head. Now I knew the fear would change sides. Now people would finally know what these jihadists were capable of. Even I hadn't thought they would be that audacious.

As I walked through Brixton up to the Elephant and Castle and across the River Thames into the City of London all I could think was that the whole world would now be on my side. Finally I would have the opportunity to start my public fight against Abu Hamza and Abu Qatada. No longer would I have to work behind closed doors. Now I could tackle these two terrorist sympathisers and recruiters head-on in the pages of the media.

Within days my phone was ringing from one end of the day to the next. People needed information and quotes from people who knew how Al Qaeda worked and I was right in the middle of it all. Journalists from places and papers I never knew existed were calling for fresh information. I like to think that I did my job properly. I made it clear to every journalist that Abu Qatada and Abu Hamza had to share some responsibility as principal recruiters for the type of people who would become terrorists who flew planes into buildings. I knew that the more of these reports that appeared, the more the British security agencies would feel compelled to do something. It was like a gift to me. All I had to explain like a mantra to journalists from the world over, passing through London, was these guys were dangerous and they had brainwashed hundreds if not thousands of young men in their mosques. From no one wanting to hear what I had to say, suddenly, it felt like everyone wanted to hear. What was clear was that everyone else was now playing catch up.

Within weeks of 9/11, Abu Qatada was arrested. It was obvious he was a big fish. Journalists were crawling all over the Fourth Feathers community centre and Finsbury Park Mosque. Once the investigations started it soon became clear that what I had been telling MI5 all along had been accurate.

Chief amongst my main complaints was that Qatada was sending young men to Afghanistan to learn how to kill people in Europe, not Afghanistan. I had told the security services that Zacarias Moussaoui – the alleged mastermind of the Twin Towers attacks – had passed through the Mosque amongst others. (Moussaoui was arrested in Minnesota in August 2001 and admitted his role in the 9/11 attacks in his 2006 trial.)

In 2006 Moussaoui was eventually sentenced to life in prison in the United States for his role in the 9/11 terrorist attacks. He was unrepentant to the end. After the judge told him he would never be released and would 'die with a whimper', Moussaoui retorted, 'God save Osama bin Laden – you will never get him (Sniffen, 2006).

I had of course told the intelligence services, until I was blue in the face, that the whole Al Qaeda edifice was sustained by criminality. At Finsbury Park Mosque there was a cottage industry manufacturing false passports and identification passes. They were laundering money and identities and organising for people to get weapons training.

When they eventually raided Finsbury Park Mosque in 2003 they found all these items and more. Abu Hamza still mocked the authorities. Despite the Mosque being closed and him being ejected, he would hold street prayer sessions every Friday in a show of complete defiance. The police were now more vigilant but they always seemed to be protecting the worshippers – in their balaclavas and military fatigues – rather than the journalists and ordinary citizens who came to gawp at the surreal scene.

Now the journalists had cottoned on to this story it was easier for me to exploit the opportunity to denounce these jihadists as much as I could. It was clear this was now having more of an impact than all of my work with the security services trying to get them to halt the spread of the Al Qaeda network. I wanted to scream from the rooftops, 'I have been telling you for years but you didn't want to listen. Now look at the mess we are in. And still you allow these people to openly propagate their hate. What is your problem?'

As far as I was concerned, if the world wanted to meet me it would now have to be on my terms and my message would be consistent. My job was to denounce these false clerics and expose them for what they were – brainwashers and jihadists bent on creating carnage in the name of their Islamist-inspired agenda.

My career as a translator had come to an abrupt end. Once again, I had been plunged into the world of the jihadist. In a very strange way I felt less exposed simply because I was now out in the open and dozens of journalist now knew what I stood for. If I disappeared they would begin to ask questions. At least that's what I convinced myself.

I returned to a healthy paranoid state determined to take care of my own security. I avoided places where the Islamists went. As a matter of principle I assumed my life was in danger and that I could be killed at any time. Frankly I was ready to die because it had become an absolute duty to expose these men of violence.

I challenged the jihadists to recognise that I too was involved in a jihad against men like them. The big difference was that my jihad wasn't about killing people – it was about saving people. Any devout Muslim knows that in our teachings we are told that if you kill one person it is the same as killing the whole of humanity. If you save one person it too is like saving the whole of humanity.

* * *

Eventually the truth will out and it appears that the message I had been trying to get across had been discovered by other means by US Military Intelligence at the Guantanamo Bay detention centre. For example, documents published on the internet by Wikileaks written by intelligence officers had concluded that for two decades Britain had effectively become a crucible of terrorism, with dozens of extremists, home-grown and from abroad who had been successfully radicalised there. Finsbury Park Mosque was singled out as a haven for extremists and it served, in their view as 'an attack planning and propaganda production base'.

The Americans went further and raised questions over why the British government and security services failed to take action sooner to tackle the capital's reputation as a staging post for terrorism which had become so established that the city was widely associated with the term 'Londonistan'.

Those same documents showed that at least thirty-five detainees at Guantanamo had passed through Britain before being sent to fight against the allied forces in Afghanistan. It was claimed this was more than from any other western nation. Of those, eighteen were originally from abroad and the other seventeen were British nationals or citizens granted residency here after claiming asylum. All were subjected to the type of indoctrination I had been begging the authorities to help stop by intervening in the work of Abu Qatada and Abu Hamza. All had been sent to terrorist training camps in Afghanistan.

Finally, after what felt like half a lifetime, Abu Hamza was arrested on 26th August 2004 for instigating acts of terrorism. For reasons that still mystify me, the charges were dropped five days later. It was difficult for other observers to make out why he had been so quickly released. The explanation from the prosecution service was that there was not enough evidence to secure a realistic conviction before a jury.

But fate intervened to prevent his release from jail. The evidence gained during interrogations at Guantanamo meant the US Federal Bureau of Investigations filed an extradition request for Abu Hamza to be sent to America to face terrorism-related charges. Furthermore the FBI, would argue in court that he must be kept in jail to secure my safety, using Hamza's fatwa against me as evidence. They argued that it was just the latest in a long string of examples that he remained a security threat and was likely, if released, to endanger other people's lives. Meanwhile the British prosecuting authorities began to look into how they might prosecute Abu Hamza in the UK courts. I knew they had enough evidence. I had provided it.

Finally Abu Hamza's outspoken 'sermons' and outrageous boasts on camera were beginning to catch up with him. In his rush to defend his cause Hamza had told a Canadian interviewer that killing a traitor was an entitlement. 'It's fine to kill them by slitting their throats, or, shooting them. Any way you can to deter them or others from doing such things.' (O'Neill, 2004)

As I was a potential witness in any proceedings against Hamza, the fact that he had identified me as a legitimate target meant that the court would not trust him to honour any bail conditions. It felt good to turn the tables on this thuggish behaviour.

The judge took the death threats against me very seriously and ruled it wouldn't be sensible to release him on bail – Abu Hamza was too dangerous. For me, it was a 'eureka' moment. I went to court to witness the spectacle. On the steps of the courthouse on the way out journalists who wanted to get a better sense of who this maverick Algerian informant was, surrounded me. I made it clear that if I needed to go to America to give evidence against Abu Hamza I was ready to get on the plane.

'I saw the trade in false documents,' I told them, 'the raising of money for terrorism, how he sent people to Afghanistan and how terrorists who committed atrocities in Algeria came to Finsbury Park and were given a safe haven. He has got away with his crimes for years.'

Of course I also told them that nothing would please me more than to see the US authorities broaden their inquiries to include Abu Hamza's involvement with Islamist terrorists who had killed thousands of innocent civilians in Algeria.

This time the British prosecutors made sure that they found enough evidence to make their charges stick. On 24th October 2004 Hamza was charged with fifteen offences, including encouraging the murder of dozens of British citizens and intent to stir up race hatred.

The trial commenced on 5th July 2005. Two days later on 7th July 2005 the unimaginable happened when Britain found itself under attack from its own citizens. What I had feared would happen all along come to pass. It was depressing, disheartening and disturbing. In some ways I felt I had failed, in others I knew now the world of 9/11 had been confirmed and Londonistan had finally come home. The British are keen to follow procedure strictly when it comes to the pursuit of justice. In yet another ironic twist Abu Hamza's case was adjourned because it was felt he could not get a fair trial in the heightened state of anxiety that the London Tube bombings provoked. But I knew he was at the heart of the network that fostered the climate to make the bombings possible. Criminal justice had caught up with him years too late.

I had told the security services over and over again, as the Colonel had told me, 'They are going to Afghanistan to train in Al Qaeda training camps and they will come back to kill you here in the UK.'

It was one of the saddest days of my life. As far as I was concerned Abu Hamza was in jail whilst his supporters carried out the bombing of London.

* * *

When the trial finally resumed on 6th January 2006 it became a battle for the judge to prevent Abu Hamza using the witness box as a soapbox. But despite doing his best to mock 'sham British justice,' as he saw it, a British jury found him guilty of eleven of the charges against him including soliciting murder, using threatening or abusive language, possessing threatening, abusive or insulting recordings designed to stir up racial hatred and of possessing an Al Qaeda handbook called the *Encyclopaedia of Afghan Jihad.*

It took just four weeks for the court to reach its verdict on 7th February 2006. Justice Antony Hughes looked across the courtroom at Hamza in the dock. 'You helped to create an atmosphere in which to kill has become regarded by some as not only a legitimate course but a moral and religious duty in pursuit of perceived justice.' He sentenced him to seven years in prison. I took the view it was too late and too little.

Again the British newspapers used my testimony to spice up their coverage of the trial. They quoted my descriptions of Finsbury Park Mosque turning from a boring place of worship into an academy for jihadist violence. Even my observations of the change of dress code for Hamza's followers were reported. Without exaggeration I could say that, 'You didn't need to go to Afghanistan, – inside the Mosque were people wearing combat clothing, it was like being in an Al Qaeda camp.' My memories of young men sleeping on the carpets of the Mosque and using its offices as bedrooms were now transformed into paragraphs of enlightenment for the newspaper readers.

As a journalist I was back!

CHAPTER 14

Letter to the Americans

IN EARLY 2002 Andrew Higgins called me from the *Wall Street Journal*. At first I had to pinch myself. For so many years I had tried to interest the Americans in the dangers of ignoring the jihadists in our midst and now Andrew wanted my help to explain to his American readers, the links between Osama Bin Laden and his right-hand man in Europe, Abu Qatada. I told him we should meet at a favourite haunt of mine for afternoon tea British style at Café Patisserie in Holborn, central London. Here was the first significant opportunity to reach out to Americans and tell them not just about Abu Qatada but how the climate of fear and hatred fostered by Abu Hamza was threatening us all and was in my view directly responsible for 9/11.

Andrew was an Englishman but worked in Moscow as the *Wall Street Journal*'s Correspondent. He had a natural interest in Londonistan because he could sense his home country was in difficult times. He also understood the importance of this story to America and above all had the platform from which to disseminate it.

He was very interested in Abu Qatada who, at that point in time, was trying to stay below the radar. The attacks on the Twin Towers and the advancing war in Afghanistan had made Qatada hot property for the security services. After about an hour's discussion I suggested to Andrew that we head down to Abu Qatada's house in West London, a short ride on the London Underground. Andrew was a little hesitant but I insisted I show him how terrorist organisers were allowed to live in London. When we arrived in Acton there was nobody in.

I suggested we go into the property to see what we could find. Andrew baulked at the idea. As far as he was concerned that was trespass and he flatly refused to entertain the idea.

But this was Abu Qatada, terrorist-in-chief and a man with blood not just on his hands, but up to his shoulders I reasoned. I decided I would look around to see if there was anything that might verify this was the address he lived at. Andrew kept his distance. I managed to retrieve some junk mail addressed to Mr Omar Osman (aka Abu Qatada) that had been left outside the front door of his home. It proved nothing beyond confirming that Abu Qatada did in fact live at the address; a mundane suburban house in peaceful London.

As well as helping Andrew identify where Abu Qatada was living, these documents enabled me to tip off my contact at the BBC, Kurt Barling, who by this time was also following up his investigation for Channel Four Television.

I explained to Andrew that he needed to make it known in the US that Qatada was an America-hater, that too little was being done to stop his murderous work, that his henchman had already tried to kill me as a traitor after one of his sermons and that the British saw his rantings as freedom of speech but really they were the fatwas of a religious fanatic who had sanctioned the killing of women, children and the elderly in my homeland of Algeria. The threat had now turned from Algeria to America and I told him I was deeply ashamed that I hadn't been able to do more to convince the authorities to do more to stop him.

Of course I couldn't let the opportunity pass to tell Andrew about the man I considered to run the Al Qaeda embassy in Europe at Finsbury Park Mosque, Abu Hamza. I told him the story of one of his bodyguards as an illustration of how ruthless the people around Hamza were.

Most of his acolytes wore combat suits or the long Arabic robe. Oussama Kassir stood out with his blond hair and athlete's body. Originally from Lebanon he had been given Swedish citizenship in 1989. Even after 9/11 he would brazenly walk around describing himself as Bin Laden's hit man. Kassir boasted openly about killing in the name of Allah. Hamza used him as a quasi-military adviser and for months new arrivals at the Mosque would be impressed by the claims of this jihadi figure.

The mantra was war against the West, it was the duty of all Muslims to fight Jews and America and moving on to the afterlife was the ultimate reward for performing these duties well in this life. Andrew listened intently and took copious notes. He was an international journalist of some repute and although he was very familiar with how the world of international poltics worked I could tell he was in a state of shock at how rooted in London the work of these terror organisers had become. For my part I finally felt I was re-finding my feet as an international journalist.

It was difficult for Andrew to understand that supporters like Haroon Aswat could openly call for attacks on America and the killing of Jews. But, as I explained, amongst his followers he walked like a hero and talked like a hero. He was an authentic mujahideen whom new arrivals looked up to. But more importantly for his story I explained that these two men had a connection to the United States. Before 9/11 in November 1999 Abu Hamza had sent these two men on a mission to America.

They flew to New York and then took a greyhound bus across America to Oregon to meet another 'graduate' of Finsbury Park Mosque, James Ujaama. They had with them several thousand pounds provided from the Mosque *Souk* funds. This was the very same Ujaama who would the following year end up in Afghanistan on behalf of Hamza. It was big talk in the Mosque that they had been dispatched to America to organise some kind of training camp. They were on their way to a town called Bly in Klamath County Oregon to meet with a radical preacher there called Semi Osman. The plan was to use a remote place called the Dog Cry Ranch to convert radicalised Americans into jihadists and to set up a military training camp, but disagreements between the three men made that venture problematic. After just two weeks at the ranch Aswat decided it was not going to work. A lack of men, materials and motivation thwarted Abu Hamza's initial foray into the American jihad. After several run-ins with the law, one of which required the written intervention of Abu Hamza himself, Ujaama decided to return to Finsbury Park Mosque to continue his website work for the Supporters of Shariah.

Oussama Kassir remained in Seattle for a few months longer but left for Europe soon after. He was arrested in 2005 on a flight from Prague to Beirut and eventually extradited to the US in 2007. He was tried in 2009 for his part in the Bly Conspiracy to set up the jihadi camp, accused of training men in the use of firearms and being in possession of some material on how to use poisons. Found guilty by a federal jury on eleven terror-related counts, he was sentenced to life in prison.

Haroon Aswat has resided in Britain's most famous high-security psychiatric hospital – Broadmoor, diagnosed with paranoid schizophrenia. The United States continued to request his extradition until the European Court of Human Rights permanently blocked his extradition on medical grounds in September 2013.

* * *

Andrew from the *Journal* wasn't the only North American journalist and journalism outlet showing interest in this story. Within a few weeks David Heath had approached me from the *Seattle Times* and a crew from the Canadian Broadcasting Corporation who were shooting a film they called 'the recruiters'.

Heath too showed a keen interest in my familiarity with Oussama Kassir and Haroon Aswat. I was one of the few people prepared to identify them as hard-core followers of Hamza who advocated violent jihad against the West. I was as explicit as I could be by telling these journalists that I had little doubt that Hamza and his supporters were umbilically linked to Al Qaeda and what was happening in Afghanistan. I think, in truth, I had a credibility problem. Despite all my years trying to gather intelligence, these American journalists couldn't quite believe that if I was being totally straight, how it was that none of these men had been arrested for wrongdoing by the British authorities. At times I wanted to scream.

A story like this spreads quickly. Once American newspapers started publishing details of my eyewitness accounts to the goings on at Finsbury Park I began getting other calls. Within days of the CBC broadcast I received a call from one of the lawyers representing some of the families of 9/11 victims, Michael Elsner. He was passing through London and wanted to meet this man who claimed Abu Hamza had had a safe haven for years in Finsbury Park Mosque and got away with his crimes. We arranged to meet in his offices in South Carolina to help him prepare his case for his clients.

Finally America was waking up to my story. It had taken me ten years, a failed marriage, near madness and living with death threats, but finally my fight against Abu Qatada and Abu Hamza seemed to be making headway. I felt with the American authorities and press on my side I was now entering an endgame of sorts. But I still had to get to America.

In the autumn of 2004 I took a call from a journalist at *Vanity Fair*. They had seen the allegations I had made about Finsbury Park Mosque in the American press and wanted to write a long article about why so many of my warnings had been ignored and whether there had been lost opportunities to prevent the 9/11 attacks. I told them 'Get me to America and I am ready to explain everything.' It had become my mantra to every US and Canadian journalist now beating a path to my door in increasing numbers.

In the end it wasn't *Vanity Fair* who got me there, though their article did appear in November 2004 (Zaman, 2004). I knew that I needed to get there to see for myself why my stance against Hamza had mattered. Above all I personally wanted to pay my respects at the scene of one of the most atrocious and audacious acts of terrorism that the world has ever seen – Ground Zero in New York.

The *Vanity Fair* article certainly opened that door for me though. In December 2004 I applied for my US visa at the Grosvenor Square Embassy in London. At first when I arrived to go through the screening process I sensed some serious reservations from embassy staff when they saw my green Algerian passport. At least that's how paranoid I had become.

In the waiting hall I felt all eyes were on me and as number after number was called I sensed that I was falling further and further to the back of the queue. Perhaps they were starting an investigation about me. My anxiety levels were rising. People who had come in after me were leaving and I was about to get up to complain when finally, after 2 hours and 10 minutes, my number came up. I went to the small cubicle to have an interview with an immigration officer. Goodness knows what he made of the sweating nervous wreck before him. I was innocent of any charge but I surely felt guiltier than Abu Hamza did.

It was clear that the immigration officer already knew who I was. It is difficult to hide when your face and opinions are all over the media. It turned out he had seen me several times on Kurt Barling's BBC reports and seemed interested in my views on Al Qaeda. So while he considered the emails that I had brought along to prove my relationship with Michael Elsner one of the attorneys for the 9/11 victims, I explained why I hated them so much and who I thought was responsible for propagating that message in Europe. It was clear that they had already made a decision and the immigration officer said he saw no reason why I shouldn't travel to the United States and he hoped I would enjoy my stay.

* * *

On 15th February 2005 I boarded a flight from London Heathrow to Washington. As I looked down at the Atlantic Ocean below, I reflected on how I had got to this point. About the friends and family I had lost in Algeria, about my failed marriage, about the future of my two children and about the fight to make the world safer without the likes of Abu Hamza and Abu Qatada on the loose. I felt a soaring sense of joy that now I was being taken seriously and my message might finally get results.

American customs officers are no shrinking violets. The excitement of finally being on American soil was tempered by the heavy duty questioning I faced after they found my bag full of videotapes of Abu Hamza. Even my explanation that I had brought them for the families of the victims of 9/11 and their lawyer cut little ice to begin with. They told me that that was an old story and no one was interested in it any more and asked why I was bringing the tapes in. After they had confirmed my story with Michael Elsner by phone I assured them that the story was a long way from over. I was exhausted but exhilarated, tomorrow the real work would begin and I could get to know America properly.

I slept fitfully and got up early, eager to see America. A colleague of Michael Elsner's came to collect me and took me to an American diner where the portions would have fed an entire Algerian family. Everyone was so friendly. Never had so many strangers greeted me in the morning with a smile and left me wishing me a good day. I really felt at home.

Michael was grateful for the videos and we went through some of the court documentation that he was preparing so I could explain to him the role that Finsbury Park had played in the build up to 9/11. It was incredible how remote the war on terror seemed to be for Americans. Finsbury Park, a small mosque in North London took on the character of an Al Qaeda hub in their eyes. Back in the UK it was seen as a little local difficulty. But that first day Elsner really wanted just to meet me and suggested I just spend the day getting over the jet lag before we set to work properly.

That first full day in America I just walked and walked around Charleston, North Carolina. A curious place to begin my acquaintance with America. It was what I had expected America to be but quieter; less hectic than in the movies and television shows pumped out all around the world. I kept asking myself – why do these extremist Arabs and Muslims hate Americans so much?

* * *

That evening I decided to pick a random bar and see for myself how Americans might react to meeting a Muslim Algerian in their midst. It was my own, very unscientific, survey of how Americans would view someone like me. I felt like I was in my own movie. It was like all those films I had watched as a child in Algeria. Man walks into a bar and causes a stir. So as I was sitting at the bar and a young lady smiled at me I asked the barman to get her the drink of her choice on my red wine tab. I'm not sure what was more fascinating – watching the barman throw the bottles in the air as he prepared the cocktail or the fact that the young woman kept smiling at me and then walked over to join me. Just like the movies. She asked me if she had seen me before. I said there was no chance of that as I was African and it was my first night in America. She said that was impossible because I had white skin.

So we began to talk about Algeria and the people who lived there. I explained not all Africans had black skin. I was amazed at her ignorance of just where Algeria was, but also surprised by her warmth. She in fact announced to the whole bar that there was an Algerian 'in the house.' I didn't pay for another drink that night. What a wonderful introduction to Americans. But it also told me that these Americans had no idea where Algeria was or the pain and suffering that we Algerians had gone through over the past decade.

For the next three days I went through the files Michael gave me to try and make sure that every piece of documentation I could help him with could be verified. Every single file was about 9/11 and it brought home to me just how far-reaching the influence of Finsbury Park Mosque had become. All my work gathering intelligence and passing it on had not been in vain.

In February 2005 of course Abu Hamza had still not been sent for trial in Britain, but seeing how the Americans were piecing together fragments of information my confidence grew with each document that even if the British didn't prosecute, then the Americans would, if they could succeed in getting him extradited to America. Some of the evidence was clearly taken from what I had been reporting from inside Finsbury Park Mosque to my British Security Service handlers

The more we worked and socialised the more I learned from Michael of how few Americans travelled abroad and how the majority of Americans had no idea what was happening outside of the United States. There was little or any understanding of the visceral hatred of their country that existed in many parts of the Middle and Far East. I was astonished.

Michael was happy and surprised at the quality of the information I was able to give him. He and his colleagues had been obliged since the 9/11 tragedy to learn fast about terrorism and they were extremely knowledgeable in a bookish sense. I of course had been dealing with it in person for sixteen years already. That was why I had come to America to work for free. I knew the costs of terrorism and it was my way of honouring the victims of 9/11.

* * *

From Charleston I had one more thing to do before ending my short but productive trip to America. I had managed to pull together my meagre savings so I could travel to New York. I couldn't return to England without seeing this place. As my plane flew over Manhattan it was already dark but the skies were clear and the view was spectacular. It was the picture that every foreigner has in his or her mind's eye of that great city.

With more haste than planning I jumped aboard a bus at La Guardia to head to downtown Manhattan and then into a yellow taxi to take me to my hotel on Times Square. I felt I was in a dream, bouncing from one iconic site to another. It was past midnight when I arrived at the hotel but I couldn't stay put – I had to walk. The bright lights, traffic and the smell of American burgers overwhelmed me. By the time I returned to put my head down I could think of nothing other than the urgent need to walk immediately to the site of the World Trade Center. Eventually I slept; I was too tired to dream.

The following morning at breakfast I met an Iranian running his business in downtown New York. London and New York are like twins; they represent the world in one city. His story was interesting but I had no time for gossip that morning, just coffee, as I could feel my heart racing with the anticipation. Perhaps it was my blood boiling more than my heart racing.

Finally arriving in New York was my chance to give my apologies and prayers to the victims for not having succeeded early enough in my mission. It is a good four miles to the site from Times Square and as I walked I found myself getting angrier and angrier. When I finally arrived at the spot I felt a cold chill as I sat there thinking about the waste of life that so many terror attacks had caused; how this tragedy in New York ultimately linked these people with all those around the world who'd experienced the terror of Al Qaeda. It linked New York to Bentalha. I'm not ashamed to say it was a painful moment and I shed a lot of tears.

At Ground Zero, all the years I had spent fighting my own fears and working for the Algerians, the French and British security services seemed for nothing. The spectacular attack that Osama Bin Laden promised came to pass at that very spot. Silly as it may read, I felt I had personally failed the American people, as I would feel again some months later with the victims of the attacks on the London Underground. If only I had gone to the CIA in 2000 when Colonel Benali had suggested it. Perhaps I hadn't tried hard enough. An American journalist writing for *Newsweek*, Stryker McGuire said of me, 'Reda Hassaïne fancies himself a spy. Like the terrorists who struck at the World Trade Center and the Pentagon, he has been undercover for half a decade, living a non-descript and outwardly unremarkable life, except in his own imagination. Rather than perpetrate terror, however, he dreams of stopping it.'

At Ground Zero the tears came as I asked myself did I dream too much and do too little?

As I wandered off to take a boat to Ellis Island and continue my short trip of discovery around New York, I consoled myself with the defence that I had refused to believe that nothing could be done. I had done my very best to warn others by going public and warning the Western world of the real dangers they were facing from these merchants of terror passing through Finsbury Park Mosque under the stewardship of Abu Hamza.

CHAPTER 15

Guilty – USA vs Mostafa Kamel Mostafa

I **WAITED FOR THE** judgment of the extradition hearing at the court house in London on 5th October 2012 with a sense of resignation. I had been disappointed so many times before in my attempts to get the British authorities to take my warnings and evidence seriously. I prepared myself psychologically to deal with the crushing disappointment of yet another decision that would let Abu Hamza off the hook.

This time though I needn't have worried. When the judgment came it was swift. Not only had Abu Hamza finally come to the end of the road for appealing against the US extradition request, the High Court's ruling was that he was to be taken directly from prison to the airport and put on a flight to America, immediately that afternoon. The speed with which the authorities acted was breathtaking and perhaps an indication of how they wanted to avoid any criticism or publicity campaign which might stall his departure.

Within hours television cameras were tracking the prison van as it sped towards the airport and a flight where US Marshals and FBI agents waited to escort Abu Hamza to meet American justice, delayed whilst he served his time following the Old Bailey trial of 2006.

By the morning of 6th October Abu Hamza had touched down on American soil. He was equally swiftly delivered to a downtown Manhattan court where United States District Judge Katherine B. Forrest had been waiting to begin the trial process of the man who had evaded US justice for eight years.

That same day Hamza appeared before Magistrate Judge Frank Maas who read the 11 charges against him. He was charged with being involved in the 1998 kidnapping in Yemen of American citizens, including providing the kidnappers with a satellite phone and taking a call from one of the gunmen who sought his direction, supporting the establishment of a terrorist camp in a town called Bly in the West Coast State of Oregon and 'facilitating violent jihad in Afghanistan'.

Hamza remained sitting whilst a lawyer turned the court papers for him. It had been decided that he would not have access to a prosthetic limb whilst he was considered a risk to himself.

Hamza's lawyers argued that he said he was physically unfit to stand trial in America and that a full evaluation would need to be made of his medical condition. Now he would finally be called to account and he knew that the seriousness of the charges could lead to him spending the rest of his life in an American maximum-security prison.

Referring to his prosthetic limbs his lawyer Sabrina Shroff argued, 'If he doesn't receive his prosthetic devices immediately, he'll need someone to take care of his daily needs or he will not be able to function in a civilized manner.'

But for all the civility of the court I could hardly believe it when I finally heard the words of the man who would be in charge of prosecuting Hamza, United States Attorney in Manhattan, Preet Bharara. These were the words I had been waiting to hear since 1998. He said, 'It makes good on a promise to the American people to use every diplomatic, legal and administrative tool to pursue and prosecute charged terrorists no matter how long it takes.'

Within three days he was back in court before Judge Forrest who conceded that although timely justice was important the scale of the job for the team of lawyers charged with defending him meant that a trial before 26th August 2013 was unreasonable. And a trial there would have to be because Abu Hamza fresh from his stint in a British prison was in no mood for compromise. He pleaded not guilty to all eleven charges laid against him. Once again I would have to have patience to see my work finally deliver results.

***

In fact the trial preparations took even longer than anticipated. Hamza was repeatedly back in court demanding extra time, more documents, greater access to his lawyers from his prison cell, he argued, in order to mount a credible defence against false charges.

Abu Hamza, now referred to in court by his real name Mostafa Kamel Mostafa, clearly wanted to still be 'the Boss' as he was at Finsbury Park Mosque. He decided from the outset of court proceedings that he would need to intervene personally by writing directly to Judge Forrest during the trial process.

American justice may seem slow by Algerian standards but at least Abu Hamza couldn't complain the judge presiding in his case was steamrollering him into court. Eventually a new trial date was set for 16th April 2014. I needed to be patient but I decided I shouldn't waste time. It was at this point that I decided with Kurt Barling that we should write my story.

✳ ✳ ✳

Abu Hamza came into court on 16th April a much smaller and more self-effacing man than the bombastic, firebrand preacher who had defied the authorities by preaching race hatred on the streets of London outside Finsbury Park Mosque. That was what he was sentenced to prison for in the Old Bailey in London, but in the United States the charges were of an entirely different nature.

Opening the case against Hamza prosecutor Edward Y. Kim claimed, 'He was a trainer of terrorists and he used the cover of religion so he could hide in plain sight in London.'

These are almost the precise words I had used to my MI5 and Special Branch handlers time and time again only to be ignored. I often asked myself what they feared most, acts of terrorism or being accused of being racists.

The American prosecutor Kim did not mince his words as he continued to characterise Hamza in a way that would have been unheard of in Britain. 'Abu Hamza didn't just talk the talk, he walked the walk. Kim continued, 'Abu Hamza was committed to war. War against non-Muslims. In support of that war he dispatched young men around the globe to train, to fight and to kill.' And all this was orchestrated from the Mosque at Finsbury Park that became his 'base of operation for his global export of violence and terror'.

Was I imagining these words in a dream? Or now sitting at home in Algeria reading my own thoughts being replayed through a prosecutor in court thousands of miles away in New York. Finally someone was making sense of the intelligence I had gathered for the Algerian, French and British security services and personally sacrificed so much for. I was beginning to feel a sense of relief.

When it came to the turn of the defence attorney to lay out the case that would be made to undermine these charges, Joshua L. Dratel told the jury Abu Hamza might have said a lot of harsh things about the United States, Israel and the West in general, but he was also critical of Al Qaeda and other terrorist groups when he disagreed with them.

So that would be his defence, I thought, he was independently minded and criticised everyone, therefore he cannot be guilty of anything in particular.

Dratel continued his opening before judge and jury saying, 'These are views, not acts. This is expression, not crimes.' That in order to reach his potential flock Hamza 'needed to be outrageous to reach the entire spectrum of his community', and offer a moderating influence, 'a third way between Osama Bin Laden on one extreme and George Bush on the other.'

Incredible I thought that a man who revelled in the massacres of women and children in my own country and I witnessed inciting others to kill people in the name of jihad, a man who claimed slitting my throat would be a heroic religious act, could claim he was somehow a peacemaker. I hoped the jury would see through this act, because they were being presented with a chameleon, a man who changes his colour and tune to serve his own objectives.

Through all this Abu Hamza sat quietly but that could not disguise the fact that he had already been assertive in his own defence by taking the decision to write directly to Judge Forrest asking that he would be allowed to testify at his trial himself. Before the jury heard the opening statements he had written a five-page letter asking that he be allowed to make his own opening statement. Perhaps mindful of allowing Hamza an opportunity to turn the courtroom into an international political platform his request was turned down.

Judge Forrest also made it clear that the law considers when words are used they also have an impact. The judge reinforced this point of law by allowing the prosecution to introduce statements made by Abu Hamza on British Television News. Hamza would now learn that he could not say one thing and then pretend he could not be held accountable for such words. The words, 'Everybody was happy when the planes hit the World Trade Center' would now come back to challenge Hamza, some might say haunt him. In effect the judge ruled these words provided 'direct and clear evidence of the defendant's state of mind as to Al Qaeda and its agenda.'

Hamza's wish to be able to give testimony was heard by Judge Forrest. When it was time for him to give evidence he would once again transform himself into a man of confidence who would give as good as he got.

But Judge Katherine Forrest gave the clearest indication very early on that Hamza would not be able to use the courtroom for political propaganda and that he would be held accountable for what he said if the court could demonstrate that there was a correlation between his words and the terrorist actions of others.

Judge Forrest is no shrinking violet. She has risen through the ranks of private legal practice despite coming from humble beginnings where by her own admission she had for a time lived on food stamps and been homeless as a child. A gifted student she had elevated herself through dedication and hard work. President Barack Obama recommended Forrest for appointment to be a district judge in May 2011. This case was the Judge's most high-profile case to date and she made it clear she placed a premium on transparency. Even when rejecting requests put in writing to her by Abu Hamza she was at pains to point out his letters had been 'read and considered'.

After the drama of the initial openings the trial settled down into presenting the jury with the picture of Abu Hamza's terror-related activities. It must have made tough listening at times but through the early evidence Abu Hamza remained a model of calmness.

The prosecutors quickly got to the issue of Hamza's vital role in the Yemen kidnappings. Although he could not conjure up the real atmosphere that I witnessed in Finsbury Park Mosque when the news came through of the kidnapping, Prosecutor Kim went for the jugular instead by focusing on the ordeal of the hostages.

Magaret Thompson – one of those hostages who was shot but survived – limped into court and the jury appeared riveted by her evidence explaining that her limp was from where she had been shot and left permanently damaged in the hostage-taking episode. She was hit in the leg with a bullet from behind which had shattered her femur. She recalled how she was with a group of tourists exploring the ancient wonders of Yemen in December 1988 when armed militants ambushed their convoy.

The tour had included teachers and university lecturers from the US, Britain and Australia. The militants collected passports and made it obvious that they were particularly interested in the Americans amongst them.

The kidnapping didn't last long as the Yemeni government decided on decisive action and sent troops in to recover the hostages in their encampment the following day. That whole episode was heavily criticised in some quarters as being rash and ill-prepared.

During the exchange of gunfire Margaret Thompson told jurors one of the militants turned to her and said, 'It's goodbye to you all.' At first she thought this meant they were to be released but soon realised to her horror and with a rising sense of panic that the hostages were being used as human shields and at that point hope turned to fear that they were all going to be killed in the firefight between government troops and militants.

The jury was reminded that Abu Hamza's motivation was family inspired as he wanted to put pressure on the Yemeni government to release a group of Britons – members of his Supporters of Shariah group – who who had been arrested earlier in the month for planning terror strikes against targets in Yemen. One of those Britons was Abu Hamza's stepson.

Margaret Thompson explained that the leader of the group Abu Hassan had told them explicitly that, 'It's not your fault that your countries bombed Iraq', and added, 'You're going to be safe. Everything is going to be Ok. We have friends in prison and we're going to keep you until they're released.'

Hamza's lawyer Joshua Dratel unsuccessfully tried to suggest that although Hamza had given a satellite phone to the kidnappers and described the kidnapping as 'justified', he was not involved in the past in any conspiracy to kidnap.

Back in December 1998 I recall the euphoria at Finsbury Park Mosque when Hamza and his band of jihadist followers suddenly realised they were at the centre of an international jihadist revival. Back then it was as if they had 'made it '.

Of course this did not now sit well with his defence that he was actually only 'an intermediary trying to negotiate the release of the hostages'. To the end, it seems, Abu Hamza has been in denial of the consequences of his own words and actions. Or perhaps he was just convinced by his own lies.

A second kidnap victim, Mary Quin, went one step further than any of the other surviving hostages by deciding in 2000 to write a book about her ordeal (Quin, 2005)

Mary Quin described to the court in graphic detail how her kidnapper had grabbed the back of her shirt and then pushed the barrel of his AK-47 assault rifle into her back. Then how she was forced to march into a hail of bullets from the government troops. When her kidnapper was wounded and fell to the ground she was able to wrestle herself free and run towards the Yemeni troops and ultimately safety.

Abu Hamza must rue the day he decided to allow her to interview him in 2000 at Finsbury Park Mosque about her ordeal. But it was at a time when he surely felt untouchable as the security services in Britain bungled the way they handled him. At that point the attention perhaps made him feel he was in control of a new international agenda. Mary Quin recorded the interview on a tape recorder that now, 14 years on, the New York jury listened to intently.

Quin described how Hamza had leant back in his chair and said to her 'I'm surprised you would come here – very surprised.' Her recollection of his brashness mirrored my own experiences with him at the time. He told her in the interview that the kidnapping of foreigners was 'Islamically a good thing to do', announcing that it was a way to undermine Yemen's non-Islamic government and remind its leaders that they could not protect their borders. He told Mary Quin in 2000 'We never thought it would be that bad', referring to the outcome of the hostage taking that left four dead and numerous others like Quin seriously harmed.

It was certainly bad for Hamza now. All he could say was that he wasn't involved in the decision to organise the kidnapping and therefore not party to the crimes in Yemen he had been charged with.

To set the scene for his defence Abu Hamza set about attempting to dispel some myths – notwithstanding that they were largely myths of his own making. When I was inside Finsbury Park Mosque it was clear to his followers that he had received his injuries, leading to the loss of his two hands and an eye, during his involvement in jihad in Afghanistan and Bosnia. They were the result, according to popular myth, of land-mine explosions whilst he was fighting the Russian occupation.

Now in court he gave a less glory-filled explanation for the loss of both hands and an eye, saying they were sustained as a result of an accident during an engineering project in Lahore, Pakistan. He realised a bottle near him was about to detonate and he picked it up at the moment it exploded. He was in a coma and lay in a hospital bed for a month and eventually returned to Britain.

He said people had treated him as a hero, adding in court 'That's exactly what happened. I am under oath.'

Abu Hamza, you exploited that myth to the detriment of others. It gave you status as a jihadist, credibility as an al-Qaeda activist and authority as a radical imam. It's no use now telling us the truth under oath now after generating untold violence from the religious platform and political authority those mythical injuries bestowed upon you and which you, of course, ruthlessly exploited.

The next important myth he wanted to deal with was his involvement with MI5 whom he said he had been working with for several years before the 9/11 attacks in New York as a force for good. His defence lawyer brandished in court a 50-page document which he said proved that Hamza had been a trusted intermediary for the British Security Services. He had been trying to calm hotheads in the Muslim community and intervene to stop violence he claimed. Judge Forrest ruled the evidence inadmissible because they didn't deal with the terrorism charges with which he had been charged.

We may never know the truth of that relationship but it confirmed to me that whilst the security services were using me to spy on Hamza in the late 1990s they were also talking to Abu Hamza himself. Seemingly incapable of putting his activities in their proper Al Qaeda context, they continued to see it as a local skirmish with a clown.

As early as 1997 an MI5 officer wrote after a meeting with Hamza that 'I reasserted the view that over the past few months in particular, he had walked a dangerous tightrope and had come close to being culpable for incitement to violence...the Security Service, in particular took a dim view of those advocating violence even if the violence was perpetrated overseas.'

So here is my question. If they recognised that in 1997 why did they leave it another eight years to prosecute him? Why did they ignore my warnings? Why did they set me up at the Fourth Feathers? Doesn't that make the British Security Services as culpable of the ensuing mayhem as those who ultimately caused it? Were they negligent in their duty to protect life despite their claims now that he faced arrest if his actions ever met the criminal threshold? Much of the evidence that was used to prosecute him in 2005 was already known by 2001.

* * *

The fireworks didn't really begin in New York until Abu Hamza took to the stand himself to defend his actions under a three-day cross-examination by prosecutors. Once again he was mostly the calm and almost self-assured preacher, repeatedly denying the charges that had been laid against him. He took notes through much of the trial using a pen attached to a prosthetic arm.

Several times Hamza had to be reminded by Judge Forrest that he was in a court of law. When Hamza intervened to accuse the prosecutor of taking statements out of context or of lacking concentration Judge Forrest reprimanded him, 'Mr Mostafa, we do need to obey the rules of cross-examination all right? Don't make speeches.' Hamza should never be under-estimated. He is your quintessential showman.

He repeated his claim that he was only a mouthpiece for Abu Hassan's kidnapping group and not their spiritual leader. In a whole series of tense exchanges he told the jury that the rejoicing about attacks on warships was not the same thing as taking civilian hostages.

But then perhaps Hamza under-estimated an American jury when challenged on his statement that 'Everybody was happy when the planes hit the World Trade Center' made in a television interview. His defence was that he called for an investigation into the trade center's collapse to determine as he put it 'how much of 9/11 belonged to Al Qaeda and how much of 9/11 belonged to the previous administration.' Deluded or paranoid, this was not Abu Hamza's finest moment.

Challenging the accepted evidence on the fate of the Twin Towers and the thousands of people who perished in them on 9/11, just a few blocks from where they once stood, was never going to endear a man defending himself against charges of terrorism to anyone in the Southern District Court of New York.

The Prosecutor picked up on Hamza's calm demeanour in court and stressed to the jury in his summing up of their case against him that 'when he spoke about jihad, he wasn't the calm man you saw on the witness stand. He was enraged. He was loud, screaming, passionate.' Ian McGinley added that Hamza 'said what he truly believed in, until it was time to be held accountable for his crimes, until it was time to come before an American jury, and then he changed his tune.'

The jury considered their verdict for four days. They did not rush to judgment on the eleven charges Abu Hamza faced. I'm pleased because it shows that beyond reasonable doubt meant just that. As the jury returned and the court listened in silence as the foreperson read out the verdicts Abu Hamza remained calm as he had through much of the trial. He had said in court that American justice 'wanted a conviction' and not a trial for the truth, which meant no doubt he fully anticipated the guilty verdicts on all eleven charges. I would like to think he had a guilty conscience.

* * *

It has been 20 years since the Algerian authorities blackmailed me into a dangerous and complicated life. But the truth is, my determination to fight against the terror that blighted my country was unshakeable. Combatting criminals who use religion to satisfy their thirst for blood was a duty for me, I suppose a kind of civic jihad.

I too believed that if I died as a martyr for the cause of democracy I would be able to take 40 people to paradise and I would reserve places there for my family and friends.

I feel exhausted, yes. But after twenty years of my life fighting terrorism and trying to expose Abu Hamza, the guilty verdict was a personal victory for me. I feel I have accomplished my mission as best I could and for the right reasons. Maybe it is time too for MI5 to apologise for what I believe they arranged for me on 21st April 2000. Perhaps now they will accept they shouldn't have tried to silence me.

* * *

After the jury delivered its eleven guilty verdicts, Judge Forrest ruled that she would need time to proceed to a sentencing which was initially set for September 2014. Kurt Barling and I completed this book in that time. But Mostafa Kamel was not yet done. He fired his defence counsel and then sought the court's help to appoint a new lawyer to prepare his legal arguments prior to sentencing. Eventually after two months of delay Judge Forrest intervened to set a new sentencing date for January 2015.

Abu Hamza has remained busy though, accusing his trial legal team of being incompetent and demanding that he be given new legal representation to prepare his papers for the sentencing. He wrote a 22-page letter to the judge which was the last thing that his soon to be sacked legal team delivered on 19th May 2014.

In it he pours scorn on the probity, efficiency and effectiveness of his defence team. Who despite this vote of no confidence, argued that his previous conviction at the Old Bailey should not form part of the Judge's considerations when determining the sentence.

At the end of his letter to Judge Forrest, which at times is simply an incoherent rant, Mostafa Kamel sums up his dissatisfaction with the defence team. Although he is very careful not to criticise either judge, jury or verdict, he appears to be blaming others for his predicament rather than his own words and deeds to the last.

'To conclude from all the above, respected Madam Judge. Throughout the past 18 months I had tried my very best to make attorney-defendant working and productive and continued to give benefits of doubts, when promises has been repeatedly broken and new were made only to be broken again, even when I am severed from visits for a long time and denied any follow-up to my instructions as to know what is really going on. However the above shortcomings are only the obvious result for such conduct and easily done to SAM inmates who have no one to turn to except the Allmighty and an honest Judge.

I would, therefore, appreciate the respected judge to allow me any other attorney for sentencing and allow me an application of retrial motion 33 (I think). I would also appreciate if this letter be included in any future related motions of legal.

I deeply apologise for the lengthy letter/app, the many mistakes or misunderstandings of points of law and how should be presented or misuse of terms and/or any other shortcomings in the letter.

Finally, I submit the letter/app to the respected madam Judge fully appreciative of any previous and future help or remedy. Thankyou.'

The 'defendant M.K. Mostafa' signed the letter.

So no longer was there any pretence of being the radical preacher Abu Hamza al-Masri. Now as he faces the reckoning for his crimes, all his pretences of importance and status within his revolutionary world have been stripped away. He is reduced to facing the consequences for his millions of words of hate and incitement, which the world now knows incontrovertibly, led to the violent actions perpetrated by his followers.

Let's not forget that British-born young men and women still travel to Syria from Britain to join in the fight with jihadist forces, encouraged by a new generation of radical preachers and their ideas of radical Islam governed under the auspices of a Caliphate .

Abu Hamza helped prise open the lid of the Pandora's box of radical Islam. For that reason he will always to me be the godfather of British jihadism. He may well have been a clown. But his clowning captured young Islamists' attention, kept it and inspired them to reach for martyrdom. In Algeria, Britain and internationally he didn't do it alone, but he was a heavyweight amongst minnows. We will now spend a generation trying to come to terms with what this means for those in the world that do not share their views. Radicalisation of young minds eager for a different way to interpret the world is far from over. Our work is not yet done.

At least, albeit belatedly, Abu Hamza has finally been held accountable for over a decade of violence and thousands of deaths inspired by his calls for violent jihad. It sends an important message that no matter how long it takes, if you act criminally you will eventually face justice in the West.

For those of us who believe in a world where dissent matters, minorities are accorded the same protection as the majority and you are not obliged to be killed because you believe in a different god – justice has been done.

Mostafa Kamal Mostafa for all these reasons I am certain that there will be no place reserved for you in Paradise.

Bibliography –
Alphabetical

Amarni, Kamel (2000) 'Comment j'ai été recruiter par la DGSE'. *Le Soir d'Algerie*. 13th November.

Author unknown (2002) 'Spy says al Qaida scouted US base'. *Jewish World Review*. 31st July.

Author unknown (2012) 'A forgotten Hamzanama'. *The Hindu*. 16th October.

Author unknown (2014) 'Abu Hamza to appeal terrorism verdict in New York'. *Telegraph.co.uk*. 20th May.

Author unknown (2014) 'Abu Hamza trial: Security services ignored warnings, says Finsbury Park mosque supergrass'.
Telegraph.co.uk. 19th May.

Author unknown (2014) 'MI5 record explodes Abu Hamza court claims'. *Mail on Sunday*. 11th May.

Author unknown (2014) 'MI5 spy ends £1million compensation fight as Abu Hamza is found guilty'. *Daily Star (Online)*. 25th May.

Barling, K. (2001) 'London lives on its nerves'. *BBC News*. 8th October.

Barling, K. (2003) 'Charity Commission bans Abu Hamza from Finsbury Park mosque'. *BBC News*. 4th February.

Barling, K. (2003) 'Rachid Ramda to be extradited?'. *BBC News*. 4th April.

Barling, K. (2003) 'London - safe haven for terrorists?'. *BBC News*. 2nd June.

Barling, K. (2005) 'Lessons from Finsbury Park Mosque'. *BBC News*. 4th August.

Barling, K. (2007) 'Finding the Bombers'. *BBC News*. 14th May.

Barling, K. (2008) 'Finally Home'. *BBC News*. 29th January.

Barling, K. (2008) 'Vulnerability of the Suicide Bomber'. *BBC News*. 1st March.

Barling, K. (2012) 'Community reacts to Abu Hamza's extradition'. *BBC News*. 5th October.

Barney, Katherine (2007) 'Mosque informer: MI5 betrayed me'. *Evening Standard*. 29th November.

Barrett, David and Robert Verkaik (2014) 'MI5 ignored warnings that Finsbury Park Mosque was a hub for al-Qaeda says spy'. *The Daily Telegraph*. 20th May.

Benramdane, D. (1999) 'Algeria accepts the unacceptable'. *Le Monde Diplomatique*. March edition.

Benmerad, Djamel (2001) 'Un journaliste algerien au service de la DGSE'. *Le Jeune Independent*. 1st July.

Burke, Jason (2001) 'How I was betrayed by the British: Réda Hassaïne risked his life infiltrating Islamic groups for police and MI5. But after two years' service he was betrayed, he tells Jason Burke'. *The Observer*. 18th February.

Burke, Jason (2001) 'MI5 and police ordered illegal break-ins at mosques'. *The Observer*. 18th February.

Burke, Jason (2001) 'MI5 and police ordered illegal raids on mosques'. *The Observer*. 18th February.

Burke, Jason (2003) *Al-Qaeda: The true story of radical Islam*. Penguin.

Casciani, D. and Sakr, S. (2006) *The battle for the mosque* BBC News online. 7th February.

Cruz, Louis D. (2012) *Unmitigated Disaster*. Xlibris Corporation.

Curtis, Mark (2011) *Secret Affairs: Britain's Collusion with Radical Islam*. Serpent's Tail.

Davenport, Justin and Keith Dovkants (2003) 'Mosque linked to key network plotting major attack'. *Evening Standard*. 21st January.

Dodd, Vikram (2006) 'Inside the mosque: an academy for holy war'. *The Guardian*. 8th February.

Dodd, Vikram (2012) 'Comment is free: In brief: Why Hamza was left alone: MI5 viewed the cleric as a harmless buffoon and a useful lure for extremists'. *The Guardian*. 26th September.

Dovkants, Keith (2005) 'I spied on Abu Qatada for MI5'. *Evening Standard*. 28th January.

Fernández-Sánchez, Pablo Antonio (2009) *International Legal Dimension of Terrorism (International Humanitarian Law)*. Brill.

Foley, Frank (2013) *Countering Terrorism in Britain and France: Institutions, Norms and the Shadow of the Past*. Cambridge University Press.

Fukuyama, Y.F. *The End of History and the Last Man, 1992, Free Press*

Gujer, Eric (2006) *Kampf an neuen Fronten*. Campus Verlag GmbH.

Hassaïne, Réda (2005) 'Under Cover Agent'. *The Sunday Times*. 17th July.

Hassaïne, Réda and Sean O'Neill (2005) 'I was tortured, says ricin plotter'. *The Times*. 9th May.

Hewitt, Steve (2010) *Snitch!: A History of the Modern Intelligence Informer*. Bloomsbury Academic.

Huntington, Samuel P. *The Clash of Civilisations and the Remaking of World Order*, 1996, Simon & Schuster

Issaki, Shimshon (2008) *Terror and Iraq: How we can better combat Islamic terrorism*. Issaki.

Laïdi, Ali (2002) *Le Jihad en Europe: Les Filières du terrorisme Islamiste*. Seuil.

Leppard, David (2001) 'MI5 knew for years of London mosque's role'. *The Times*. 25th November.

Leppard, David (2001) 'MI5 knew for years of London mosque's role'. *The Sunday Times*. 25th November.

Leppard, David (2003) 'Bio-war suits found in mosque'. *The Sunday Times*. 6th January.

Leppard, David (2006) 'Agent says MI5 dismissed Hamza as "harmless clown"'. *The Sunday Times*. 12th February.

Leppard, David (2006). 'How liberal Britain let hate flourish'. *The Sunday Times*. 12th February.

Leppard, David and Nick Fielding (2005) 'The Hate'. *The Sunday Times*. 10th July.

Leppard, David, Gareth Walsh and Paul Nuki (2000) 'Dirty-tricks trail of a Muslim mole'. *The Sunday Times*. 8th October.

McGrory, Daniel (2003) 'A haven for faithful hijacked by extremists'. *The Times*. 21st January.

Moore-Bridger, Benedict (2012) 'MI5 spy beaten up by Qatada thugs "is suing handlers"'. *Evening Standard*. 24th February.

Morey, Peter and Amina Yaqin (2011) *Framing Muslims: Stereotyping and Representation after 9/11*. Harvard University Press.

Napoleoni, Loretta (2003) *Modern Jihad: Tracing the Dollars Behind the Terror Networks*. Pluto Press.

Napoleoni, Loretta (2010) *Terrorism and the Economy: How the War on Terror is Bankrupting the World*. Seven Stories Press.

O'Neill, Sean (2001) 'Why France lived in fear of "Londonistan" Evidence on extremists ignored'. *The Daily Telegraph*. 13th October.

O'Neill, Sean (2003) 'Mosque has been source of concern over terrorism since 1996'. *The Daily Telegraph*. 21st January.

O'Neill, Sean (2003) 'Terrorism and ID cards'. *The Times*. 22nd January.

O'Neill, Sean (2004) 'Death threats made against key witness'. *The Times*. 4ᵗʰ June.

O'Neill, Sean (2007) 'Informant who risked his life to fight extremists "betrayed by MI5"'. *The Times*. 29ᵗʰ November.

O'Neill, Sean (2008) 'Proud day for spy who infiltrated mosque'. *The Times*. 28ᵗʰ January.

O'Neill, Sean and Daniel McGrory (2006) 'Kill and be killed: how cleric raised generation of terrorists'. *The Times*. 8ᵗʰ February.

O'Neill, Sean and Daniel McGrory (2006) *The Suicide Factory: Abu Hamza and the Finsbury Park Mosque*. Harper Perennial.

O'Neill, Sean and Réda Hassaïne (2001) '"My son was brought up to abhor terrorists" Man accused of training the September 11 hijackers never knew them, say his mother'. *The Daily Telegraph*. 1ˢᵗ November.

O'Neill, Sean and Réda Hassaïne (2001) 'I did nothing wrong. I'm just a Muslim and a student of flying'. *The Daily Telegraph*. 28ᵗʰ November.

Parry, Tom and Tom McTague (2012) 'Qatada Spy: I'm living in fear: MI5 agent's assassin's nightmare'. *Daily Mirror*. 14ᵗʰ November.

Phillips, John and Martin Evans (2008) *Algeria: Anger of the Dispossessed*. Yale University Press.

Phillips, Melanie (2012) *Londonistan*. Gibson Square Books.

Quin, Mary (2005) *Kidnapped in Yemen: One Woman's Amazing Escape from Terrorist Captivity*. Mainstream Publishing.

Radu, Michael (2010) *Europe's Ghost: Tolerance, Jihadism, and the Crisis in the West*. Encounter Books.

Reid, Sue (2005) 'So how many more martyrs did he create?'. *Daily Mail*. 3ʳᵈ September.

Reid, Sue (2005) 'The lethal web; just log on to find the enemy within who despise the British infidels'. *Daily Mail*. 8ᵗʰ July.

Reid, Sue (2007) 'And still they're preaching poison; New laws were meant to stop radical clerics stirring up racial hatred in mosques. But as this disturbing Mail investigation reveals, they are still pouring out their vitriol'. *Daily Mail*. 13ᵗʰ January.

Reid, Sue (2012) 'The brave agent who exposed Hamza only to be betrayed by MI5'. *Daily Mail*. 11ᵗʰ April.

Reid, Sue, Sinead Macintyre and James Tozer (2005) 'The Enemy Within; Yesterday Tony Blair promised tough new measures to contain the preachers of hate in our midst. But as this Mail investigation has discovered, it may already be too late'. *Daily Mail*. 6ᵗʰ August.

Robin, Jean (2000) 'La vengeance de l'agent secret'. *Le Parisien*. 9ᵗʰ October.

Robin, Jean (2000) 'J'ai aide les francais'. *Le Parisien.* 10th October.

Schanzer, Jonathan (2001) *Al-Qaeda's Armies: Middle East Affiliate Groups & The Next Generation of Terror.* S.P.I. Books.

Sherwell, Philip and David Barrett (2014) 'Guilty: Hamza will die in US Jail'. *The Daily Telegraph.* 20th May.

SK (2000) 'Un algerien au service de l'espionnage francais a Londres'. *Le Quotidien d'Oran.* 8th October.

Sniffen, M.J. (2006) 'America, you lost – I won: Moussaoui sentenced to life in prison'. *Chicago Sun Times.* 4th May.

Tapper, Jake (2003) 'Muslim spy who infiltrated Bin Laden's terror network in London'. *The Times.* 16th January.

Taylor, Ben (2005) 'Terror suspects "likely to get free homes"' *Daily Mail.* 29th January.

Thomas, Dominique (2003) *Le Londonistan: La Voix du djihad.* Michalon.

Thompson, Paul (2004) *The Terror Timeline: Year by Year, Day by Day, Minute by Minute: A Comprehensive Chronicle of the Road to 9/11– and America's Response.* HarperCollins.

Todd, Paul, Jonathan Bloch and Patrick Fitzgerald (2009) *Spies, Lies and the War on Terror.* Zed Books.

Waugh, Paul and Oliver Finegold (2005) 'British Camp X-Ray suspect "confessed to training with Bin Laden"; US documents allege Guantanamo bay detainees were at al Qaeda military base'. *Evening Standard.* 28th January.

Wells, Tom (2012) 'Qatada smiled as his evil thugs beat me up for being MI5 spy: Mole inside hate mosque sues UK for Pounds 1M'. *The Sun.* 26th February.

Woods, Richard and David Leppard (2006) 'How liberal Britain let hate flourish'. *The Sunday Times.* 12th February.

Woods, Richard, David Leppard and Michael Smith (2005) 'Tangled web that still leaves worrying loose ends'. *The Sunday Times.* 31st July.

Zaman, Ned, David Wise, David Rose and Bryan Burrough (2004) 'The Price of Failure: The path to 9/11: Lost warnings and fatal errors'. *Vanity Fair.* November Edition.

Bibliography by Type and Date (most recent first)

Books drawing on Réda Hassaïne testimony

Foley, Frank (2013) *Countering Terrorism in Britain and France: Institutions, Norms and the Shadow of the Past.* Cambridge University Press.

Cruz, Louis D. (2012) *Unmitigated Disaster.* Xlibris Corporation.

Phillips, Melanie (2012) *Londonistan.* Gibson Square Books.

Curtis, Mark (2011) *Secret Affairs: Britain's Collusion with Radical Islam.* Serpent's Tail.

Morey, Peter and Amina Yaqin (2011) *Framing Muslims: Stereotyping and Representation after 9/11.* Harvard University Press.

Hewitt, Steve (2010) *Snitch!: A History of the Modern Intelligence Informer.* Bloomsbury Academic.

Napoleoni, Loretta (2010) *Terrorism and the Economy: How the War on Terror is Bankrupting the World.* Seven Stories Press.

Radu, Michael (2010) *Europe's Ghost: Tolerance, Jihadism, and the Crisis in the West.* Encounter Books.

Fernández-Sánchez, Pablo Antonio (2009) *International Legal Dimension of Terrorism (International Humanitarian Law).* Brill.

Todd, Paul, Jonathan Bloch and Patrick Fitzgerald (2009) *Spies, Lies and the War on Terror.* Zed Books.

Issaki, Shimshon (2008) *Terror and Iraq: How we can better combat Islamic terrorism.* Issaki.

Phillips, John and Martin Evans (2008) *Algeria: Anger of the Dispossessed.* Yale University Press.

Gujer, Eric (2006) *Kampf an neuen Fronten.* Campus Verlag GmbH.

O'Neill, Sean and Daniel McGrory (2006) *The Suicide Factory: Abu Hamza and the Finsbury Park Mosque*. Harper Perennial.

Quin, Mary (2005) *Kidnapped in Yemen: One Woman's Amazing Escape from Terrorist Captivity*. Mainstream Publishing.

Thompson, Paul (2004) *The Terror Timeline: Year by Year, Day by Day, Minute by Minute: A Comprehensive Chronicle of the Road to 9/11-- and America's Response*. HarperCollins.

Burke, Jason (2003) *Al-Qaeda: The true story of radical Islam*. Penguin.

Napoleoni, Loretta (2003) *Modern Jihad: Tracing the Dollars Behind the Terror Networks*. Pluto Press.

Thomas, Dominique (2003) *Le Londonistan: La Voix du djihad*. Michalon.

Laïdi, Ali (2002) *Le Jihad en Europe: Les Filières du terrorisme Islamiste*. Seuil.

Schanzer, Jonathan (2001) *Al-Qaeda's Armies: Middle East Affiliate Groups & The Next Generation of Terror*. S.P.I. Books.

Benramdane, D. (1999) 'Algeria accepts the unacceptable'. *Le Monde Diplomatique*. March edition.

Newspaper articles drawing on Réda Hassaïne testimony

Author unknown (2014) MI5 spy ends £1million compensation fight as Abu Hamza is found guilty. *Daily Star (Online)*. 25th May.

Author unknown (2014) 'Abu Hamza to appeal terrorism verdict in New York'. *Telegraph.co.uk*. 20th May.

Barrett, David and Robert Verkaik (2014) 'MI5 ignored warnings that Finsbury Park Mosque was a hub for al-Qaeda says spy'. *The Daily Telegraph*. 20th May.

Sherwell, Philip and David Barrett (2014) 'Guilty: Hamza will die in US Jail'. *The Daily Telegraph*. 20th May.

Author unknown (2014) 'Abu Hamza trial: Security services ignored warnings, says Finsbury Park mosque supergrass'. *Telegraph.co.uk*. 19th May.

Author unknown (2014) 'MI5 record explodes Abu Hamza court claims'. *Mail on Sunday*. 11th May

Parry, Tom and Tom McTague (2012) 'Qatada Spy: I'm living in fear: MI5 agent's assassin's nightmare'. *Daily Mirror*. 14th November.

Author unknown (2012) 'A forgotten Hamzanama'. *The Hindu*. 16th October.

Barling, K. (2012) 'Community reacts to Abu Hamza's extradition'. *BBC News*, 5th October

Dodd, Vikram (2012) 'Comment is free: In brief: Why Hamza was left alone: MI5 viewed the cleric as a harmless buffoon and a useful lure for extremists'. *The Guardian*. 26th September.

Reid, Sue (2012) 'The brave agent who exposed Hamza only to be betrayed by MI5'. *Daily Mail*. 11th April.

Wells, Tom (2012) 'Qatada smiled as his evil thugs beat me up for being MI5 spy: Mole inside hate mosque sues UK for Pounds 1M'. *The Sun*. 26th February.

Moore-Bridger, Benedict (2012) 'MI5 spy beaten up by Qatada thugs "is suing handlers"'. *Evening Standard*. 24th February.

Barling, K. (2008) 'Vulnerability of the Suicide Bomber'. *BBC News*, 1st March

Barling, K. (2008) 'Finally Home'. *BBC News*, 29th January

O'Neill, Sean (2008) 'Proud day for spy who infiltrated mosque'. *The Times*. 28th January.

Barney, Katherine (2007) 'Mosque informer: MI5 betrayed me'. *Evening Standard*. 29th November.

O'Neill, Sean (2007) 'Informant who risked his life to fight extremists "betrayed by MI5"'. *The Times*. 29th November.

Barling, K. (2007) 'Finding the Bombers'. *BBC News*, 14th May.

Reid, Sue (2007) 'And still they're preaching poison; New laws were meant to stop radical clerics stirring up racial hatred in mosques. But as this disturbing Mail investigation reveals, they are still pouring out their vitriol'. *Daily Mail*. 13th January.

Sniffen, M.J. (2006) 'America, you lost – I won: Moussaoui sentenced to life in prison'. *Chicago Sun Times*. 4th May.

Leppard, David (2006) Agent says MI5 dismissed Hamza as 'harmless clown'. *The Sunday Times*. 12th February.

Woods, Richard and David Leppard (2006) 'How liberal Britain let hate flourish'. *The Sunday Times*. 12th February.

Dodd, Vikram (2006) 'Inside the mosque: an academy for holy war'. *The Guardian*. 8th February.

O'Neill, Sean and Daniel McGrory (2006) 'Kill and be killed: how cleric raised generation of terrorists'. *The Times*. 8th February.

Casciani, D. and Sakr, S. (2006) *The battle for the mosque* BBC News online. 7th February.

Leppard, David (2006). 'How liberal Britain let hate flourish'. *The Sunday Times*. 12th February.

Reid, Sue (2005) 'So how many more martyrs did he create?'. *Daily Mail*. 3rd September.

Reid, Sue, Sinead Macintyre and James Tozer (2005) 'The Enemy Within; Yesterday Tony Blair promised tough new measures to contain the preachers of hate in our midst. But as this Mail investigation has discovered, it may already be too late'. *Daily Mail*. 6th August.

Barling, K. (2005) 'Lessons from Finsbury Park Mosque'. *BBC News*, 4th August.

Woods, Richard, David Leppard and Michael Smith (2005) 'Tangled web that still leaves worrying loose ends'. *The Sunday Times*. 31st July.

Hassaïne, Réda (2005) 'Under Cover Agent'. *The Sunday Times*. 17th July.

Leppard, David and Nick Fielding (2005) 'The Hate'. *The Sunday Times*. 10th July.

Reid, Sue (2005) 'The lethal web; just log on to find the enemy within who despise the British infidels'. *Daily Mail*. 8th July.

Hassaïne, Réda and Sean O'Neill (2005) 'I was tortured, says ricin plotter'. *The Times*. 9th May.

Taylor, Ben (2005) 'Terror suspects "likely to get free homes"' *Daily Mail*. 29th January.

Waugh, Paul and Oliver Finegold (2005) 'British Camp X-Ray suspect "confessed to training with Bin Laden"; US documents allege Guantanamo bay detainees were at al Qaeda military base'. *Evening Standard*. 28th January.

Dovkants, Keith (2005) 'I spied on Abu Qatada for MI5'. *Evening Standard*. 28th January.

Zaman, Ned, David Wise, David Rose and Bryan Burrough (2004) 'The Price of Failure: The path to 9/11: Lost warnings and fatal errors'. *Vanity Fair*. November Edition.

O'Neill, Sean (2004), 'Death threats made against key witness'. *The Times*. 4th June.

Barling, K. (2003) 'London - safe haven for terrorists?'. *BBC News*. 2nd June.

Barling, K. (2003) 'Rachid Ramda to be extradited?'. *BBC News*, 4th April.

Barling, K. (2003) 'Charity Commission bans Abu Hamza from Finsbury Park Mosque'. *BBC News*, 4th February.

O'Neill, Sean (2003) 'Terrorism and ID cards'. *The Times*. 22nd January.

Leppard, David (2003) 'Bio-war suits found in mosque'. *The Sunday Times*. 6th January.

McGrory, Daniel (2003) 'A haven for faithful hijacked by extremists'. *The Times*. 21st January.

Davenport, Justin and Keith Dovkants (2003) 'Mosque linked to key network plotting major attack'. *Evening Standard*. 21st January.

O'Neill, Sean (2003) 'Mosque has been source of concern over terrorism since 1996'. *The Daily Telegraph*. 21st January.

Tapper, Jake (2003) 'Muslim spy who infiltrated Bin Laden's terror network in London'. *The Times*. 16th January.

Author unknown (2002) 'Spy says al Qaida scouted US base'. *Jewish World Review*. 31st July.

O'Neill, Sean and Réda Hassaïne (2001) <I did nothing wrong. I>m just a Muslim and a student of flying>. *The Daily Telegraph*. 28th November.

Leppard, David (2001) 'MI5 knew for years of London mosque's role'. *The Times*. 25th November.

O'Neill, Sean and Réda Hassaïne (2001) '"My son was brought up to abhor terrorists" Man accused of training the September 11 hijackers never knew them, say his mother'. *The Daily Telegraph*. 1st November.

O'Neill, Sean (2001) 'Why France lived in fear of "Londonistan" Evidence on extremists ignored'. *The Daily Telegraph*. 13th October.

Barling, K. (2001) 'London lives on its nerves'. *BBC News*, 8th October.

Benmerad, Djamel (2001) 'Un journaliste algerien au service de la DGSE'. *Le Jeune Independent*. 1st July.

Burke, Jason (2001) 'MI5 and police ordered illegal raids on mosques'. *The Observer*. 18th February.

Burke, Jason (2001) 'How I was betrayed by the British: Réda Hassaïne risked his life infiltrating Islamic groups for police and MI5. But after two years service he was betrayed, he tells Jason Burke'. *The Observer*. 18th February.

Burke, Jason (2001) MI5 and police ordered illegal break-ins at mosques. *The Observer*. 18th February.

Leppard, David (2001) 'MI5 knew for years of London mosque's role'. *The Sunday Times*. 25th November.

Amarni, Kamel (2000) 'Comment j'ai été recruiter par la DGSE'. *Le Soir d'Algerie*. 13th November.

Leppard, David, Gareth Walsh and Paul Nuki (2000) 'Dirty-tricks trail of a Muslim mole'. *The Sunday Times*. 8th October.

Robin, Jean (2000) 'J'ai aide les francais'. *Le Parisien*. 10th October.

Robin, Jean (2000) 'La vengeance de l''agent secret'. *Le Parisien*. 9th October.

SK (2000) 'Un algerien au service de l'espionnage francais a Londres'. *Le Quotidien d'Oran*. 8th October.

Further Reading

Fukuyama, Y.F. (1992) *The End of History and the Last Man, Free Press*.

Huntington, Samuel P. (1996) *The Clash of Civilisations and the Remaking of World Order*. Simon & Schuster.

Husain, Ed. (2007) *The Islamist*. Penguin.

Nawaz, Maajid (2012) *Radical: My journey from Islamist extremism to a democratic awakening*. Ebury Publishing.